Y. Doroshinskaya, V. Kruchina-Bogdanov

LENINGRAD
AND ITS ENVIRONS

GUIDEBOOK

Progress Publishers
Moscow

Y. Doroshinskaya, V. Kruchina-Bogdanov

LENINGRAD
and Its Environs
A Guide

Елена Дорошинская, Вадим Кручина-Богданов
Ленинград и его пригороды
Путеводитель
На английском языке
Редакция литературы по спорту и туризму

Translated from the Russian
Editor of the Russian text **I. Rakhmanina**
Designed by Mikhail Zanegin

Art Editor **V. Zavadovskaya**
Maps by **V. Sokolov**

Updated to January 1, 1977

20904-000
Д 014 (01)-80 102-79   1905040100

CONTENTS

Welcome to Leningrad!

Pick up any guidebook on our city—Soviet or foreign, it doesn't make any difference—and you will inevitably come across this sentence in every one of them: 'Leningrad is one of the world's most beautiful cities.' We hope that you will soon be convinced of the truth of this statement yourself.

In terms of world history Leningrad is a young city. Less than three centuries have passed since its first structures were raised on the banks of the River Neva. Here you will not find monuments carved out of the depths of antiquity; you will be charmed and captivated by other things. Do you know, for instance, that our city is often called the 'Venice of the North'? Visitors to Leningrad are struck by the bright glimmer of water everywhere in this city built on dozens of islands. They are struck by the soft shimmer of the canals and their inimitably poetic and colourful bridges, by the ripple of small rivers and the ferries and row-boats that ease down them, by the expanse of the city's main river, the forever restless Neva, and finally, by the Gulf of Finland, whose shores today's Leningrad reaches.

The city is spread over a wide area with many large squares and long broad avenues. Its streets are so wide that it would seem our ancestors had an inkling of how busy these thorough-fares would eventually become. Thanks to the moist maritime climate, parks and gardens always have a pleasant verdant freshness, even in the hottest weather.

Lovers of history have another name for the city—the 'Palmyra of the North'—a name surfacing from the depths of the

7

ancient world that has remained in the memory of mankind as a symbol of magnificent architectural monuments.

Leningrad is like a huge architectural museum. There are so many architectural masterpieces here that to this day they defy the imagination. One can stand for hours admiring the austere plastic forms of the 18th century. The festive palatial buildings, built in the so-called Russian baroque style, are resplendent with decorative brilliance. Russian classicism flourished along the banks of the Neva where it combined the principles of antique architecture with the development of a national architectural heritage. The accomplishments of contemporary urban development are embodied in the structures erected today by Soviet architects.

The inherent unity of two arts—architecture and sculpture—is what gives Leningrad its unique look. Sculptured figures grace palaces, residential buildings, triumphal arches, bridges, parks and streets.

Monuments on Leningrad's streets, squares, and gardens immortalise the memory of outstanding statesmen, revolutionaries, military leaders, scientists, writers, composers and artists, not to mention the fact that they beautify the city. Not only do these monuments reflect the life of the country, they are a universal tribute to man's genius as well. Here one may meet Descartes, Darwin, Lomonosov, Mechnikov, Pasteur, Roentgen . . ..

Leningrad is also a 'museum of bridges'. There are around 400 in the city. It is also a 'museum of fences', which adorn riverbanks, streets, gardens, cathedrals and bridges. Finally, there are the street and park lamps, weather-vanes, coats-of-arms of the city, even the grille and lattice work—all of which are the words and stanzas of the poem that is Leningrad.

Leningrad is more than a treasury of the arts past and present; it is more than a city connected with the dawn and the subsequent milestones of Russian science, industry and the arts. Leningrad will unveil for you the most important pages in history of the country—the history of the people's struggle against autocracy, feudalism, and social and political oppression in tsarist Russia. The City on the Neva was witness to the activity of revolutionaries at different periods of the Russian liberation movement. Leningrad was the cradle of the proletarian revolution.

It was here that Lenin began his revolutionary activity at the turn of the century. He headed Marxist circles in the industrial areas of the city, moulding the most progressive workers into professional revolutionaries. It was here that Lenin laid the foundation of the Communist Party. It was in the City on the Neva that Lenin announced the victory of the Socialist Revolution and the birth of the world's first workers' and peasants' state. And it was here that Lenin proclaimed the peace policy of the Soviet Union, the same course steadfastly pursued by the Communist Party and the Soviet Government ever since.

The city was first called St. Petersburg, and later Petrograd. After the leader of the October Revolution died in 1924, the city's workers decided to rename the city after the great Lenin.

Leningrad is a city exemplifying the glorious revolutionary, labour and military traditions of the Soviet people.

For its military heroism and its economic achievements Leningrad was twice awarded the Order of Lenin, the Order of the October Revolution, the Order of the Red Banner and the Hero-City Gold Star.

During the years of the Second World War Leningrad was surrounded by fascist troops, but the courageous city withstood an excruciating 900 day siege. The enemy did not set one foot inside the city. Leningrad became the first city to receive the title Hero-City.

Everything that had been destroyed during the war was restored a long time ago. The city is becoming larger now and even more beautiful. Leningrad's particular contribution to the country's postwar development has been its production of rare machinery, its scientific discoveries and its vast housing construction. Leningrad is one of the largest centres of technological progress and culture in the country today. The present concept of the 'sights of Leningrad' includes not only monuments of the past, but buildings of industrial enterprises, institutes, schools, hospitals, new palaces of culture, sports facilities and whole areas of building developments.

Of course it's impossible to say everything there is to say about Leningrad in one book. Six volumes bearing the unassuming title 'Essays on the History of Leningrad' have been recently published—each a thousand pages long. There also exists an artistic chronicle dedicated to the city of Leningrad—works of prose and poetry, paintings, sketches, musical works and other forms of art, which have become masterpieces of national culture. Many new names and works are constantly being added to this chronicle. A few years ago a public organisation was formed in Leningrad called the 'Club of Specialists on the City'. Its members make an in-depth study of the life of the city, bringing to light forgotten or little known facts and details about its past. The bibliography of fictional, scientific and reference literature on Leningrad is boundless.

Dear guests of Leningrad! We hope you will read this guidebook in preparation for a trip to this city or just for the sake of knowing a little more about it. It should come in handy during your stay in Leningrad.

And now a more detailed account of the city's biography.

THE HISTORY OF LENINGRAD

*Every stone here is a chronicle
unto itself.*

MIKHAIL DUDIN

The Neva delta region, which is the site of present-day Leningrad and its environs, was settled by Slavic tribes more than a thousand years ago. In the 10th century these tribes became part oi Kiev Rus, an early feudal state which had arisen in Eastern Europe at the turn of the 9th century. The River Neva, which pours into the Gulf of Finland of the Baltic Sea, had long been part of a trade route linking Rus with other European countries and provided it with an exit to the sea.

Since the end of the 12th century Rus' neighbours to the north had made numerous though unsuccessful attempts to seize this area by the Neva. In the early 17th century, however, the Kingdom of Sweden managed to take these lands. Diplomatic efforts to have the seized territory returned to Russia proved fruitless. In 1700 the war broke out between Russia and Sweden, which the history books call the Great Northern War. While the war was going on, this ancient Russian territory was won back, and the country once again had its exit to the sea. However, with the war still in progress and the threat of attack still a reality, tsar Peter the Great ordered that a fort be built on one of the islands. The Peter and Paul Fortress was completed on May 16 (May 27 new style), 1703, and this day is considered the date of the founding of the city of St. Petersburg. It took all of one year under the shield of the fortress' cannon fire to build the first streets of the young city. In 1712 Peter the Great transferred the highest governmental institutions

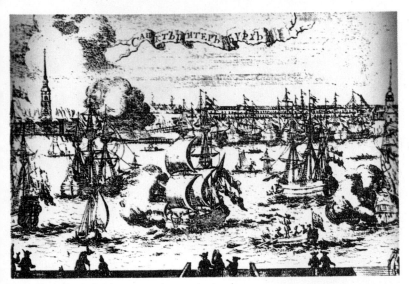

Petersburg in the 18th century (engraving)

from Moscow to this city on the Neva. St. Petersburg became Russia's capital. The city was built on such a wide scale, that in twenty or thirty years it would be competing with the greatest cities of Europe.

The tremendous task of creating a huge capital city was shouldered by hundreds of thousands of peasants who were resettled here for this specific purpose.

From its very outset the building of St. Petersburg followed one single design. Not only was the mapping out and the width of the city's main arteries regulated, but also the architectural make-up of homes of people of different social strata, and later even the heights of buildings were regulated.

During Peter's reign architects formulated designs (to use contemporary terminology) for subsequent urban development. Commissions were set up in the early 18th century which set standards on construction in the city.

In the first third of the 19th century St. Petersburg assumed an appearance of which the great Russian poet Alexander Pushkin wrote:

> *I love thee, Peter's proud creation,*
> *Thy princely stateliness of line,*
> *The regal coursing, patient,*
> *Twixt sober walls of massive stone ...*

Peter the Great's Cottage

The Admiralty

St. Petersburg quickly became built up as a seaport and an industrial centre. By the end of the 1820s almost all of Russia's foreign maritime trade was concentrated in this city. Its first industrial enterprises were shipyards, brickworks, arms and gunpowder plants and large manufactures.

Printing offices were opened in the new city, followed by the founding of the Maritime Academy (1715), the School of Engineering (1719), the first museum (1719), the Academy of Sciences (1725), and the country's first public theatre (1756). By the middle of the 18th century the city's main centre with its magnificent architectural ensembles had taken shape, and royal residencies with palaces and gardens were built in the suburbs.

Outstanding architects and sculptors had a hand in creating these true works of art. Some were foreign artisans who embraced Russia as their second country. Their work reflects the traditions and characteristics of Russian culture.

History will never forget the names of such brilliant architects as Vassili Bazhenov, Andrei Voronikhin, Andrean Zakharov, Giacomo Quarenghi, Bartolomeo Rastrelli, Carlo Rossi and Ivan Starov. It has recorded the names of several talented folk artisans as well—Samson Sukhanov, Vassili Yakovlev and Ivan Yevstifeyev. Thousands of other craftsmen—common people—never knew fame, but it was they who had embodied the designs of brilliant architects.

14

Griboyedov Canal

In the second half of the 19th century the city became a large industrial and cultural centre of Russia.

The country's first major railroad was built connecting St. Petersburg and Moscow, followed by the Maritime Canal which allowed the new port at the mouth of the River Neva to handle bigger ships with deeper hulls. The Mariinskaya and Tikhvinskaya waterway systems were constructed, linking the Neva and the Volga.

At the beginning of the 20th century St. Petersburg was producing nearly one-half of the country's chemical products, one-quarter of its plant and machinery, and one-sixth of its textile goods. Approximately one out of every five inhabitants of the city was a factory worker.

The Russian capital became an important scientific and technical centre. Many outstanding scientists lived and worked in the city, such as Mikhail Lomonosov, Vassili Petrov, Ivan Kruzenstern, Emil Lentz, Alexander Popov, Sergei Botkin, Nikolai Pirogov and many others. The world's first electrically powered vessel was launched from a shipyard on the Neva. In St. Petersburg Dmitri Mendeleyev discovered the periodic table of the elements. The world's first incandescent electric bulb was lit here; the design for a jet aircraft was developed here; radio communication was invented; a television image was received with the aid of an electron-ray tube, and the first multi-engined airplane—the 'Russian Vityaz'—was built. The findings of the Pulkovo Astronomical Observatory attained international renown. The St. Petersburg mathe-

15

Senate Square on December 14, 1825 (watercolour)

matical school, whose luminaries included Pafnuti Chebyshev and Leonard Eiuler, was famous all over the world.

A national school of painting came into being in St. Petersburg. Such masters as Karl Bryullov, Orest Kiprensky, Ivan Kramskoi, Ilya Repin and Valentin Serov created their masterpieces here. The names of great composers are connected with the city—Pyotr Tchaikovsky, Mikhail Glinka, Nikolai Rimsky-Korsakov, Modest Mussorgsky, Alexander Borodin—and the classics of Russian literature.

> *The poet has long immortalised the Neva,*
> *The pages of Gogol are steeped in Nevsky,*
> *Onegin was inspired by the Summer Gardens,*
> *Blok was enraptured by the city's islands*
> *But along Razyezhaya Street roamed Dostoyevsky.*
>
> *SAMUIL MARSHAK*

In the middle of the 19th century urban planners stopped adhering to one set design. Even in the centre of the city rather nondescript housing developments began to be erected—so-called 'dokhodniye doma' (profit homes). As the price of land skyrocketed, the dense housing greatly exceeded admissible limits.

Bolsheviks speaking at a meeting of workers and soldiers in Petrograd in 1917

Construction on the outskirts of the city followed a spontaneous course. In industrial areas housing construction mainly took the form of uninviting hostels and rooming houses. Workers lived in unbelievably crowded conditions. The centre of the city had been already enjoying achievements of modern civilisation such as electric lighting, plumbing, sewage and paved streets, but the outskirts wallowed in dirt and darkness. Municipal authorities purposely wrote many areas off the official geographical confines of the city so that they wouldn't have to worry about making improvements in such neighbourhoods. The mortality rate in the outskirts was two times higher than in the centre, and St. Petersburg as a whole was said to have the highest mortality rate in all of Europe. The Russian writer Fyodor Dostoyevsky used the adjective 'sick' in describing this city.

This city of social contrasts, this city which Russia's autocratic rulers called the bulwark of the monarchical system, became the hub of progressive thought and the centre of the Russian revolutionary movement.

It was here that an uprising was staged on December 14, 1825, by the Decembrists, a faction of revolution-inclined nobility. Several decades later a second wave of the liberation movement arose, this time headed by revolutionary democrats in whose views the idea of a peasant revolution was combined with utopian socialism. The first Marxist

17

The cruiser *Aurora*

Leningrad during the blockade

organisations came into being in the 1880s. In the autumn of 1895 all Marxist circles in St. Petersburg were united under the leadership of Lenin into one 'League of the Struggle for the Emancipation of the Working Class'. The League began to fuse the ideas of scientific socialism with the proletarian movement. That was the first political Organisation which became the nucleus of the revolutionary Marxist party, and it relied on the mass working-class movement.

Then came the 20th century, and with it three Russian revolutions. All of them had their roots in the city on the Neva. The first was the Revolution of 1905, a bourgeois-democratic movement of the masses. The revolution was crushed, but it awakened the political awareness of millions. The second revolution, which took place in February 1917, destroyed the monarchical system. The revolutionary proletariat, headed by the Bolshevik Party, steered a course towards developing the bourgeois-democratic revolution into a socialist revolution. The Great October Socialist Revolution was victorious in October 1917. As a result, the world's first socialist state was formed. This important event in history will be discussed in greater detail in the chapter on relics of the revolution and places in the city associated with Lenin.

Until November 1919, Petrograd workers took up arms and together with Red Army troops defended their city against internal counter-revolutionary forces and foreign intervention. While repulsing mili-

The monument to the heroic defenders of Leningrad on Victory Square

The Palace Bridge

tary danger, the young Soviet Republic had to combat hunger, epidemics and dislocation. It had liquidated the last hotbeds of civil war and foreign intervention by November 1922. In 1925 the Party, in keeping with the behests of Lenin, embarked upon the socialist industrialisation of the country. Leningrad played an extremely important role in resolving this problem.

By 1927 the city had reattained prewar industrial levels. It began manufacturing the first Soviet-made tractors and aviation engines and the country's first turbines and generators for power stations, timber-carriers and weaving looms. The first Soviet blooming mill was built in 1931 at the Izhorsky Works in a record time—8 months and 28 days. In 1935 the Admiralty Works built the world's first welded ice-breaker.

The first Soviet scientific research institutes were opened. By the end of the first decade of Soviet power there were four times as many museums in the city than before the Revolution. New theatres opened, and the first Palaces of Culture appeared.

People began to arrive in Leningrad from all parts of the country: there was enough work for them all. An urgent solution to the housing problem had to be found.

In 1917, immediately after the victory of the Great October Socialist Revolution private ownership of houses as a source of income was abolished by a decree of the Soviet government. As a result, it was

19

already possible in 1918-1919 to improve the housing situation of more than 300 thousand people, who until then had lived in exceptionally bad conditions.

However, during the civil war, not much could be done. The building of the outskirts began after the end of the civil war. As well as living quarters, the city built schools, clubhouses, hospitals, children's establishments, stadiums—things workers in these areas had never known before the Revolution.

In 1935 the first Soviet draft of the General Urban Development Plan for Leningrad was drawn up, and work was begun soon afterward. Many of its ideas, however, did not have time to be effected. The Soviet Union was invaded by Hitler Germany. The Great Patriotic War (1941-1945) of the Soviet people against fascism began.

In September of 1941 German forces advanced to the very limits of the city. For 900 days the city was subjected to massive air raids and artillery bombardments. There are few examples in history that could measure up to the horror of the Leningrad blockade—or to the courage of the city's defenders. More than one million of its people gave their lives in the fight against the fascists; it was only through these tremendous sacrifices that the city could be saved. 'We fought for Leningrad; now we will make it greater and more beautiful than ever'—this was the slogan with which hundreds of thousands of people participated in the restoration of their city.

Tourists arriving in Leningrad occasionally ask in surprise: 'Where are the ruins of the blockade?', 'Was it really that bad?' The chapter, '900 Days—The Heroic Defence of Leningrad', will explain the hell the city went through during the siege.

The city healed the wounds caused by the war. The echo of those years might be heard only in the names of streets, squares and avenues: Anti-Aircraft Gunners Street (Úlitsa Zen'itchikov), Courage Square (Plóshchad Múzhestva), Avenue of the Unconquered (Prospékt Nepokoryónnykh). More than fifty new streets and squares have been named after soldiers who defended Leningrad. Two magnificent Victory Parks have been laid—the Moscow Victory Park and the Maritime Victory Park.

There are the unseen wounds—the ones in the hearts of the people—that never heal. It's hard to find a Leningrad family who didn't suffer the loss of a loved one during the war. To this day one of the city's newspapers prints letters under the heading 'Please Respond'. These letters are written by people who are hoping beyond hope to hear from loved ones and friends whom the war separated from them. There is a special account in the State Bank entitled the 'Peace Fund'. The people of Leningrad constantly make voluntary contributions to it as they understand better than anyone else the meaning of the word 'peace'.

The next chapter will acquaint you with the postwar Leningrad—the city as it is today.

LENINGRAD TODAY
AND TOMORROW

**Geography,
Climate,
Territory**

Leningrad is situated on the eastern shore of the Gulf of Finland of the Baltic Sea. It is the northern-most of all cities with population of over one million, and is located on the same latitude as the southern part of Alaska and the southern tip of Greenland.

At present the city is situated on 44 islands in the delta of the River Neva, the largest of which (Vasilyevsky Island) covers an area of 10 sq km. The islands have a plain relief and almost all are oval-shaped.

Leningrad has about 50 rivers, streams, channels and canals totalling over 160 km. The city's main river is the Neva, which divides the city in two approximately equal parts. Each part consists of old sections (toward the centre) and never ones on the outskirts. The river splits up into five arms and spills into the Gulf of Finland. Leningrad's 'Blue Map' corresponds to about one-tenth of its total area.

Leningrad has a maritime, moderate *climate,* the most temperate for this northern parallel in the entire country. This is due to the influence of the Gulfstream. Meteorological observations show that July is the warmest month with a 17.8°C mean temperature and January the coldest, averaging −7.9°C.

On the average, the temperature rises above zero 222 days out of the year. It rains an average of 126 days a year. The most precipitation is in August, and the least in March. Long-standing weather data indicate that the snowy season as a rule lasts from the beginning of November to the middle of April, but there have been winters with very little snowfall. The windiest times of the year are during autumn and winter, with south, southeast and southwest winds predominating.

Leningrad weather is famous for its changeability. It's not unusual for the temperature and the atmospheric pressure to take a nosedive or the wind velocity and direction to change drastically—all in one day. Different areas in the city can have a divergence in temperature of up to 8-10°C.

The bathing season along the coastline of the Gulf of Finland lasts from the middle of June through the end of August. Water temperature during the summer is usually 10°C to 24°C. The Neva is about 2 or 3 degrees cooler than the Gulf.

22

The twenty-fifth of May is considered to be the start of White ights, when night never comes and the evening twilight melts into awn. White Nights are the 'whitest' from June 11 to July 2, and they d around the twentieth of July.

The territory of Leningrad covers an area of 660 sq. km.; with the burbs included—more than 1,400 sq. km. There are over two thousand streets and squares. If you were to combine these streets into one raight line you would get a road stretching 2,632 km; in other words, vering all the city's streets would be the equivalent of going from, t's say, Leningrad to Bordeaux or Leningrad to Reykjavik. Leninrad's farthest suburb is about 65 km from the centre of the city.

dministrative ivision, overnment, he Population

Leningrad proper is comprised of *sixteen administrative districts.* Greater Leningrad includes five suburban districts as well.

Leningrad is governed by the City Soviet of the People's Deputies nd the districts by the District Soviets of the People's Deputies.

Like all other local Soviets in the USSR, the Leningrad City Soviet xecutes the laws and decrees issued by the Soviet government and it andles such projects as organisation of public services, the building of ouses and cultural facilities and the formulation and maintenance of city budget. The deputies of the Leningrad City Soviet are among the ost upstanding citizens in the community: workers, engineers, technians, scientists, figures of arts and culture, students — in effect, people om all strata of the population.

The Leningrad City Soviet consists of 654 deputies, of which about ne half are women.

The work of the Soviets is constantly under the control of the

The Executive Committee of the Leningrad Soviet of People's Deputies (Mariinsky Palace)

people. Deputies systematically report to their constituents and may be recalled at any time if they do not fulfill their responsibilities.

Sessions of the City Soviet are held four times a year. During the intervals between sessions a 24-man Executive Committee of the Leningrad City Soviet acts as the governing body. The Soviets maintain close contact with such voluntary organisations as home and block committees, people's voluntary detachments, retirees' councils, library councils, children's clubs, etc. Over 450,000 people in the Greater Leningrad area assist the local Soviets in their activities.

The population of Leningrad, including the towns and settlements under the city's jurisdiction is more than four and a half million. The population is made up of over 100 different nationalities and ethnic groups. Russians make up the majority of the population. 30,000 weddings take place every year in the city, and 50,000 new citizens are born here yearly.

In 1964 a commemorative 'Born in Leningrad' medal was designed which is ceremoniously awarded to parents when their newborn is registered. The baby's name and date of birth are inscribed on the medal.

New buildings in Leningrad

The House of Youth

The Annual City Budget

Leningrad's yearly budget is upwards of billion roubles. City taxes comprise little more than 8 per cent of its revenue. The budget is basically funded by allocations from government institutions and enterprises, more than half of which as been earmarked for the municipal economy, and over 40 per ent—to health, education and social maintenance. A great deal of ocial and cultural projects are also funded out of central government nd republican budgets and from trade unions and other public organi- ations, institutions and enterprises.

**Housing Construction
and Organisation
of Public Services**

About one-fifth of the city's housing
was completely destroyed or heavily
damaged during the blockade. Even
with the enemy at the gates of the city
a group of architects were completing designs for the city's restoration
and future development. Two months later, on March 29, 1944, when
the siege was lifted, the Soviet government decided to take urgent
measures to revive the industrial and economic life of the city. New
housing constructions began. All restoration work was completed
in 1950.

In the first two decades after the war alone (1946-1965), the city
constructed housing totalling an area of 20,000,000 sq. m.—almost the
same amount built during the city's 214-year history before the Revolution. Leningrad has 2.5 times more housing facilities today than it did
before 1917. Every ten minutes a new apartment is built; every day two
new apartment buildings go up. Rent never makes up more than 4
per cent of the family budget, and hasn't been raised since 1926. The
cost of one kilowatt of electricity is 4 kopecks.

Leningrad has all the fresh water it needs and more. It is taken from
the deepest point of the Neva in the city and funneled through an
extensive filtering process. Each city dweller uses an average of over
360 litres of water a day.

There are many parks, gardens and boulevards in Leningrad. They
are not spread equally, however, throughout the city: the northern
areas have more greenery than the southern. Thanks to a planned system of horticulture, lawns and gardens are appearing in the central
sections of the city as land is cleared after reconstruction of homes and
blocks. In new areas builders are required to plant trees, shrubs and
flowers near the apartment buildings. Every small cluster of buildings is
provided with a garden, as well as a park for the whole neighbourhood.

Every year the appearance of the city is enhanced by the planting
of 200,000 new trees. In the near future each city dweller is to 'own' 20
sq. m. of the city's park area.

In keeping with pollution control standards, dozens of industrial
enterprises have either been shut down, re-equipped or relocated outside the city limits. There are over 1,600 machines for sweeping and
hosing down streets and removing snow. More than 100 special vessels
purify the water in the city's canals.

Health Care

There are 1,455 active health care institutions in the city—hospitals, separate polyclinics for adults and children, maternity consultation centres, outdoor patient clinics. More than twenty research institutes and medical educational establishments have their own clinics. The number of doctors in Leningrad have increased elevenfold in the years of Soviet power. There are more and more health resorts being built in Leningrad's suburbs. New large medical facilities have been built or are soon to be commissioned, such as a specialised emergency hospital, a cardiological centre and others.

As is well known, medical care in the Soviet Union is free.

Education

Every one out of three inhabitants of Leningrad is studying. To make a comparison, 20 per cent of the population of the pre-revolutionary capital of the Russian Empire was illiterate. Today more than half a million people are enrolled in the city's general education and vocational schools. The latter schools provide the students with a general secondary education plus a trade.

For those who work and wish to continue their education without leaving their jobs, night schools and correspondence schools are available as well as branches of specialised secondary schools and institutions of higher learning. Those who study in this fashion receive 30-or 0-day paid holidays to prepare for exams, a four-month paid holiday to defend a graduation thesis; a discount of 50 per cent of the cost of the ticket during the examination period, if the correspondence-course student is studying in another city; an extra day off for senior students and many other privileges. Enterprises have the right to send their workers to institutes and specialised secondary schools and pay them grants exceeding state scholarships by 15 per cent.

More than a quarter of a million students are enrolled in the city's 1 institutions of higher learning. The major ones are: The State University (over 20,000 students), The Northwest Correspondence Polytechnical Institute (approximately 20,000 young industrial and office workers are enrolled here while holding down jobs), The Polytechnical

A new building of Leningrad University

A reading room in th
M. Saltykov-Shchedrin public librar

Institute (over 17,500 students), the Institute of Railway Enginee
(13,000 students) and the Forestry Academy (over 10,000 students
Leningrad institutions of higher learning train specialists in 425 profe
sions. All graduates are guaranteed a job.

Almost one out of every ten people in Leningrad have a diplom
from an institution of higher learning.

Some 450,000 people a year are studying in their factories or offic
to raise their qualifications or to take up a new profession.

Education in the USSR is free.

Palaces and houses of culture, museums and institutions of high
learning have lecturing bureaus which organise readings on the wide
of topics in the fields of science and the arts. These lectures attra
knowledge seekers of all ages and trades.

People's universities are becoming more and more popular as pu
lic educational organisations promoting self learning and, hence, tl
cultural enrichment of working people. They attract some 70,00
people wishing to improve themselves in such fields as social and pol
ical science and technology, law, economics and physical training.

The public library as seen from the outside

Leningrad — a Centre of Industry, Science and Culture

The blockade during the war dealt a tremendous blow to *Leningrad's industry* — about a thousand industrial enterprises were destroyed. Already in 949, however, it reached the pre-war level. Today the city produces ine times as much as it did before the war.

Mechanical engineering and metal-working account for a significant proportion of Leningrad's industrial output. Leningrad enterprises maufacture turbines and generators for most of the country's power staions. The world's first nuclear icebreaker, the *Lenin,* was built here in 959, and in 1974 and 1977 two more powerful nuclear-powered vesels were constructed — the *Arktika* and the *Sibir.* The *Kirovets,* a powrful multi-purpose tractor, is well known in many foreign countries. Ever new achievements of Leningrad's industry (instrument making, machine tool construction, electronics, radioengineering) reaffirm the city's right to consider itself an international as well as national manuacturer. Almost two-thirds of all Leningrad's industrial output is produced by production associations. This type of organisation allows researchers, designers and manufacturers to better coordinate their efforts and achievements for developing and producing up-to-date plant nd machinery.

The whole country knows the products of Leningrad's light and

29

The atomic-powered icebreaker *Arktika*

food industries. Approximately one out of every eight pairs of shoe and one out of every ten garments manufactured in the country com from this city's factories.

Leningrad ranks second to Moscow as the leading scientific centr of the country. There are over 450 research institutes and research an development organisations in the city. Its scientists and techniciar have worked out processes for obtaining synthetic rubber, for produc ing aluminium, and they have created the first optical glass. Leningra scientists are well known for their work in the fields of mathematic geology, shipbuilding, physiology, high-energy physics, oceanograph etc. Among the institutions enjoying wide international recognition ar the Main Astronomical Observatory of the USSR Academy of Sc ences, which is referred to as the 'astronomy capital of the world', th Joffe Institute of Physics and Technology, the Pavlov Institute of Phys ology, the Petrov Institute of Cancer Research, the Komarov Botanic Institute, the Institute of Arctic and Antarctic Studies and many other

There are sixteen theatres with permanent companies in Leningra Among them are three music theatres, the country's largest studer

The large concert hall of the Shostakovich Leningrad Philharmonic

music theatre, the Conservatoire Opera Studio, five concert halls, a circus, music hall, and so on.

Leningrad's professional theatres alone are frequented by 30 million people a year.

These are the words of an Intourist guide:

'Tonight I'd like to take you to all the places I myself enjoy going to. I'm sure you'll have an unforgettably wonderful evening.

'We are now on Theatre Square. For me this is a square of music. The Conservatoire practically takes up a whole block. The square echoes with the music of Anton Rubinstein, Mikhail Glinka, Alexander Glazunov, Pyotr Tchaikovsky and Sergei Prokofyev.

'I love to arrive early at the Kirov Theatre of Opera and Ballet, which is located across the street from the Conservatoire. The inside of the theatre is light blue with gold trimming. It's just beautiful. I hope that whatever show you see in this theatre, you'll enjoy it and remember it for a long time.

'If you prefer modern opera and ballet, may I suggest our Maly Theatre. Its presentations are always a unique experience. The Maly Opera and Ballet Theatre is situated on one of the most beautiful squares in Leningrad. It has every right to be called Arts Square. It is also the site of the Philharmonic Society and the Theatre of Musical Comedy. I don't admire a musical comedy, but

this doesn't take away from its popularity among the many love[ ]
of this art genre. If you like the temperamental Kalman, if y[ ]
prefer the graceful style of Strauss, or if the operettas of Sov[ ]
composers interest you, then you should spend your evenings he[ ]
in the Theatre of Musical Comedy.

'If I were actually your guide, I would love to accompany y[ ]
to the Philharmonic Society. This hall with its white marble c[ ]
umns stands out not only for its grand elegance but also for [ ]
high acoustic qualities. Conducted for several decades now [ ]
Yevgeni Mravinsky, the Leningrad Philharmonic Symphony O[ ]
chestra is famous all over the world.

The monument to V. I. Lenin on the square adjoining the Finland Station
The Summer Gardens in winter
Arts Square
Winter Canal
A sphinx on University Embankment
The Admiralty
The Smolny
V. I. Lenin's apartment and study in Smolny
The Winter Palace
St. Isaac's Cathedral
Architect Rossi Street
The monument to the Motherland in the Piskaryovskoye Memorial Cemetery
Nevsky Prospekt
A Leningrad scene
A holiday on the Neva
The Green Belt of Glory
Bank Bridge

*'You have sensed, I'm sure, that I am partial towards music.
But it wouldn't be fair of me not to mention Leningrad marvellous
drama theatres. The Gorky Bolshoi Theatre of Drama is one of
them. I do not know of a more talented company of actors. Each
and every one of them is absolutely brilliant. Every premiere of
the company is always a big event. Other theatres are the Pushkin
Academic Theatre of Drama, the Lensoviet Theatre, the Komissarzhevskaya Theatre of Drama and the Children's Theatre. It
would be an almost impossible task for me to write even a few
words about what each one of them is noted for.*

*'How little I've managed to tell you. In Leningrad there are
dozens of theatres, concert halls and palaces of culture. Each one
has its own traditions and its own inimitable characteristics.'*

The city's more than 200 palaces and houses of culture and clubs
are situated mainly in areas built up after revolution. Auditoriums of
many clubhouses are more spacious than the old theatre halls. The
Lensoviet and Maxim Gorky Palaces of Culture, for example, have
a seating capacity of more than 2,000 persons each. The stages of these
and other large palaces of culture are often provided to Soviet and
foreign artists performing in Leningrad.

There are a considerable number of studios and circles affiliated
with palaces and houses of culture. Several amateur groups are so
good they're almost on a level with the professionals. There are seventeen of these so-called People's Theatres in Leningrad: opera and ballet theatres, musical comedy theatres, drama theatres, and the young
viewers' theatre. There is also an amateur circus.

The recently built Palace of Youth stands on the colourful bank of
the Little Neva (Málaya Névka). Some 5,000 people take up enjoyable
activities here. The Palace of Youth organises athletic competitions
and many kinds of contests, talks and discussions by the young people
having similar professions and performances by amateur and professional artists. Young people of Leningrad have at their disposal
exhibition, dancing and music halls, a rec-room, indoor swimming pool,
library and restaurants. There is a 700-room hotel for the young townspeople's guests.

Another Leningrad club is the 'House of Nature', where members of

The A. Pushkin Drama Theatre. The monument to Catherine II

the Environmentalist Society may attend lectures, see films and visit exhibitions.

The Chigorin Chess Club was named after the founder of the Russian school of chess. Russia's first chess club was formed right here in the City on the Neva in the middle of the 18th century.

Some 200,000 people visit Leningrad's movie theatres daily. In addition to movie theatres there are also hundreds of movie halls in all palaces and houses of culture and clubs throughout the city.

Authors of guidebooks and guides can't seem to get together on the exact number of museums in Leningrad. Some justly feel that each museum open for public viewing should be treated separately. Others no less righteously adhere to the principle of the administrative subordination of certain museums considered to be branches of larger ones. In addition, there exists a large number of exhibits and museums at enterprises, schools and theatres in operation all the time.

Whatever the answer to this question may be, it would take not one week, but months and years to visit all of Leningrad's museums.

It's been estimated that if you spent just half a minute viewing each object in the Hermitage, it would take you ten years to get through the whole museum. More than twenty million people visit Leningrad's museums every year. The most frequently visited ones are the State Hermitage Museum and the Museum of the History of Leningrad and its

The ballet 'Chopiniana' at the S. Kirov Theatre of Opera and Ballet

branches. The Leningrad Branch of the Lenin Central Museum is visited by some two million people yearly.

There are about 2,500 libraries in Leningrad, housing over
50,000,000 books and journals. The Saltykov-Shchedrin Public Library
with a collection of 20,000,000 books and journals is the largest library
in Leningrad and the second largest in the country.

*Leningrad is one of the largest publishing centres in the Soviet
Union,* with over thirty publishing houses in operation here. The yearly
volume of books and pamphlets printed exceed 55,000,000 copies.

An average of 200,000 books and pamphlets are sold daily. The
Leningrad Branch of the All-Union Book Lovers' Society has been
formed here.

There are approximately 400 magazines and other periodicals published in the city, such as the literary and political journals *Zvezdá,
Nevá, Avróra,* and for schoolchildren *Kostyór* and *Ískorka.* The city's
newspapers are *Leningrádskaya právda, Vechérni Leningrád, Sména,
Leningrádsky rabóchi,* and for the young *Léninskye ískry,* etc.

The armoured car 'Enemy of Capital', a relic of the Revolution

Leningrad and Sports

Leningrad has a long tradition in sports. The country's first sailboat races were held here way back in the 18th century. By the way, Tsar Peter I was one of Russia's first yachtsmen.

Leningrad's inhabitants participate in more than fifty kinds of sports. Winter sports and water sports are especially popular. Approximately one out of every five people belongs to a sports club, such as *Dynamo, Spartak, Zenit, Burevestnik,* etc.

Leningrad athletes have participated in every national and the majority of international competitions. Fifty-nine Olympic champions hail from Leningrad. Lyudmila Pinayeva won three Olympic gold medals for rowing, other Olympic heroes from Leningrad are Galina Stepanskaya and Yevgeni Kulikov (skating-race), Nina Baldycheva (skiing), Nadezhda Chizhova (shot putting), Gennadi Shatkov (boxing), Tatyana Kazankina (track and field) and many others.

There are 34 large stadiums in the city. The largest open air arena is Kirov Stadium, with a seating capacity of 100,000. This stadium is slated to host the soccer preliminaries of the 1980 Summer Olympics. The Lenin Stadium seats 30,000 spectators. The indoor Jubilee Sports Palace with its two artificial ice rinks seats 6,000 fans. The Winter Stadium

The main staircase in the Hermitage

The monument to A. Pushkin on Arts Square

holds 5,000 spectators. The newly built 25,000-seat Sports Palace is a unique facility with a regular size indoor soccer field. An all-purpose indoor sports arena with facilities for 17 different kinds of sports is scheduled for completion by 1980.

Approximately 30 km from Leningrad is the town of Kavgolovo, the skiing capital of the country, where international competitions are held. Kavgolovo's biggest ski-jump is 70 metres high.

The city has more than 300 soccer fields, 1,700 basketball, volleyball and tennis courts, 22 swimming pools, 12 rowboat houses, over 300 skating rinks, etc. These statistics far from tell the whole story, as it's practically impossible to get a full count of all sports facilities. They are also to be found in factories, office buildings, schools and in almost every backyard.

All educational establishments also have their own gyms, playgrounds and suburban ski areas.

The *Yubileiny* Sports Palace

Public Transport

The tracks of the Leningrad metro system stretch out a total of more than 50 km. According to the General Urban Development Plan, the metro is to become the main form of public transportation. Today, however, trams, trolleys and buses are as popular as ever. Many people prefer riding a 'route taxi'—a 10-seat minibus. Every day tens of thousands of people use city cabs. The inhabitants of Greater Leningrad find the suburban electric trains convenient, since all the city's railway stations are in the centre of the city and next to metro stations.

National and International Transportation Facilities

After Moscow, *Leningrad is the USSR's leading centre of passenger rail communication.* The railway system connects Leningrad with all major cities in the country. More than half the passengers travelling long distances use the newly reconstructed Moscow Railway Station. The Finland Station has been completely rebuilt. The Vitebsk Railway Station is scheduled to undergo major reconstruction, and the Baltic is to be assigned the routes of one of the city's oldest terminals, the Warsaw Station. The reason all these measures are being taken is that passen-

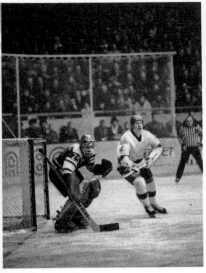

A hockey match

A shop at the S. Kirov Elektrosila
industrial complex

ger flow is expected to more than double by the mid-1980s. Travelling by train has always been one of the main forms of tourism.

The Leningrad Seaport is the largest in the country, and is a maritime centre of international stature. The Gulf of Finland freezes over in winter, but icebreakers make navigation possible all year round.

Some four to five thousand ships from 50 countries arrive at this port yearly. Vessels docking in Leningrad Harbour are met by pilot boats and given navigational assistance, since the eastern part of the Gulf of Finland is rather shallow. The Maritime Canal built in 1875-1885 begins 30 km before the entrance into the harbour. The canal bed was dredged along the bottom of the Gulf of Finland. Its width is 80-120 m.

Regular passenger lines connect Leningrad with Europe's biggest ports. Many tourists come to Leningrad by ship.

Leningrad is the start of the Volga-Baltic Canal—part of a deep-water transport system of rivers, lakes and canals connecting the Baltic and White Seas in the north with the Caspian, Azov and Black Seas in the south. Passenger ships and freight vessels intended for river-sea navigation run this Volga-Baltic route.

Leningrad's new River Terminal meets all the needs of present-day navigation. Tens of thousands of tourists embark on cruises along the rivers and lakes of the European part of the USSR from this terminal. This type of tourism is becoming more and more popular, and tourists from abroad find river cruises especially interesting.

Thirty-five air routes of Soviet planes and 26 routes flown by foreign airlines connect Leningrad with 16 European countries and 105 cities in the Soviet Union. Pulkovo Airport, one of the largest in the country, provides passengers with a maximum of comfort. Coming to Leningrad on chartered flights is popular among tourists today.

Highways branch out from Leningrad in eleven different directions, connecting the City on the Neva with other Soviet cities and foreign countries as well.

Leningrad's International Ties

Leningrad is a member of the World Federation of Twinned Cities, an organisation founded in 1957 and recognised by the UN and UNESCO. Leningrad's mayor has repeatedly been elected Chairman of the Presidium of the Association for relations between Soviet and foreign cities, which is a collective member of the Federation. Every last Sunday in April the citizens of Leningrad observe International Twinned Cities' Day. Among Leningrad's twinned cities are: Bombay (India), Dresden (GDR), Gdansk (Poland), Göteborg (Sweden), Havre (France), Manchester (England), Milan (Italy), Osaka (Japan), Rotterdam (The Netherlands), Santiago de Cuba (Cuba), Turku (Finland), Zagreb (Yugoslavia) — more than thirty cities in all. This is probably where these Leningrad street names come from: Drezdenskaya, Gdanskaya, Manchesterskaya, Havrskaya and Zagrebsky Boulevard. Leningrad maintains ties with twinned cities on many levels, such as municipal government, culture, sports and tourism. These cities traditionally celebrate Leningrad Day, and Leningrad sets aside a day in honour of any one of its twinned cities.

Almost every day Leningrad receives a number of delegations from foreign governments, parties, parliaments, municipalities and trade unions. Friendship Delegations arrive here by ship from Denmark, Finland, German Democratic Republic, Norway, the Polish People's Republic, Sweden, the USA, etc.

Almost all the leading enterprises of the city have in their portfolios orders from foreign companies. Krasny Oktyabr pianos are marketed in many European countries. France imports our colour TV sets and videotape recorders. The products of the Petrodvorets Watch Factory are also popular abroad. The print fabrics manufactured by the Slutskaya Factory are well known in 25 countries. Perfume and Russian folk stringed instruments are also among the goods Leningrad exports to over 100 foreign countries. Leningrad is now exporting more goods of different types to more countries than ever before and these exports will increase with each year to come.

Leningrad is a big importer of industrial equipment and consumer goods.

The city conducts direct trade operations with its nearest neighbour, Finland, through the All-Union Import-Export Association Lenfintorg.

Leningrad holds traditional international fur auctions, which are well known all over the world. Now they are being conducted three times a year—in January, July and a special auction of astrakhan fur in October. The 75th International Fur Auction in 1977 was attended by 250 merchants from 22 countries.

Leningrad design and construction organisations fill orders of foreign countries for building plants, factories, power stations, dams and mines.

The city maintains many various international scientific ties. The

Institutes of the USSR Academy of Sciences are affiliated with 100 scientific institutions all over the world. Joint research is conducted in the fields of medicine and technology as well as a systematic exchange of information and scientific publications. In recent years Leningrad has hosted such scientific forums as the International Symposium on Solar-Terrestrial Physics, the International Congress on Limnology, the International Conference on Luminescence, the International Botanical Congress, the General Conference of the International Council of Museums, the International Congress on Navigation, and the International Symposium on Ethnography.

About 6,000 foreign students from 100 countries study in the city's institutions of higher learning.

One of the most popular tourist spots in the country, Leningrad receives, not counting Soviet tourists, hundreds of thousands of foreign visitors a year. Tourism is blossoming partly because the number of tourist activities has been increased. Right now there are more than twenty types of tours in the Soviet Union which have been very popular: motor tours by car or bus with accommodation in camping grounds, medical treatment and rest at health resorts, tours for hunting and fishing trips, tours to international symposiums, exhibitions, art festivals, sports contests, business tours, 'friendship trains', student tours, etc.

On one of the most beautiful houses in Leningrad there is a tablet with the inscription 'House of Friendship and Peace with the Peoples of Foreign Countries'. Here in its magnificent halls and drawing rooms citizens of Leningrad hold receptions for foreign delegations. All kinds of exhibitions, films and concerts help the hosts and guests get to know one another better.

The Leningrad of Tomorrow

The General Urban Development Plan for Leningrad for the next 20-25 years was approved by the Council of Ministers of the USSR in 1966. This document was drawn up by architects, sociologists, engineers, economists, doctors and representatives of many other professions.

The Plan has found practical application of the ideas set forth in the Programme of the CPSU: to provide the best conditions for living, working, resting and satisfying the material and intellectual needs of the people.

In accordance with the Plan, a number of plants and factories will be moved outside the city limits. Some scientific and research institutes will also be relocated in the suburbs. There they can operate with greater ease and efficiency. Housing developments, schools, children's establishments and stores are also planned for the outskirts of Greater Leningrad. All these measures will allow to control the partial population flow from Leningrad and prevent it from turning into a giant city in which, as other big cities in the world have shown, it would be difficult to provide optimal living conditions.

In keeping with the Plan, the city is being developed concentrically in all directions from its historical nucleus. New thoroughfares are being built onto already existing ones. Cultural and service projects are being constructed along with new housing. The following structures have been erected in the city in recent years: the Oktyabrsky Concert Hall, the Jubilee Sports Palace, the House of Fashion, the *Oktyabr-*

The monument on Victory Square ▶

skaya, Leningrad, Moskva and *Rechnaya* Hotels, the River Terminal, the exhibition facilities in the Harbour and the House of Youth. Pulkovo Airport and the Children's Sports School on Vasilyevsky Island have been recipients of the State Prize. Much attention is given to the architectural appearance of public buildings and various types of enterprises. These ornately architectured structures predominate in entire municipal districts.

Apartment houses being built today are from 9 to 16 storeys high. The city's Main Architectural Planning Board is very cautious about higher buildings. These are to be constructed far from the centre, so as not to clash with the classical architectural design of the central area of the city which urban planners are trying so hard to preserve.

Present-day architects are carrying on the tradition of creating structures along the Neva which are easily visible from far off. Plans are being drawn up for erecting embankments higher up the river, as well as laying out squares by the river's bridges.

The newer areas of the city will preserve its traditional rectilinear design and its soothing architectural silhouette accentuated by separate buildings.

Partial reconstruction of certain blocks in the city built before the Revolution is under way. When major restoration is done, every effort is made to have the buildings' façades retain their original appearance. Wings and annexes in yards, however, are being taken down so as to make room for flower beds, trees and play areas for children. Approximately 200 old apartment buildings are being modernised annually.

More than 1,000 architectural and historical treasures, statues and parks in the city and its many bridges, fountains and iron fences are under government protection. Monuments of the past in the Soviet Union are protected by law. The Leningrad *Restavrator* firm systematically inspects and restores the city's historical and architectural monuments.

The General Urban Development Plan is set to provide the city with a direct exit to the sea. This will eliminate the paradox which has historically plagued Leningrad: although the city has hundred of kilometres of beautiful river embankments and is situated close to the sea, it has no sea embankment. Years ago, boggy sandbanks stretched along the shores of the Gulf of Finland. Before the Revolution, industrial enterprises, warehouses and harbours had been built in areas where the seacoast was a little higher, and these structures weren't particularly noted for their great beauty. Today plans are in the works for creating an imposing seaside façade of the city.

Putting these plans into effect will not be an easy thing. In many areas of the Gulf of Finland the shoreline is so low that it is immediately covered when the tide starts to come in. These areas have to be raised to more than 3 metres above sea-level. This city will thus receive a territory suitable for building four times the size of Vasilyevsky Island.

If you tour The New Maritime District on Vasilyevsky Island, you can see its western part where the landfall has already been completed. There you can see Leningrad's shoreline façade taking shape. The new structure can be seen from as far as Lakhta township, located along Maritime (Primórskoye) Higway and from aboard excursion boats cruising from Leningrad to Petrodvorets.

WHEN SHOULD YOU COME TO LENINGRAD
HOW TO MAKE A TRIP TO LENINGRAD
YOU'VE ARRIVED IN THE CITY
(The Tourist's Notebook)

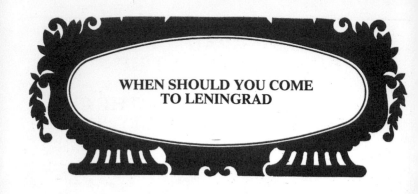

WHEN SHOULD YOU COME TO LENINGRAD

It doesn't make any difference when you come to Leningrad—early in the morning or late at night, early spring or late autumn—if the spirit of the fine and the beautiful breathes within you, you can't help but be charmed by our city. Perhaps you might like to come to Leningrad at midday in January— then you will be greeted by a city robed in a silvery ermine veil of snow, a city austere yet graceful, magnificent and proud...

Incidentally, I hope you will be able to visit the City on the Neva in the second half of June, so you can see Leningrad's most famous wonder, White Nights...

LEV USPENSKY

All in all, Leningrad is a 'city for all seasons'. It has something to offer at any time of the year.

Spring lasts from approximately the 17th of March to 1st of June.

Winds are rarely as strong in spring as they are in winter, and there is less dampness in the air as well. Mornings are still frosty, and at times it can get pretty cool, but as the day wears on, it warms up. The sun shines more often in spring than at any other time of the year, and the winter-hardened people of Leningrad love to soak up its invigorating rays, sunning themselves by the walls of the Peter and Paul Fortress even with ice floes still coursing down the Neva.

The ice on the Neva starts breaking up during the second half of April. The river ice flows about 3 to 5 days, and then for about 10 days, on the average, thick ice-floes of all shapes and designs make their way from Lake Ladoga down the Neva. It's a rarity for anyone from Leningrad not to visit the Neva at this time of the year. It's really a sight to see. The best place to observe everything is from the Vasilyevsky Island Spit (strélka Vasílyevskovo óstrova).

Every April the city sponsors a music festival in which guests from all over the country and abroad join the artists of Leningrad. In this festival only new musical compositions may be performed. There are also discussions on music among the artists, musical critics and the audience. At this time a 'Week of Music for the Children' is held as well.

May 1st is International Workers' Solidarity Day, and a huge holiday demonstration is held in Palace Square (Dvortsóvaya plóshchad).

The Piskaryovskoye Memorial
Cemetery on Victory Day, May 9

Among the participants in the demonstration are foreign students and working people from other countries visiting Leningrad, and in the stands—guests from twinned cities. In the evening parades are held in squares and parks and the city is all lit up.

May 2nd is traditionally accompanied by sports events in honour of the celebration. Bicycle races are held on a track 2.5 km in circumference in the vicinity of Palace Square. Track and field competitions take place in the city's stadiums. Oarsmen compete along the River Malaya Nevka. A great sports festival is held in Kirov Stadium.

May 9th is Victory Day. From early in the morning an endless stream of vehicular and pedestrian traffic makes its way toward Piskaryovskoye Cemetery, where the people of the city come to honour the memory of the soldiers and civilians who perished during the blockade. A cortege of motorcycles accompanies a line of vehicles bearing city and military banners. The banners are lowered and heads are bowed in a moment of silence. Innumerable wreaths and bouquets of flowers are laid at the foot of the Monument to the Motherland.

On this day large crowds gather around the Monument to the Heroic Defenders of Leningrad, which was erected in 1975 in Victory Square. Former soldiers who defended the world from fascism designate places where they can get together with their buddies from the same outfit. Newspapers print announcements to this effect entitled 'Veterans, let's get together!'

Every May 9th a converging-race is held. Palace (Dvortsóvaya) Square is the finish line of this 8-kilometre run. In the evening there are fireworks in honour of the holiday. Multi-coloured rockets are shot up into the sky from the Neva embankments, Maritime Glory Square (Plóshchad Morskóy slávy) and from other streets and squares in the city.

Every spring a forever-young Leningrad invites its guests to see its festive ceremonies, its sports and cultural celebrations, and simply to stroll along its bright, spring sun-drenched avenues.

Summer lasts from approximately the 2nd of June to the 11th of September.

The sun hardly descends beyond the horizon before it rises again. It is so bright, that there is no need for street lamps; as a matter of fact they are not used for two months before July 20 or thereabouts.

> *It's midnight and it's still light outside. See how inexpressibly distinct, imposing and aloof the spires of the Peter and Paul Fortress and its twin the Admiralty stand out silhouetted in this white radiance. It seems these White Nights of Leningrad were created just for connoisseurs of architecture—every architectural detail becomes so clear and expressive in their light: how the bell towers pierce the sky; how the opal waters of the Neva glimmer; how wide these two fiery wings stretch over the city, these summer lights of morning and evening almost seem to touch ends.*
> *You haven't seen this? What you're missing out on!*

LEV USPENSKY

The poetic White Nights coincide with school proms, after which the former schoolchildren stroll over to the Neva. At the beginning of July a youth festival is traditionally held, symbolically called 'Crimson Sails' (Áliye parusá). A romantic novel by the Russian writer Alexander Grin entitled *Crimson Sails* (1923) speaks of a happiness that comes to those who believe in dreaming. On this festive night, the Neva from the area of the Palace (Dvortsóvy) Bridge to the Kirov Bridge is transformed into a giant theatrical stage. Hundreds of boats fill the river, some rigged up like old schooners. Ships' cannons fire, rockets flare, and powerful streams of water from moving fountains soar into the air.

During White Nights, Leningrad's townfolk love to take boatrides along the waterways of the city. The silhouettes of the shores in the pale light are just breathtaking.

In 1958 the city initiated the annual *White Nights Festival of the Arts*. It lasts from June 21st to the 29th. At this time Leningrad's theatres and concert halls present the finest the city has to offer. Leningrad's music and stage stars make sure they are in their home town for this festival. Any concert during the White Nights Festival is considered a big event. In Petrodvorets you can see a truly enchanting spectacle: artists of the famed Leningrad Ballet Company performing to a background of rainbow-like streams of water—creating a truly magic effect.

Thousands of Soviet and foreign tourists come to the White Nights Festival. All you have to do is buy the appropriate tour, and you will be able to see all the interesting things going on in Leningrad at this time.

Autumn lasts from approximately September 12th to December 4th.

In September the Leningrad weather is very mild, but it gets much colder in October. Of course, it rains a lot, too. October often experiences an 'Indian Summer' when warm, sunny and calm weather returns for

Pavlovsk Park

a while. Leningrad's environs are quite nice at this time, especially in Petrodvorets, Pushkin and Pavlovsk Parks.

Autumn marks the end of the Leningrad sports season. According to a tradition more than fifty years old, a 30-kilometre marathon race is held at the end of September or the beginning of October which starts in the town of Pushkin and winds up in Leningrad's Palace Square. In recent years Finnish athletes have also participated in this competition.

Autumn is the time when Leningrad along with the rest of the country celebrates the biggest Soviet holiday—the anniversary of the Great October Socialist Revolution. Leningrad has its own way of observing this event. Before the official ceremonies begin, ships from the Baltic Fleet enter the Neva. At night their silhouettes are outlined by a string of electric lights. The Neva glimmers with the fiery torches high atop the Rostral Columns and the Peter and Paul Fortress.

On November 7th a traditional military parade is held in Palace Square, followed by a mass demonstration. In front march veterans who actually took part in the Revolution.

52

The festivities conclude with a fireworks display at night and artillery salutes in honour of this national holiday.

The autumnal days grow shorter and shorter. When it gets dark the monuments, palaces and cathedrals create a special effect all lit up.

Autumn has its advantages. This is the time of year when Leningrad welcomes its theatre-goers and music lovers to the opening of the new season.

Winter lasts from about the 5th of December to the 16th of March.

The first half of winter is usually warmer than the second half. The sun does not shine often, and when it does, it does not rise high over the horizon; this type of light gives a special warm colouration to the façades of buildings. Leningrad is magnificent in its snowy mantle. Because of the fickle weather, severe frosts are sometimes followed by warm spells. Then the walls of massive buildings, park fences and bare black tree branches become covered with long (several centimetres) silver icicles. Leningrad looks like a real fairy-tale town.

The people of Leningrad love winter, and they prepare themselves for its coming. The canals are covered with snow and ice, but the Neva is kept clear by ice-breakers working around the clock: the river must carry away the snow that's removed from the city's streets to the Gulf of Finland.

Homes are always warm—there is central heating everywhere. But many people prefer keeping active in their spare time rather than sitting at home. They spend their free moments walking or engaging in every type of winter sports imaginable.

Skiing is most popular. It is a rare family that does not own at least one pair of skis. Many enterprises and organisations have their own ski lodges outside the city where people come without equipment and get everything they need. On weekends special trains called Ski Lines take sportsmen to their favourite slopes and later bring them back to the city.

Stadiums, parks and yards turn into ice-skating rinks. The many schools and clubs where children of all ages—even tots—are taught how to skate are very popular.

In winter yachtsmen change over to ice-boats—sailboats on gigantic ice-skates.

Motor races are also held on ice-tracks.

Other kinds of winter sports are popular as well, such as ice-fishing. Fishermen walk a good distance—a few kilometres—out onto the Gulf of Finland, or they pick out one of the many suburban lakes. There is a reservoir with a fishing club which organises a contest every winter for the most fish caught.

It is not surprising to see people swimming in the Neva during the most severe frost. Small areas of the river are cleared of ice, and the 'health nuts' who swim in them are called 'Walruses', since like real walruses who inhabit the Polar regions, these people are not afraid of icy water. There are over five hundred 'Walruses', and they belong to the *Bolshaya Neva* Swimming Club.

The *Russian Winter* Festival is held in the Kirov Central Park of Culture and Rest, with its traditional troika rides and other Russian folk customs.

HOW TO MAKE A TRIP TO LENINGRAD

INTERNATIONAL RAILROAD LINES TO LENINGRAD:

Point of Departure	Travel Time
Berlin	32 hrs., 43 min.
Budapest	44 hrs., 05 min.
Bucharest	44 hrs., 40 min.
Dresden	33 hrs., 00 min.
Helsinki	12 hrs., 40 min.
Paris	48 hrs., 10 min.

Pulkovo Airport

Prague	49 hrs., 00 min.
Sofia	55 hrs., 29 min.
Warsaw	22 hrs., 26 min.

FLYING TIME TO LENINGRAD FROM EUROPE'S LARGEST CITIES:

Point of Departure	Travel Time
Amsterdam (via Stockholm)	4 hrs., 35 min.
Belgrade	3 hrs., 15 min.
Berlin	2 hrs., 25 min.
Budapest	2 hrs., 40 min.
Budapest (via Warsaw)	4 hrs., 00 min.
Burgas	2 hrs., 25 min.
Copenhagen	1 hr., 45 min.
Hamburg	2 hrs., 25 min.
Helsinki	1 hr., 05 min.
London (via Copenhagen)	4 hrs., 40 min.
Moscow	1 hr., 00 min.
Oslo (via Stockholm)	3 hrs., 25 min.
Paris	3 hrs., 20 min.
Sofia	3 hrs., 20 min.
Stockholm	1 hr., 25 min.
Warsaw	1 hr., 55 min.
Zurich	3 hrs., 30 min.

REGULAR PASSENGER SHIP ROUTES

Leningrad — Bremerhaven
Leningrad — Havre
Leningrad — Copenhagen
Leningrad — London
Leningrad — Stockholm
Leningrad — Helsinki
Leningrad — Montreal (via Bremerhaven, London, Havre)
Leningrad — New York (via Bremerhaven, London, Havre)

Tourists coming to Leningrad by water are accommodated on board ship during their stay in the city.

ENTRY AND EXIT BORDER POINTS FOR MOTOR TOURISTS

The following cities bordering Finland, Poland, Czechoslovakia, Hungary and Ru-

54

Palace Square

...mania are year-round entry points for tourists travelling by car: Vyborg (Torfyanovka, Brusnichnoye), Nuijamaa, Brest, Shegini, Uzhgorod, Chop, Porubnoye and Lyasheny.

Foreign tourists are allowed travel in the Soviet Union in private cars or foreign firms' motor-coaches, or they can rent a car or motor-coach from Intourist.

CUSTOMS AND CURRENCY REGULATIONS

Like any other country, the Soviet Union has certain regulations regarding customs and currency. Strict adherence to them will keep you from any unwanted misunderstandings and difficulties that may arise from not knowing or from misinterpreting these regulations.

The official currency of the USSR is the rouble. Bringing in or taking out and sending Soviet currency in or out of the country is strictly forbidden. An exception is made for citizens of socialist countries visiting the Soviet Union, who may carry in specific amounts of Soviet currency obtained in their respective countries' banks and may carry out any unspent Soviet money to return it to their respective countries' banks.

Foreign tourists may bring into the USSR any amount of declared foreign currency in cash or payment vouchers, precious metals (gold, silver, platinum and platiniferous metals in bullion, scrap or raw), precious stones, pearls and articles manufactured therefrom with the exception of gold coins. The Customs Declaration blank in which all foreign currency and valuables are listed is the basis for the free and unimpeded conveyance of the said currency and valuables out of the country, as well as for concluding other transactions with imported valuables within the USSR.

Any transaction with foreign currency or valuables other than through state banking agencies is strictly forbidden on Soviet territory.

Foreign currency and checks may be exchanged into roubles at the Bank for Foreign Trade of the USSR, its branches, and exchange offices and at exchange offices of the USSR State Bank, which are located practically all over the country. Any cashing foreign currency accepted by the USSR State Bank may be exchanged. Foreign currency is exchanged at the official exchange rates of the USSR State Bank which are published every month.

When exchanging foreign currency into roubles on the basis of the customs declaration, the tourist is given a registration receipt enabling him to re-exchange any unspent roubles back into foreign currency upon departure.

Tourists are allowed to bring duty-free into the USSR items intended solely for personal use: clothes, footwear, underwear and linen, tourist and sports accessories, perfume, cosmetics, etc., in amounts appropriate for their length of stay in the country and according to season. In addition, tourists may bring duty-free (per person): one camera and one non-professional movie camera with accessories, one portable typewriter and inexpensive souvenirs in reasonable quantities.

Tourists coming to the USSR for hunting may take along hunting weapons. To do this they must have a voucher from Intourist or any foreign tourist agency confirming the purpose of the trip and the existence of the hunting weapons. Any hunting weapons brought into the country must be taken out.

Tourists coming to the USSR by auto pay no duty for their vehicles, but they are under obligation to take them out when leaving the country.

Tourists are allowed to take out of the country any objects bought in shops with Soviet currency obtained from the Bank for Foreign Trade of the USSR or branches of the USSR State Bank in exchange for foreign currency. Goods bought by foreign tourists in specialized shops and at other trade organisations with foreign currency may be taken out of the USSR without restriction. For such objects tourists should keep a corresponding shop bill or shop certificate.

The following items are forbidden to be brought into the USSR: fire- and side arms and ammunition therefore, gun powder and explosives, virulent poisons opium, hashish and other narcotics, device for smoking these drugs, pornographic literature and pictures, books, photographic and movie films, gramophone records, manuscripts, etc., which are politically and economically harmful to the USSR.

The following items are forbidden to be taken out of the USSR: fire- and side arms and ammunition therefore, gun powder and explosives, virulent poisons opium, hashish and other narcotics, device for smoking them, cancelled securities. Antiques and works of art (paintings, sculpture, icons, carpets, furniture, fabrics, ornaments, manuscripts, books, etc.) may be taken out of the country only by special permission from the USSR Ministry of Culture and are subject to a customs tax of 100 per cent of the price indicated in the exit licence. Detailed information about customs and currency regulations can be found in the General Rates and Regulations for Foreign Tourists annually issued by Intourist.

One of the embankments

YOU'VE ARRIVED IN THE CITY
(The Tourist's Notebook)

USEFUL INFORMATION

If you've come as a tourist, you will be met by representatives of Intourist or the *Sputnik* International Youth Travel Bureau. If it's a business tour, you will be met by representatives of the organisation or firm you will be working in conjunction with. Whatever the case, these people will help you get through the necessary formalities and will take care of your baggage, transportation and the hotel.

If by any chance there should be a foul-up and you are not met when you arrive, approach any airport, rail or seaport clerk or militiaman and say the word 'Intourist'. Someone will either take you to Intourist personnel or call one of the numbers listed below. These telephones are manned by people who speak foreign languages.

Pulkovo Airport (24 hours a day) — 291-85-90.

Moscow Railway Station (from 9 a.m. to midnight — 219-46-45.

The Passenger Maritime Port on Vasilyvsky Island — 217-03-20.

The address of the *Central Service Department of the Leningrad Amalgamation of the USSR Company for Foreign Travel 'Intourist':* 11 St. Isaac's Square (opposite the *Astoria* Hotel), tel.:211-51-29.

The address of the *Leningrad Branch of the Sputnik International Youth Travel Bureau:* 4 Chapygin Str. *(Druzhba* Hotel), tel.: 238-34-02.

ADDRESSES OF RECOMMENDED HOTELS
Intourist hotels are marked with an asterisk.

* *Astoria* — 39 Herzen Str. Nearest Metro station — Nevsky Prospekt.

Baltiyskaya — 57 Nevsky Prospekt. Nearest Metro station — Mayakovskaya.

Druzhba — 4 Chapygin Str. Nearest Metro station — Petrogradskaya.

* *Karelia* — Tukhachevsky Str. (in the Harbour area).

Kievskaya — 49 Dnepropetrovskaya Str.

Ladoga — 26 Shaumyan Avenue.

* *Leningrad* — 5/2 Pirogov Emb. Nearest Metro station — Ploshchad Lenina.

Mir — 17-19 Gastello Str. Nearest Metro station — Párk Pobédy (Victory Park).

The *Leningrad* Hotel

* *Moskva* — Nevsky Prospekt. Nearest Metro station — Ploshchad Alexandra Nevskovo.

Moskovskaya — 43/45 Ligovo Avenue. Nearest Metro station — Ploshchad Vosstaniya.

Oktyabrskaya — 10 Ligovo Avenue. Nearest Metro station — Ploshchad Vosstaniya.

* *Pribaltiiskaya* — Tukhachevsky Str. (in the Harbour area).

Rossiya — 163 Moskovsky Avenue. Nearest Metro station — Párk Pobédy.

Sovetskaya — 43 Lermontovsky Avenue. Nearest Metro station — Baltíisky Vokzál (Baltic Station).

Sputnik — 34 Moris Thorez Avenue. Nearest Metro station — Ploshchad Muzhestva.

Vyborgskaya — 3 Torzhkovskaya Str.

* *Yevropeiskaya* — 1/7 Brodsky Str. Nearest Metro station — Nevsky Prospekt.

Zarya — 40 Kurskaya Str.

> *Where do you go with your thousand and one questions? To your hotel's service bureau, of course!*

In whatever hotel you are staying, the service bureau will answer any questions you may have regarding your stay in the USSR and render all assistance in connection with tourist services. It will arrange excursions for you through the city and its environs, to museums; it will arrange transportation as well. In addition, the service bureau can order tickets to the theatre, circus, concerts and sports events. It will supply you with information about where to shop, where to have a camera or watch fixed, or what to do if you've misplaced or forgotten something, etc.

The hotel service bureau is open from 9 a.m. to 9 p.m. At any other time, see the hotel manager or the floor clerk.

FOREIGN CURRENCY EXCHANGE

Foreign currency may be exchanged at the airport, the Maritime Port and in the *Astoria, Yevropeiskaya, Karelia, Leningrad, Moskva* and *Pribaltiiskaya* hotels daily from 9 a.m. to 8 p.m. (closed during lunch hour — 2-3 p.m.) You may exchange any unspent money at the airport or the Maritime Port.

Soviet Currency Denominations:
Bank-notes: 100, 50, 25, 10, 5, 3, 1 (roubles)
Nickel coins: 1 rouble piece, 50, 20, 15, 10 (kopecks)
Bronze coins: 5, 3, 2, 1 (kopecks)
There are 100 kopecks in a rouble.

THE POST OFFICE, TELEGRAPH AND TELEPHONE

Postcards, stamps, and envelopes are sold at news-stands and post offices. Mail boxes come in two colours — red, for local (Leningrad) mail and blue, for mail going to all other destinations. Special delivery letters, printed matter and telegrams may be sent through the hotel post office or another branch of the city post office.

The Leningrad Central Post Office — 9 Communications Union Str.

The Leningrad Central Telegraph — 1 Communications Union Str. Packages to other countries may be sent at three post offices:

Post Office Branch C-400 (6 Nevsky Prospekt.) Open 10 a.m. - 8 p.m., 7 day a week. Handles all postal and telegraph transactions as well as international phone calls to every country.

Clerks at this post office speak foreign languages. This is where all correspondence comes for foreign guests staying in Leningrad when the hotel is not readily known or when the addressee himself has indicated his address as 'Leningrad, C-400 General Delivery'. Letters are kept for 30 days, telegrams — 45 days.

Central Post Office (9 Communication Union Str.) Open 9 a.m.-9p.m., Sundays – 10 a.m.-8 p.m.

Oktyabrskaya Hotel Post Office (10 Ligovo Avenue, opposite the Moscow Railway Station). Open 9 a.m.-10 p.m., Sundays 9 a.m.-4 p.m. (Telegrams on Sunday — 9 a.m.-10 p.m.)

The Soviet Union has certain regulations on objects which may be sent abroad by mail. The following may not be mailed: jewellery, amber pieces, antiques, all types of film, unused and cancelled postal stamps, etc. If you have any questions in this regard, call the C-400 Post Office (Tel.: 219-74-94). Foreign postal and telegraph rates may vary with different countries depending on the agreements the Soviet Union has with these countries.

Telephone calls to other Soviet cities and abroad may be ordered through the service bureau of your hotel, and you can talk straight from your room. If you wish, you can place long-distance phone calls yourself at a call office; a full list of call offices is available at the hotel service bureau. A four minute local call from a public phone booth costs two kopecks.

Leningrad also has a 'Home Service' through which you can have the following mailed out: telegrams, special delivery and registered mail and printed matter, cash remittances and parcels. You can phone for these services from 8 a.m. to 7 p.m. (Tel.: 273-01-36).

PUBLIC TRANSPORT: HOURS OF OPERATION, FARES

Type of Transport	Hours of Operation	Fares	Charge per Piece of Baggage over 30 kg or 60 × 40 × 20 cm.
Bus	6 a.m. — 1 a.m.	5 kopecks	10 kopecks
Trolleybus	6 a.m. — 1 a.m.	4 kopecks	10 kopecks
Tram	5.30 a.m. — 1 a.m.	3 kopecks	10 kopecks
Metro	6 a.m. — 1 a.m.	5 kopecks	two 5-kopecks pieces
Route Taxi		15 kopecks	no extra charge
City Taxi	24 hours a day	40 kopecks for first kilometre; 20 kopecks for each additional kilometre	no extra charge

Children up to seven years of age ride free on all forms of transportation.

All forms of ground transportation operate without a conductor.

Buses, trolleybuses and trams have special money boxes where you drop the fare in and take a ticket. One ticket is good for one ride the whole length of the route in one direction. You should hold onto the ticket until the end of the trip.

In route taxis the fare is collected by the driver.

Vestibules of metro stations have coin machines for changing 20-, 15-, and 10-kopeck pieces into 5-kopeck pieces. You can travel to any point on the metro without paying an extra fare for changes.

On any form of ground transportation you can ask the driver for transit coupons (ten to a pack). When you get on a bus, tram or trolley, you date one of these coupons with a special punch usually located next to the ticket box.

The best way to order a taxi is through the service bureau of your hotel or take one at a taxi stand. Cruising taxis have a green light on the windshield. If a taxi with the green light on does not stop when you hail it, it means the driver is answering a radio call.

The taxi fare is registered on a meter.

IF YOU HAVE YOUR OWN CAR

You are probably aware that traffic flows on the right-hand side of the street. It goes without saying, drinking and driving don't mix.

Honking is not allowed in the city (except, of course, in emergencies, such as preventing an accident).

International traffic signs are used.

Unless otherwise indicated, the city speed limit is 60 km per hour, 80 km per hour in the suburbs. In areas where the speed limit is lifted, there are special signs posted to this effect.

Parking is free, and allowed except at bus and trolleybus stops and in areas indicated by 'No Parking' signs. There are also parking lots requiring payment. They are in operation around the clock. (Daily rates for cars — 30 kopecks, for buses — 50 kopecks.)

If you do not insure your car when you cross the border, you may still do so in Leningrad, at the Ingosstrakh Foreign Insurance Agency (17 Kalyayev Str.). You may insure your vehicle against civil liability arising from damage or injury to third persons when travelling on Soviet territory, as well as against accidents.

Addresses of recommended parking lots: St. Isaac's Square (near the *Astoria* Hotel), tel. 212-20-42; Moscow Avenue (near the *Rossiya* Hotel), tel. 298-76-74; 5 Pérvaya Staroderevénskaya Str. (entering the city from the direction of Vyborg), tel 239-20-50; Torzhkovskaya Str. (near the *Vyborgskaya* Hotel not far from Maritime Highway), tel. 46-39-52. We recommend the Service Station nearby the *Olgino* camping site (19 kilometres on Maritime Highway) They do repair work and towing, and have parts for Soviet-made cars in stock. Payments for repair work are made in accordance with set price standards.

The *Olgino* and *Repino* camping sites on Maritime Highway are open from May through August. If you plan to stop over here, be sure to make reservations in advance.

The newly-built *Olgino* motel and camping site is situated on the shore of the Gulf of Finland. Vacationers at the *Repino* camping site have use of the *Dyuny* Holiday Hotel beach.

Tourists are given space for pitching tents, or if they prefer, they may stay in a bungalow or regular cottage. For those who prefer to do their own cooking, there are kitchens equipped with gas stoves and refrigerators. Other conveniences provided for motoring tourists are: postal and telegraph services, news-stands with the latest newspapers and magazines in Russian and foreign languages, sports grounds, and restaurants and cafés featuring national dishes etc.

RULES FOR TAKING MOVIES AND PICTURES

In Leningrad tourists may take snapshots and moving film of architectural places of interest, public buildings, theatres, apartment buildings, museums, streets and squares. However, like other countries, the Soviet Union has certain ethical standards and regulations regarding picture taking, adherence to which will prevent any possible misunderstandings.

In taking pictures of people bear in mind that many people do not like to be photographed unless you first ask their permission to do so. Photographs and movies at factories, farms, offices and educational establishments may be taken only with the permission of the administration of the organisation concerned.

It is forbidden to take pictures of military objects and installations, seaports, airports, rail terminals, bridges, tunnels, radio stations and similar structures. No pictures may be taken from on board aircraft.

WORKDAYS AND HOLIDAYS

As in other Soviet cities, Leningrad's factory and office workers have a five-day work week. Saturdays and Sundays are days off.

The workday in offices starts at 9 or 10 in the morning.

The following are (non-working) holidays in the USSR: January 1 (New Year), March 8 (International Women's Day), May 1-2 (International Workers' Solidarity Day), May 9 (Victory Day), October 7 (Constitution Day), November 7-8 (the anniversary of the Great October Socialist Revolution).

SHOPS

Department Stores in the Centre of the City:

Gostiny Dvor — 67 Nevsky Prospekt; *Leningrad Commerce House* (Dom Leningrádskoi torgóvli) —21-23 Zhelyabov Str.; *Passage* (ladies' goods) —48 Nevsky Prospekt.

Specialty Shops

Records (Grammplastínki) —32-34 Nevsky Prospekt; *Paintings, sculptures, objects of applied art* —8 and 45 Nevsky Prospekt; *Souvenirs* (Suveniry) — 26 Nevsky Prospekt; *Photographic Goods* (Fototovary) —61 Litéiny Avenue and 92 Nevsky Prospekt; *Watches* ('Kosmos') —57 Nevsky Prospekt; *'Beryozka'* Shop —26 Herzen Str.; 43 Lermontov Avenue, in the *Sovietskaya* Hotel.

Bookshops

Akademkniga (run by the USSR Academy of Sciences) —57 Liteiny Avenue; *Book House (Dom knigi)* —28 Nevsky Prospekt; *World (Mir)* (books produced by the socialist countries) — 16 Nevsky Prospekt; *Sheet Music (Noty)* —26 Nevsky Prospekt; *Slides ('Globus')* —78 Nevsky Prospekt; *Prints, reproductions* — 72 Nevsky Prospekt.

BON APÉTIT

If real Russian cooking is what you want, visit the *Sadko* Restaurant (1/7 Brodsky Str.). At the *Fregat* (39/14 Grand Avenue, Vasilyevsky Island) you can also try traditional Russian dishes.

For those with a flair for the exotic we suggest the *Kronwerk* Restaurant. It is situated on a three-masted ship anchored by the walls of the Peter and Paul Fortress in Kronwerk Strait.

For your further dining pleasure may we recommend:

Restaurants:

Astoria —2 St. Isaac's Sq.
Baku —12/23 Garden Str. (Sadóvaya)
Kavkazsky —25 Nevsky Prospekt
Leningrad —5 Pirogov Emb.
Metropol —22 Garden Str.
Moskva —49 Nevsky Prospekt
Neva —46 Nevsky Prospekt

The *Kronwerk* Restaurant

Olen —71 Maritime (Primorsky) Avenue, town of Zelenogorsk
Sovietsky —43 Lermontov Avenue
Yevropeisky —1/7 Brodsky Str.

Cafés:

Avrora —60 Nevsky Prospekt
Beliye Nochi —41 Mayorov Str.
Lakomka —22 Garden Str.
Leningrad —96 Nevsky Prospekt
Ogonyok —24 Nevsky Prospekt
Pogrebok —7 Gogol Str.
Svetlyachok —100 Nevsky Prospekt
Ulybka —79 Nevsky Prospekt

**SOME STATE
AND PUBLIC ORGANISATIONS
AND AGENCIES DEALING
WITH FOREIGN VISITORS:**

The Leningrad Branch of the Bank for Foreign Trade of the USSR —2 Brodsky Str.

The Leningrad Amalgamation of the USSR Company for Foreign Travel Intourist —11 St. Isaac's Sq.

The Ingosstrakh (Foreign Insurance Agency) —17 Kalyayev Str.

The Leningrad Branch of the Union of Societies for Friendship and Cultural Ties with the Peoples of Foreign Countries —21 Fontanka Emb.

The Leningrad Branch of the Sputnik International Youth Travel Bureau —4 Chapygin Str.

The Culture Centre

At the initiative of the Intourist Leningrad Amalgamation, a Culture Centre has been set up for foreign tourists in the city, which is in operation from the beginning of May through October. At present this centre is located in the *Nevsky* Palace of Culture—an edifice built for the personnel of the Nevsky Engineering Factory named after Lenin.

Discussions are held here for foreign tourists about life in the Soviet Union. Leningrad's guests can watch documentary films, newsreels and movies in foreign languages, and attend performances of top vocal and choreographic ensembles. Address of the Culture Centre: 32, Obúkhovskaya oboróna Avenue. *Public transport.* Bus—70; Trams—7, 8, 17, 27, 38, 44 to the *Nevsky* Culture Palace. Tel. 265-13-70.

THEATRES AND CONCERT HALLS

Ballet on Ice—Yubileiny Sports Palace, 18 Dobrolyubov Avenue. *Public transport.* Trolleybuses—6, 7, 12; Bus—49; Trams—1, 6, 8, 18, 21, 33, 37, 40.
Created in 1967. Repertoire includes choreographic miniatures and dancing.

Bolshoi Puppet Theatre—10 Nekrasov Str. 517 seats. *Public transport:* Trolleybuses—3, 8, 11, 13, 15, 19, 23; Buses—6, 7, 22, 43; Trams—5, 7, 9, 12, 13, 14, 17, 19, 24, 25, 28, 32, 34.
Founded in 1931. Shows for children and adults.

The Childrens' Theatre—46/48 Suburban Avenue. 998 seats. *Public transport:* Trolleybuses—2, 3, 8, 9, 11, 13, 15; Buses—30, 45; Trams—9, 11, 27, 28, 34; Metro station—Pushkinskaya.
One of the country's first theatres for children. Founded in 1922.

The Circus—3 River Fontanka Emb. 2,465 seats. *Public transport:* Trolleybuses—3, 8, 11, 13, 15, 19; Buses—23, 25; Trams—2, 3, 5, 7, 9, 13, 14, 19, 22, 24, 28, 34.

The country's oldest circus. The Leningrad Circus has a Museum of Circus Art (see the section on 'Museums').

Shows start at 7 p. m., concerts at 7.30 p. m.

The Comedy Theatre—56 Nevsky Prospekt. 900 seats. *Public transport:* Trolleybuses—1, 5, 7, 14, 22; Buses—3, 4, 6, 7, 14, 22, 25, 27, 43, 45, 70, 90; Trams—2, 3, 5, 13, 14, 24; Metro stations—Nevsky Prospekt, Gostiny Dvor.

For further information, see the chapter 'The Main Thorougfare—Nevsky Prospekt'.

The Glinka Academic Capelle—11 Zhelyabov Str., 20 River Moika Emb. 803 seats. *Public transport:* Trolleybuses—1, 5, 7, 10, 14, 22; Buses—2, 3, 4, 6, 7, 14, 22, 44, 45, 47, 100.

In the building of the Capelle you can hear both choral and instrumental concerts. The building was reconstructed between 1866 and 1889. Architect—L. Benoit.

The Gorky Bolshoi Theatre of Drama—65 River Fontanka Emb. 1,412 seats. *Public transport:* Trolleybuses—2, 3, 8, 9, 11, 13, 15; Buses—14, 25, 30, 43; Trams—2, 3, 5, 9, 11, 13, 14, 24, 27, 28, 34.

The first drama theatre created in Petrograd. Opened in 1919 as a 'theatre of tragedy, romantic drama and high comedy'. Its head director since 1956—People's Artist of the USSR G. Tovstonogov. The theatre's repertoire includes Russian, Soviet and foreign classics and works of contemporary playwrights. Characteristic of this theatre is its tendency to portray the sharp struggles and clashes of life in a vividly realistic form, as well as a tendency toward broad socio-historical generalisations.

The building was constructed in the 1870s. Architect—L. Fontana.

The Kirov Theatre of Opera and Ballet—1 Theatre Sq. 1,774 seats. *Public*

transport: Buses—2, 3, 22, 43, 49, 50, 90, 100; Trams—1, 5, 8, 11, 15, 21, 24, 31, 33, 36, 42.

For further information, see the chapter 'Theatre Square and Places of Interest in the Vicinity'.

The Komissarzhevskaya Theatre of Drama—19 Rakov Str. 916 seats. *Public transport:* Trolleybuses—1, 5, 7, 10, 14, 22; Buses—3, 4, 6, 7, 14, 22, 23, 25, 44, 45, 70, 90; Trams—2, 3, 5, 7, 12, 13, 14, 24, 34; Metro stations—Nevsky Prospekt, Gostiny Dvor.

For further information, see the chapter 'The Main Thoroughfare—Nevsky Prospekt'.

The Lenin Komsomol Theatre—4 Lenin Park. 1,520 seats. *Public transport:* Buses—10, 25, 45; Trams—3, 6, 12, 25, 26, 31, 34; Metro station—Gorkovskaya.

A theatre for young people. Founded in 1936. Building constructed in 1939. Architects—N. Miturich and V. Makashev.

The Lensoviet Theatre—12 Vladimirsky Avenue. 1,024 seats. *Public transport:* Trolleybuses—1, 3, 5, 7, 8, 10, 11, 13, 14, 15, 19, 22, 23; Buses—3, 4, 6, 7, 22, 27, 43, 44, 45; Trams—9, 11, 22, 28, 34; Metro station—Vladimirskaya.

Founded in 1939. Repertoire includes Russian, Soviet and foreign classics and works of modern playwrights.

Building constructed in the 1820s. Architect—A. Mikhailov.

The Maly Theatre of Opera and Ballet—1 Arts Sq. 1,212 seats. *Public transport:* Trolleybuses—1, 5, 7, 10, 14, 22; Buses—3, 4, 6, 7, 14, 22, 23, 25, 44, 45, 70, 90; Trams—2, 3, 5, 7, 12, 13, 14, 24, 34; Metro stations—Nevsky Prospekt, Gostiny Dvor.

For further information, see the chapter 'The Main Thoroughfare—Nevsky Prospekt'.

The Music Hall. The Lensoviet Palace of Culture—42 Kirov Avenue. *Public transport:* Trolleybuses—1, 31; Buses—23, 25, 46, 65, 80; Metro station—Petrogradskaya.

Opened in 1967, Troupe often tours the cities of the Soviet Union and abroad: France, GDR, Poland, etc.

The Oktyabrsky Concert Hall—6 Ligovo Avenue. 4,000 seats. *Public transport:* Trolleybuses—1, 5, 7, 10, 14, 22; Buses—3, 6, 7, 22, 27, 30, 44, 46, 85, 120; Trams— 10, 16, 19, 25, 27, 44, 49; Metro station—Ploshchad Vosstaniya.

The largest concert hall in Leningrad.

The building (1967). Architect—V. Kamensky and others. The frieze on the façade by M. Anikushin.

The Puppet Theatre—52 Nevsky Prospekt. 271 seats. *Public transport:* Trolleybuses—1, 5, 7, 14, 22; Buses—3, 4, 6, 7, 14, 22, 25, 27, 43, 45, 70, 90; Trams—2, 3, 5, 13, 14, 24; Metro stations—Nevsky Prospekt, Gostiny Dvor.

One of the oldest puppet theatres in the country. Founded in 1918. Shows mainly for younger children.

The Pushkin Academic Theatre of Drama—2 Ostrovsky Sq. 1,372 seats. *Public transport:* Trolleybuses—1, 5, 7, 14, 22; Buses—3, 4, 6, 7, 14, 22, 25, 27, 43, 45, 70, 90; Trams—2, 3, 5, 13, 14, 24; Metro stations—Nevsky Prospekt, Gostiny Dvor.

For further information, see the chapter 'The Main Thoroughfare—Nevsky Prospekt'.

The Rimsky-Korsakov Leningrad Conservatoire Opera Studio—3 Theatre Sq. 1,718 seats. *Public transport:* Buses—2, 3, 22, 43, 49, 50, 90, 100; Trams—1, 5, 8, 11, 15, 21, 24, 31, 33, 36, 42.

For further information, see the chapter 'Theatre Square and Places of Interest in the Vicinity'.

The Shostakovich Leningrad Philharmonic. Bolshoi Hall—2 Brodsky Str. 1,318 seats. *The Glinka Maly Hall*—30 Nevsky Prospekt. 475 seats. *Public transport:* Trolleybuses—1, 5, 7, 10, 14, 22; Buses—3, 4, 6, 7, 14, 22, 23, 25, 44, 45, 70, 90; Trams—2, 3, 5, 7, 12, 13, 14, 24, 34; Metro stations—Nevsky Prospekt, Gostiny Dvor.

For further information, see the chapter 'The Main Thoroughfare—Nevsky Prospekt'.

The Theatre of Musical Comedy— 13 Rakov Str. 1,592 seats. *Public transport:*

Trolleybuses—1, 5, 7, 10, 14, 22; Buses—3, 4 6, 7, 14, 22, 23, 25, 44, 45, 70, 90; Trams—2, 3 5, 7, 12, 13, 14, 24, 34; Metro stations— Nevsky Prospekt, Gostiny Dvor.

For further information, see the chapter 'The Main Thoroughfare—Nevsky Prospekt'.

The Variety Theatre—27 Zhelyabov Str 652 seats. *Public transport:* Trolleybuses—1, 5, 7, 10, 14, 22; Buses—2, 3, 4, 6, 7 14, 22, 44, 45, 47, 100.

Founded in 1938. The main stage for the Leningrad Revue Theatre (founded 1939) directed by People's Artist of the USSR Arkadi Raikin.

CINEMAS IN THE CENTRE OF THE CITY

Avróra—60 Nevsky Prospekt
Barricáda—15 Nevsky Prospekt
Khudózhestvenny—67 Nevsky Prospekt
Koliséi—100 Nevsky Prospekt
Leningrad—4 Potyomkin Str.
Molodyózhny—12 Garden Str.
Nevá—108 Nevsky Prospekt
Nóvosti dnyá—88 Nevsky Prospekt (news reels)
Oktyábr—80 Nevsky Prospekt
Ródina—12 Tolmachev Str.
Stereokino—4 Lenin Park
Titán—47 Nevsky Prospekt
Velikán—4 Lenin Park (the city's larges movie theatre)
Znániye—72 Nevsky Prospekt (documentary and science fiction films)

You can get a complete listing of Leningrad's movie theatres and find out what's on at the service bureau of your hotel or at any one of the city's bill-boards. The service bureau can also give you information about where to see films in foreign languages.

The majority of the city's cinemas are open all day long from 9 or 10 in the morning. A film show usually lasts about 1 hou and 40 minutes. Seats are numbered (rov and seat numbers are indicated on tickets'

No one is admitted after the show has begun. Tickets may be obtained at the ticket window or through the hotel service bureau.

Tickets to evening shows cost 30 to 50 kopecks, cinerama and wide-screen films — 50 to 70 kopecks, and newsreels — 10 kopecks. Matinees are about 20 to 25 per cent cheaper than evening showings.

SPORTS FACILITIES, SPORTS CLUBS, LARGEST STADIUMS

The Army Sports Club Swimming Pool — 1 Kondratiev Str.

The Burevéstnik Sports Society Cycle Track — 81 Engels Avenue

The Chigorin Chess Club — 25 Zhelyabov Str.

The Children's and Youth's Sports School — Vernost Str.

The Children's Sports School — 66 Maly pereulok, Vasilyevsky Island

The Dynamo Stadium Tennis Court — 44 Dynamo Avenue

Kirov Stadium — 1 Marine Avenue

Lenin Stadium — 2g Petrovsky Island

Major Arena — Moskovsky Victory Park

The Spartak Swimming Pool — 1 Kondratiev Str.

Speedway Stadium — 67 Olginskaya Str.

The Sport Games Palace — Butlerov Str.

The Trud Sports Society Yacht Club — 7 Petrovskaya kosa

The Vódnik Sports Society Yacht Club — 92 Martynov Emb.

The Winter Stadium — 11 Inzhenernaya Str.

The Young Pioneers' Palace Tennis Court — 21 Krestovsky Avenue

The Yubiléiny Sports Palace — 18 Dobrolyubov Avenue

The Známya Rowing Club — 4 Vyazovaya Str.

MUSEUMS

Museums of the History of the Revolution

The Cruiser Aurora Museum. A branch of the Central Naval Museum — Petrogradskaya Emb., opposite No.4. Free admission and excursions. Group tours by advance request.

For further information, see the chapter 'Lenin Memorial Places. Relics of the Revolution.'

Lenin Museum-Flats (listing given in accordance with chronicle of events). Free admission and excursions.

7 Ilyich Pereulok, Flat 13. *Public transport:* Trolleybuses — 2, 3, 8, 9, 11, 13, 15; Bus — 30; Trams — 9, 11, 28, 34; Metro station-Pushkinskaya.

Open Tuesday from 11 a.m. to 4 p.m., other days from 11 a.m. to 6 p.m.; closed: Wednesday.

Lenin lived and worked in this apartment during the first period of his revolutionary activity in St.Petersburg, from February 14 (26), 1894, to April 25 (May 7), 1895. Here he wrote the work *What the 'Friends of the People' Are and How They Fight the Social-Democrats.*

52, Lenin Str., Flat 24. *Public transport:* Trolleybuses — 6, 9; Trams — 3, 17, 18, 21, 30, 31, 37, 40. Open: Tuesday from 11 a.m. to 4 p.m., other days from 11 a.m. to 6 p.m. Closed: Wednesday.

Lenin's sister Anna Ulyanova-Yelizarova and her husband Mark Yelizarov lived here. Upon his return from exile Lenin and his wife, Nadezhda Krupskaya, lived here from April 4 (17), 1917, till early July 1917. The museum was opened November 6, 1927. It was founded with the participation of Nadezhda Krupskaya and Anna Ulyanova and Maria Ulyanova.

10th Sovietskaya Str., 17-a, Flat 20. public transport: Trolleybus — 10; Bus — 21; Trams — 6, 10, 12, 16, 28, 32, 38. Open: Tuesday from 11 a.m. to 4 p.m., other days from 11 a.m. to 6 p.m.; closed: Wednesday.

This apartment of the Bolshevik worker

S. Alliluyev was one of the first secret places of the latter underground period. Lenin lived here from July 7 (20) to July 9 (22), 1917. On the night of July 10 (23) he left this apartment for Razliv Station.

For further information, see the chapter 'Razliv'.

The 'Sarai' Memorial Museum in Razliv. Razliv Station, 2 Yemelyanov Str.

The 'Shalash' Memorial Museum. Tarkhovka Station. Open daily from 11 a.m. to 5 p.m., Tuesday: from 11 a.m. to 4 p.m.; closed: Wednesday.

For further information, see the chapter 'Razliv'.

32, River Karpovka Emb., Flat 31, Public transport: Trolleybuses—1, 6, 9; Buses—10, 19, 23, 25; Trams—3, 17, 18, 20, 21, 30, 31, 37, 40; Metro station—Petrogradskaya. Open Tuesday from 11 a.m. to 4 p.m., other days: from 11 a.m. to 5 p.m.; closed: Wednesday.

An historic session of the Party Central Committee headed by Lenin took place here on October 10 (23), 1917, at which the decision to stage the armed uprising was made.

For further information, see the chapter 'Lenin Memorial Places. Relics of the Revolution'.

1, Serdobolskaya Str., Flat 20. Public transport: Trolleybus—31; Buses—99, 273; Trams—2, 18, 20, 21, 22, 23, 26, 40. Open Tuesday from 11 a.m. to 4 p.m., other days from 11 a.m. to 5 p.m.; closed: Wednesday.

The 'Sarai' Memorial Museum in Razliv

Lenin's last secret address. He lived and worked here after returning from Finland until October 24 (Nov. 6), 1917. From here Lenin directed the immediate preparation for the October armed uprising and late on the night of October 24 he left for Smolny—the headquarters of the Revolution.

For more information, see the chapter 'Lenin Memorial Places. Relics of the Revolution'.

5, Kherson Str., Flat 9. Public transport: Trolleybuses—1, 10, 14, 16, 22; Buses—2, 58; Trams—10, 13, 17, 24, 44, 46, 48, 4. Open Tuesday from 11 a.m. to 4 p.m., other days from 11 a.m. to 6 p.m.; closed Wednesday.

Lenin often visited his friend and colleague V. Bonch-Bruyevich in this apartment in 1917. It was here that on the night of October 25 into the following day of October 26 (Nov. 7-8), 1917 that Lenin wrote the draft of one of the first decrees of Soviet Power—the Decree on Land.

*Smolny. The Assembly Hall. Lenin's first study and living room at Smolny—Proletarian Dictatorship (Proletárskaya diktatura) Sq.

Group tours by advance request.

For further information, see the chapter 'Lenin Memorial Places. Relics of the Revolution'.

*The Leningrad Branch of the Lenin Central Museum—*5/1 Khalturin Str. Free admission and excursions. Open every day except Wednesday, from 10.30 a.m. to p.m.

For further information, see the chapter 'Lenin Memorial Places. Relics of the Revolution'.

*The Museum of the Great October Socialist Revolution—*4 Kuibyshev Str. Free admission and excursions. Open Monday and Friday from 12 to 7. p.m.; Tuesday, Wednesday and Saturday from 11 a.m. 7 p.m.; closed: Thursday.

For further information, see the chapter 'Lenin Memorial Places. Relics of the Revolution.'

History Museums

Artillery, Engineers and Signals Museum—7 Lenin Park. *Public transport:* Buses—1, 23, 25, 46, 65, 80; Trams—2, 3, 12, 22, 25, 26, 30, 34, 51; Metro station—Gorkovskaya. Free admission. Open daily from 1.30 a.m. to 6.30 p.m. Sunday from 11.30 a.m. to 6 p.m.; closed: Tuesday.

The building (1850-1860, the architect—P. Tamansky) was intended for an arsenal. One of the sections housed the Artillery Museum founded in 1765. In 1963 the Central Military-Engineering Historical Museum was opened in this building. Since 1965—Artillery, Engineers and Signals Museum.

On display is a wide collection of fire- and side-arms, fortification facilities, signal equipment, uniforms from ancient times up to the present day. The museum boasts a vast collection of military relics, equipment, munition, banners and Russian and foreign orders and medals.

The Central Naval Museum—4 Pushkin Sq. Free admission. Open Monday and Wednesday from 11 a.m. to 6 p.m.; Thursday from 1 p.m. to 8 p.m.; Friday from 11 a.m. to 4 p.m.; closed: Tuesday.

The History of Leningrad Museum—44 Red Fleet Emb. Free admission and excursions. Open Monday and Friday from 1 p.m. to 8 p.m., Tuesday from 11 a.m. to 4 p.m., Thursday, Saturday and Sunday from 11 a.m. to 7 p.m.

This museum collects, preserves and displays documents associated with the history of St. Petersburg—Petrograd—Leningrad from the time of the city's founding to the present. The museum keeps an historical diary of present-day Leningrad, recording all important events connected with the life of the city.

For more information about the exposition 'Leningrad During the Years of the Great Patriotic War', see the chapter '900 Days—The Heroic Defence of Leningrad'.

The Museum of the History of Religion and Atheism—2 Kazan Sq. Free admission

and excursions. Open Monday and Friday from 12 to 6 p.m., Thursday from 1 p.m. to 8 p.m., Wednesday, Saturday and Sunday from 11 a.m. to 6 p.m.

For further information, see the chapter 'The Main Thoroughfare—Nevsky Prospekt'.

Peter the Great's Cottage in the Summer Gardens, a Museum—5 Petrovskaya Emb. Open (from May 1 to November 10) daily from 12 to 7 p.m.; closed: Tuesday.

For further information, see the chapter 'The Peter and Paul Fortress. The Summer Gardens'.

Peter the Great's Summer Palace. Open daily from 3 p.m. to 8 p.m.; Sunday from 11 a.m. to 12; closed: Tuesday.

For further information, see the chapter 'The Peter and Paul Fortress. The Summer Gardens'.

The Peter and Paul Fortress—Revolution Sq. Open Tuesday from 11 a.m. to 4 p.m.; other days from 11 a.m. to 6 p.m.; closed: Wednesday.

For further information, see the chapter 'The Peter and Paul Fortress. The Summer Gardens'.

The Piskaryovskoye Memorial Cemetery—72 Avenue of the Unconquered. Open daily from 11 a.m. to 6 p.m.

For further information, see the chapter '900 Days—The Heroic Defence of Leningrad'.

The St. Isaac's Cathedral, Memorial Museum—St. Isaac's Sq. Open daily from 11 a.m. to 6 p.m., Tuesday from 11 a.m. to 4 p.m.; closed: Wednesday.

For further information, see the chapter 'The Central Squares'.

Suvorov History of the Armed Forces Museum—41-b Saltykov-Shchedrin Str. *Public transport:* Trolleybuses—11, 15, 25; Bus—1. Free admission and excursions. Open daily from 11 a.m. to 6 p.m.; Monday from 12 to 6 p.m.; closed: Wednesday.

This exposition includes many effects connected with the life of the famed Russian military leader, military relics, weaponry, maps and other documents, paintings, sculptures and engravings. Materials with regard to the military activity of Soviet Army units awarded the Order of Suvorov during the Great Patriotic War (1941-1945) are also on display.

Art, Literature and Theatrical Museums

The Brodsky Museum-Flat—3 Arts Sq. Free admission. Open every day except Monday and Tuesday from 11 a.m. to 6.30 p.m.

For further information, see the chapter 'The Main Thoroughfare—Nevsky Prospekt'.

The Dostoyevsky Museum-Flat—5/2 Kuznechny pereulok. *Public transport:* Trolleybuses—3, 8, 11, 13, 15, 23; Trams—9, 11, 27, 28, 34, 44, 49; Metro station—Vladimirskaya. Open every day except Monday from 10.30 a.m. to 6.30 p.m.

The Hermitage—34/36 Palace Emb. Open daily from 11 a.m. to 6 p.m.; during the summer from 10 a.m. to 5 p.m.; closed: Monday.

For further information, see the chapter 'The Central Squares'.

'Literatorskiye Mostki' Nekropolis. Branch of the Museum of Urban Sculpture—30 Insurrection Sq. *Public transport:* Buses—14, 36, 44; Trams—10, 25, 44. Open daily from 9 a.m. to 5 p.m. (May through September); from 11 a.m. to 6 p.m. (October through April); closed: Thursday.

Buried here are prominent statesmen and figures from the world of science, literature and the arts: Vissarion Belinsky, Alexander Blok, Dmitry Mendeleyev, Ivan Pavlov, Georgi Plekhanov, Ivan Turgenev and others. This is the final resting place of the Ulyanov family, where Lenin's mother, sisters and the husband of his sister Anna, the outstanding revolutionary Mark Yelizarov, are buried.

The Lomonosov Museum. The Kunstkammer building—4 University Emb. Free admission and excursions (group tours b advance request). Open every day excep Saturday from 11 a.m. to 5 p.m.

For further information, see the chapte 'The Embankments of Vasilyevsky Islan

The Museum of Artistic Decoration Russian Palaces at the End of the 18 and Beginning of the 19th Century—Tow of Pavlovsk. Open every day except Frida from 10 a.m. to 6 p.m.

For further information, see the chapte 'Pushkin and Pavlovsk'.

The Museum of Circus Art—3 Rive Fontanka Emb. *Public transport:* Trolle buses—3, 8, 11, 13, 15, 19, 23; Trams—5, 12, 13, 14, 20, 24, 28, 34. Open every da except Sunday from 12 to 5 p.m. Grou tours by advance request.

The only museum of its kind in the wor More than 80,000 exhibits—circus prop the personal effects of famed masters the arena, scale models of circus acts, pos ers, documents, photographs, and liter ture on the history of the circus. The m seum not only collects, but also designs m terials for creating new acts.

The Museum of Decorative and Applie Art of the Mukhina Higher School of I dustrial Art Design—13 Solyanoi pereulo *Public transport:* Trolleybuses—3, 8, 11, 1 15, 19, 23; Buses—14, 25, 26; Trams—2, 3, 12, 14, 17, 19, 20, 25. Free admission. Ope daily from 11 a.m. to 4.30 p.m.; Saturda from 11 a.m. to 2.30 p.m.; closed: Sunday.

On display are the finest works of th School's students and teachers, as well ceramics, artistic glass and leather prod ucts, furniture, fabric, metal engraving etc., characteristic of the history of decor tive, applied and commercial art from th 17th through the 20th century. There is als a unique collection of artistic tiled stov and fireplaces.

The Museum of Literature, run by th USSR Academy of Sciences Russian L erature Institute—4 Makarov Emb., Vasi yevsky Island. Free admission and excu sions. Open every day except Monday an Tuesday from 11 a.m. to 6 p.m.

For more information, see the chapter 'The Embankments of Vasilyevsky Island'.

The Museum of Musical Instruments—5 t.Isaac's Sq. Free admission. Open Wednesday, Friday and Sunday from 12 to p.m.

Over 3,000 musical instruments from the 6th to the 20th century from various counties comprise this collection which is the largest of its kind in the world. Also on display are the personal instruments of outstanding Russian composers and performers.

The Museum of Theatrical Art—6 Ostrovsky Sq. Free admission and excursions. *Public transport:* Trolleybuses—1, 5, 7, 10, 14, 22; Buses—3, 6, 7, 14, 22, 25, 43, 44, 45, 0; Metro stations—Gostiny Dvor, Nevsky Prospekt. Open Monday from 12 to 7 p.m.; Wednesday from 2 p.m. to 9 p.m.; closed: Tuesday.

This museum houses over 300,000 exhibits from the history of the Russian and Soviet theatre: stage props, documents, photographs, playbills, programmes, sound recordings, sketches and models of decorations and portraits and busts of theatrical figures.

The Museum of Urban Sculpture—Alexander Nevsky Sq. *Public transport:* trolleybuses—1, 14, 16, 22, 28; Buses—8, 21, 6, 30, 70, 120; Trams—7, 13, 17, 24, 27, 38, 4, 46, 48, 49; Metro station—Ploshchad Alexandra Nevskovo. Open daily from 11 m. to 6 p.m. (from May through October—from 11 a.m. to 7 p.m.); closed: Thursday.

The Alexander Nevsky Monastery, one of Leningrad's oldest architectural monuments, is situated at the end of Nevsky Prospekt. The Monastery was built in 1710 in memory of the Russian statesman and military leader of the 13th century, Alexander Nevsky.

The Museum of Urban Sculpture now situated in the Monastery studies and participates in the restoration of statues and monuments standing on the city's streets and squares. The exposition in the Annunciation (Blagovéshchensky) Church consists of collection of authors' models, engravings, drawings, drafts and photographs of Leningrad's most significant sculptures and monuments. The exposition is also dedicated to the implementation of the sculptured monuments propaganda programme advanced by Lenin.

Memorial cemeteries are located near the entrance to the Monastery grounds. Outstanding figures in Russian science and culture are buried here: the 18th century scholar Mikhail Lomonosov; the architects Andrian Zakharov, Andrei Voronikhin, Carlo Rossi, Giacomo Quarenghi; the composers Mikhail Glinka, Pyotr Tchaikovsky, Anton Rubinstein; the writers Ivan Krylov, Fyodor Dostoyevsky and many others. Created by famous Russian architects and sculptors, many tombstones here are of great artistic value.

The National Pushkin Museum and Its Branches—Town of Pushkin. Open daily from 11 a.m. to 6 p.m.; closed: Tuesday.

For further information, see the chapter 'Pushkin and Pavlovsk'.

The Pavlov Museum-Flat—1/2 Lieutenant Schmidt Emb. Admission and excursions by advance notice. Open every day except Saturday and Sunday from 11 a.m. to 7 p.m.

For further information, see the chapter 'The Embankments of Vasilyevsky Island'.

The Palace-Museums in the Parks of Petrodvorets. Open daily from 11 a.m. to 6 p.m. The Grand Palace is closed on Monday, the Monplaisir on Wednesday, and the Hermitage is closed on Thursday.

For further information, see the chapter 'Petrodvorets—a Town of Fountains'.

The 'Penaty' Repin Museum-Estate—Railway station—Repino. Open every day except Tuesday from 10 a.m. to 6 p.m.

For further information, see the chapter 'The Karelian Isthmus'.

The Pushkin Museum-Flat—12 River Moika Emb. *Public transport:* Trolleybuses—1, 5, 7, 9, 10, 14, 22; Buses—2, 3, 4, 6, 7, 14, 22, 26, 27, 44, 45, 47; Trams—7, 8, 21,

22, 26, 31, 51. Free admissions and excursions. Open daily from 11 a.m. to 6 p.m.; Monday from 11 a.m. to 4 p.m.; closed: Tuesday.

For further information, see the chapter 'The Central Squares'.

The Rimsky-Korsakov Museum-Flat, a branch of the Theatrical Museum-28, Zagorodny prospekt. *Public transport:* Trolleybuses—2, 3, 8, 11, 13, 15; Buses—9, 11, 27, 28, 34. Open daily from 12 to 6 p.m.; closed: Monday, Tuesday.

The Russian Museum—4/2 Engineers' Str., Arts Sq. Open daily from 11 a.m. to 6 p.m.; Monday from 11 a.m. to 4 p.m.; closed: Tuesday.

For further information, see the chapter 'The Main Thoroughfare—Nevsky Prospekt'.

The USSR Academy of the Arts Scientific Research Museum—17 University Emb. Open every day except Monday and Tuesday from 11 a.m. to 6.30 p.m.

For further information, see the chapter 'The Embankments of Vasilyevsky Island'.

Natural Science and Technological Museums

The Academician Chernyshev Central Geological Museum—72-b Srédni proyézd Vasilyevsky Island. *Public transport:* Trolleybuses—10, 12; Buses—35, 60; Trams—? 11, 18, 40, 42. Free admission and excursions. Open every day except Sunday from 10 a.m. to 4 p.m.

The museum's exposition consists of sections of regional geology and mineral resources and a section devoted to preserving and displaying monographic collections (over 1,000 paleontological collections are of world significance). The museum houses about 80,000 species of minerals and fossil fauna.

The Arctic and Antarctic Museum—24-a Marat Str. *Public transport:* Trolleybuses—3, 8, 11, 13, 15, 19, 22, 23; Trams—? 11, 28, 34; Metro station—Vladimirskaya. Open every day except Monday and Tuesday from 10 a.m. to 6 p.m.

The only museum in the world dealing with the nature of the polar lands, the history of their discovery, exploration and settlement, and the life of the peoples of the Far North. There is a large display of materials on the Soviet Antarctic expeditions.

The Botanical Museum of the Komarov Institute of Botany. The Botanical Garden of the USSR Academy of Sciences—2 Professor Popov Str. *Public transport:* Buses—10, 19, 23, 25, 33, 46, 71, 9 Trams—17, 18, 30; Metro station—Petrogradskaya. Open every day except Friday from 11 a.m. to 4 p.m. Greenhouse open in summer from 11 a.m. to 4 p.m.

This museum was founded in 1823. Its collection includes some 60,000 species of plants of the Soviet Union and other countries.

An exhibition entitled 'Plants from Around the World' has been opened in a special museum building erected on the grounds of the Botanical Gardens.

Open for viewing are the park with plants of the USSR and foreign countries a greenhouse with over 3,000 species of tropical and subtropical plants, flora of various continents and collections of cacti, rhododendrons, conifers, etc.

The Dokuchayev Central Soil Science Museum—6 Birzhevói proyézd. Free admission and excursions. Open every day except Saturday and Sunday from 9.15 a.m. to 6 p.m.

For further information, see the chapter 'The Embankments of Vasilyevsky Island'.

The House of Scientific and Technological Information—58 Nevsky Prospekt. *Public transport:* Trolleybuses—1, 5, 7, 10, 14, 22; Buses—3, 6, 7, 22, 27, 43, 44, 45, 70; Trams—2, 3, 13, 14, 24; Metro stations—Nevsky Prospekt, Gostiny Dvor. Free admission. Open Monday, Wednesday and Friday from 11 a.m. to 6 p.m.; Saturday from 11 a.m. to 3 p.m.; closed: Tuesday, Thursday and Sunday.

A methods and organisational centre of information on the latest achievements in science and industry. A permanent exhibition shows the technological progress of Leningrad's industry. There are exhibitions on particular subjects where many tools and machines are demonstrated in action. Specialists are on hand to answer questions.

The House of Scientific and Technological Information maintains ties with experts from 10,000 enterprises in the Soviet Union and abroad.

The Military-Medical Museum—2 Lazarétny pereúlok. *Public transport:* Trolleybuses—2, 3, 8, 9, 11, 13, 15; Trams—9, 11, 27, 28, 34; Metro station—Pushkinskaya. Free admission and excursions. Open every day except Friday from 11 a.m. to 6 p.m.

This exposition is devoted to the history of the country's military-medical science from its inception to the present day. On display are documents, manuscripts of outstanding medical scholars, apparatus, instruments, pictures, sculptures and photographs.

The Mining Museum of the Plekhanov Mining Institute—45 University Emb. Free

admission and excursions. Open daily from 10 a.m. to 4 p.m.; Wednesday from 1 p.m. to 8 p.m.; Saturday from 10 a.m. to 2 p.m.; closed: Sunday.

For further information, see the chapter 'The Embankments of Vasilyevsky Island'.

The Museum of Ethnography of the Peoples of the USSR—4/1 Engineers' Str. open daily from 11 a.m. to 6 p.m.; Saturday from 12 to 6 p.m.; in summer—Tuesday and Wednesday from 1 p.m. to 9 p.m.; Thursday, Saturday and Sunday from 11 a.m. to 5 p.m.; closed: Monday.

For further information, see the chapter 'The Main Thoroughfare—Nevsky Prospekt'.

The Museum of Public Health of the House of Sanitary Education—25 Rakov Str. *Public transport:* Trolleybuses—1, 5, 7, 10, 14, 22; Buses—3, 6, 7, 22, 43, 45; Trams—2, 3, 5, 12, 13, 14; Metro stations—Nevsky Prospekt, Gostiny Dvor. Free admission and excursions. Open every day except Monday from 11 a.m. to 6 p.m.

Founded in 1918 for the purpose of instructing the population in the fields of hygienics and health care.

The museum has on display numerous specimens, skilfully constructed models, the latest discoveries of medical science and the achievements of Soviet medicine in the fight to save lives. There are many exhibits dealing with the work of the country's leading medical researchers.

The Peter the Great Museum of Anthropology and Ethnography—3 University Emb. Free admission and excursions (group excursions by advance request). Open every day except Friday and Saturday from 11 a.m. to 5 p.m.

For further information, see the chapter 'The Embankments of Vasilyevsky Island'.

The Popov Central Communications Museum—4 Podbelsky pereúlok. *Public transport:* Trolleybuses—5, 14; Buses—2, 3, 22, 26, 27; Trams—21, 26, 31. Free admission. Open daily from 12 to 6 p.m.; Thursday from 12 to 7 p.m.; closed: Monday.

One of the oldest technological museums

in the country. Authentic apparatus, documents, pictures and photographs illustrate the history of the post, telegraph, telephone, radio and the development of TV technique and communication apparatus produced by Soviet industry.

Over three million postal stamps from every country are kept in the museum. Thematic and jubilee stamps selected from this collection, as well as the latest Soviet stamps are on permanent display.

The Railway Museum—50 Garden Str. *Public transport:* Trolleybuses—3, 17; Buses—43, 50, 90; Trams—2, 3, 5, 13, 14, 24; Metro station—Plóshchad Míra. Free admission. Open every day except Saturday and Sunday from 11 a.m. to 5.30 p.m.

The collections of this museum include documents, model trains, working scale replicas of all types of railroad technology, tracks, bridges, signalling, automatic devices and telemechanics of the country's railroads, from the time of the first Russian steam locomotive to the present.

The Zoological Museum of the USSR Academy of Sciences—1 University Emb. Free admission and excursions (group excursions by advance request). Open daily from 11 a.m. to 5 p.m.; Tuesday from 11 a.m. to 4 p.m.; closed: Monday.

For further information, see the chapter 'The Embankments of Vasilyevsky Island'.

The Zoological Park—1 Lenin Park. *Public transport:* Buses—1, 10, 25, 45, 46, 80; Trams—6, 26, 31, 34. Open daily from 10 a.m. to 7 p.m.

The Leningrad Zoo is an important scientific and educational institution. 360 species of animals from many countries are kept here.

HOW TO FAMILIARISE YOURSELF WITH THE CITY

SIGHTSEEING ROUTES AROUND LENINGRAD

SEEING THE CITY IN ONE DAY

HOW TO FAMILIARISE
YOURSELF WITH THE CITY

Since Leningrad is located on a plain, and lightly rolling hills are only to be found at its outskirts, there is no natural elevation in the city proper from which you can have a bird's eye view of the town.

In order to get a general idea of Leningrad's unique appearance and design, as well as the layout of its historical and architectural points of interest, we suggest you visit the Vasilyevsky Island Spit. To get there you can travel part of the first tour route suggested in this book—the Embankments of Vasilyevsky Island. There is no other place in the city from which you can see so much all at once.

It would be a good idea to arrange for a sightseeing tour of the city in car or bus through the Intourist Service Department. You will get a chance to see various areas of the city and get an impression of its size and its historic and revolutionary past. You will see present-day Leningrad as one of the largest centres of industry, science and the arts. You will see the breadth of housing construction. You will see the dawn of a new tomorrow being forged today.

And if you have any time left, we suggest you visit any one of the city's museums, and at night go to the theatre or to a concert, or simply stroll along the city's streets and embankments and try to feel its atmosphere and special beauty.

SEEING THE CITY IN TWO DAYS, THREE DAYS, A WEEK

Pick out what you feel are the most interesting of the thirteen tour routes of Leningrad and its environs suggested in this book. But keep in mind that even if you love to walk, it's a bit difficult getting around Leningrad without using public transport. Many architectural and historic monuments mentioned in any one specific tour may be as much as 10 or 15 kilometres apart.

The tours we have suggested are very flexible. If you wish, you can of course strike out on your own and charter your own course of exploring the city and its places of interest.

It's hard to get lost in Leningrad because of the city's strict geometrical design. You can use the wide River Neva (which is impossible to confuse with any other river in the city) as a guide, as well as some of the city's tall structures which are visible from far away, such as the TV tower, the bell-tower of the Peter and Paul Fortress cathedral, the spire of the Admiralty and the gold dome of St.Isaac's Cathedral.

Even if you can't find your hotel or any particular street, square or museum, any citizen of Leningrad will gladly show you the way or will tell you what bus, tram, trolleybus, etc. to take. The people of Leningrad are famous for their hospitality and are proud of their city and love it dearly. But keep in mind one thing: during the height of the tourist season there will be a lot of visitors to the city who know their way around town no better than you!

Foreign tourists staying in Leningrad more than four days might want to avail themselves of the excursion 'Along the Rivers and Canals of Leningrad'. The tour lasts 1 hour and 15 minutes. It begins at the Hermitage Pier. Tourists become acquainted with the architecture and the past and recent history of certain areas of the centre of the city. The guides tell them about the palaces, parks, monuments, bridges, embankments, establishments of higher learning, theatres, associated with the names of famous people, with major historical events, and with today's fast paced world.

SIGHTSEEING ROUTES AROUND LENINGRAD

First Acquaintance
(The Embankment
of Vasilyevsky Island)

We suggest that for your first excursion in Leningrad you follow an itinerary beginning at the Spit of Vasilyevsky Island (Strélka Vasilyevskovo óstrova), proceeding on to University Embankment (Universitétskaya náberezhnaya) and concluding with Lieutenant Schmidt Embankment (náberezhnaya Leitenánta Schmidta).

The sights on this tour are not far from one another, but the Spit of Vasilyevsky Island, where your excursion starts, is quite a distance away from the Lieutenant Schmidt Embankment, to which the route we recommend will bring you. Just in case, here is some information on public transport, which you can use to

—start your tour from Pushkin Square: Trolleybuses—1, 6, 7, 9; Buses—7, 10, 30, 44, 45, 47, 60; Trams—21, 26, 31

—ride down University Embankment: Trolleybus—6; Buses—7, 10, 30, 44, 47, 60

—return to the centre of town from Lieutenant Schmidt Embankment: Bus—60; Trams—15, 26

the sequence indicated by their numerical designations on our maps. The addresses of the architectural and historical sights which are the subject of this chapter are shown in the captions to the maps. The descriptions following below include mention of the museums which you can visit during your excursion, should you so desire.

Both in this and in subsequent chapters, monuments are on the whole designated in accordance with their original names and functions.

VASILYEVSKY ISLAND (Vasílyevsky óstrov)

Two of the island's sides are washed by the Greater and Little Neva (branches of the Neva), which throw themselves into the Gulf, and its

77

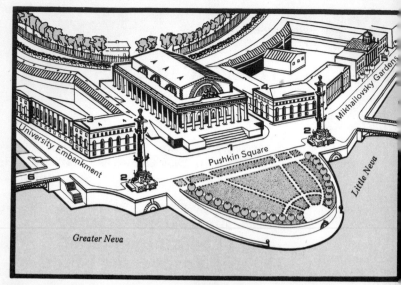

1. Stock Exchange Central Naval Museum—4, Pushkin Sq. 2. Rostral Columns 3. Southern Warehouse Zoological Institute Zoological Museum of the USSR Academy of Sciences—1, University Emb. 4. Northern Warehouse Dokuchayev Central Soil Science Museum—2 Makarov Emb. 5. Customs House Institute of Russian Literature of the USSR Academy of Sciences *(Pushkin House)*—4, Makarov Emb. Museum of Literature—4, Makarov Emb. 6. Palace Bridge

western side is bathed by the waters of the Gulf itself. The Greater (Bolsháya) and Little (Málaya) Neva are separated by Vasilyevsky Island's eastern promontory, the Spit (Strelka).

The island's advantageous geographical position was immediately appreciated by Peter I, who decided to station the new capital's administrative centre here.

Two plans for the city which were drawn up one after the other—one in 1716 by the architect Domenico Trezzini and the other in 1717 by the architect Jean-Baptiste Leblond—while Peter I was still living (he died in 1725) envisaged the creation of a network of canals on Vasilyevsky Island. But laying the canals turned out to be too complicated and difficult, and only an insignificant portion of them was dug. Although Trezzini and Leblond's plans remained unrealized, they influenced the way Vasilyevsky Island was built up. In the first half of the 18th century the governor's residential palace, the houses of grandees and premises for trading—the Gostiny dvor (arcade)—were built here; construction was also begun of the building of the 'Twelve Collegiums', in which it was proposed to accomodate the highest administrative organs, and of the city's and country's first public museum.

Peter the Great issued many decrees instructing the city's inhabitants to settle this particular island first. Yet the absence of bridges across the Greater and Little Neva and the fact that the island was cut

Petersburg in the 18th century. A view of Vasilyevsky Island (watercolour)

off from the rest of the city during the freezing over and thawing of the rivers and during storms played a decisive role in its fate.

The idea of establishing the administrative centre here had been definitely rejected by the middle of the 18th century. The core of the city began to take shape on the left bank of the Neva, to which the main roads from the other areas of the country led. The artificial channels on Vasilyevsky Island had to be filled up. But the clear-cut, right-angle planning of this part of the future city was inherited from Peter's time. Three avenues—the Grand (Bolshói), the Middle (Srédnii) and the Little (Mályi)—lie parallel to the Neva in place of the main canals. Streets called 'lines' intersect them at right angles. Each side of these streets is designated by a separate ordinal number, recalling the embankments of narrow canals which were planned under Peter the Great. There are altogether 29 such lines, excluding one which does not cross Grand Avenue at right angle and is therefore simply called Slanting Line (Kosáya líniya).

In 1733 the Sea Port was transferred to the Spit of Vasilyevsky Island, where it remained until 1855. A commercial centre was built near the new port, with an Exchange (Bírzha), warehouses and a Customs House. This is how the ensemble on the Spit arose.

In time the island which did not manage to turn into the city's main administrative district became one of its principal cultural and scientific centres. The Spit is sometimes called the 'Museum Quarter'. Eight museums, four institutions of higher learning, including the University, many establishments under the USSR Academy of Sciences, and scientific and research institutes are located there.

Then the main buildings were being erected on the Spit of Vasilyevsky Island, the Kirov (formerly Trinity) Bridge did not yet exist. But the Spit's axis is so situated that one has the best overall view of its ensemble precisely from this bridge, and particularly from its centre.

> ... I ran to the Palace Embankment and up along it till Trinity Bridge from which I had been advised to look at the city. This was the best piece of advice I've been given in my life.
> I really don't know whether there is any view in the whole world which can be compared with the panorama which unfolded before my eyes...
> If one turns one's back to the fortress and walks upstream, the view changes, but still remains grandiose.
>
> A. DUMAS

The River Neva reaches one of its widest points—up to 600 m—near the Spit. Only at its mouth it is wider. From the Spit one can see how the Neva splits into two arms—the Little and Greater Neva.

THE RIVER NEVA

It has its source in Lake Ladoga and empties into the Gulf of Finland. Its length is 74 km, for 32 km of which (the distance keeps increasing as the city grows) it flows within the limits of Leningrad. Its average width is from 400 to 600 m, and it reaches a depth of up to 24 m, although its prevailing depth is from 8 to 11 metres. It is navigable over its entire extent, and is free of ice 200 or so days of the year

The Neva immediately 'explains' the city's architectural planning and composition in their historical development.

The city began to go up in a few places simultaneously along the banks of the Neva, stretched to the river's very mouth and moved far upstream. Its mightiest waterway became its 'main street'. In 1716 an edict was issued requiring that only stone buildings be erected along the river. Gradually solid lines of buildings rose on both sides of the Neva. They were made up of the city's most beautiful houses, which were linked by a common artistic scheme and formed the city's architectural centre.

The splendid appearance of the city's main river has been sung by many poets. The Neva has been called 'eternal', 'boundless', 'wide-open', 'mysterious'... Yet scientists as well as poets have written and are still writing about the Neva. It would be hard to find a river which has been the subject of so many scientific studies—over 250. The reason lies in the Neva's 'difficult' character. It is always deep and carries as much water to the sea as the Nile. Since the city's founding the Neva's waters have more than 300 times risen over one and a half metres above their normal level and a few times they have risen to such an extent as to cause catastrophic floods. There were numerous projects for protecting the city from floods. At present a project for the cardinal protection of Leningrad from this natural calamity has been worked out; it is described in somewhat more detail in the chapter 'The New Maritime District on Vasilyevsky Island'.

THE PANORAMA OF THE NEVA BANKS

Standing in the centre of the Spit's embankment facing the Neva, you will see the long, grey, seemingly squat walls of the Peter and Paul (Petropávlovskaya) Fortress straight ahead. Inside the fortress rises the famous bell tower of the St. Peter and St. Paul Gathedral with its fine gold spire. 122.5 metres high, it was until the middle of the 20th century the highest structure in the city. While the bell tower was still under construction, Peter I used to climb up its scaffolding with a spy-glass to admire the view of the growing city.

Now the city's tallest structure is the 321-metre-high TV Centre tower. Its open-work design is visible, when the sky is clear, in the distance to the left of the fortress.

To the right of the fortress you can see one of the nine bridges over the Neva—the *Kirov Bridge* (Kírovsky móst). (Built 1903. Raisable span reconstructed 1965-1967. Length of the bridge—600 m. Width of the navigable span—43.2 m.) It is the second largest bridge in the city (the longest is the 905-meter-long *Alexander Nevsky Bridge* (móst Aleksándra Névskovo), which lies upstream at a bend of the river. In the smoothness of its contours and its architectural design, the Kirov Bridge is among the most beautiful structures of its kind. It is one of Leningrad's 22 drawbridges.

In the distance beyond Kirov Bridge rises the twelve-storey building of the *Intourist Hotel Leningrad.* (Built 1970. The group of architects headed by S. Speransky who designed it were awarded the State Prize in 1973.) The large edifice with its granite ramps and stairways which lead to the embankment organically merges with its surroundings. You will be able to have a look at the *Leningrad* Hotel during your other excursions around the city.

On the left bank of the Neva the Kirov Bridge gives onto the Palace Embankment. A detailed acquaintance with the latter's architectural ensembles is in store for you. But looking at it from here, the Spit, you will see many of the sights covered in future tours.

On the Palace Embankment near Kirov Bridge, to the right, a grey three-storey building with light pilasters starting at the first floor draws one's attention. It is the so-called Marble Palace (Mrámorny dvoréts), which now houses the Leningrad Branch of the Central Lenin Museum.

If you walk a little ways to the right of the centre of the semicircular terrace on the Spit, you will find yourself next to the Palace Bridge (Dvortsóvy móst). (Built 1908-1914. The cast-iron grille was added in 1939. Reconstructed 1977. Its length is 250 m and its width is 27.8 m. The size of its raisable span makes it one of the most imposing structures of its kind.) From the Palace Bridge you will see the buildings of the Winter Palace (Zímny Dvoréts) and the Hermitage on the other bank.

Beyond Palace Bridge, on the next left-bank embankment—the Admiralty (Admiraltéiskaya)—one can see the side wings of the Main Admiralty, surmounted by the thin spire with the tiny boat at its summit which crowns the building's main block.

However much you may subsequently wander around the centre of the town, however much you may admire its embankments and avenues, the uncommonly beautiful Admiralty spire will stick in your memory as one of the city's best ornaments. It is the subject of Pushkin's immortal lines:

> *That in my chamber 'thout a light*
> *I write or sit a book perusing*
> *Whilst, luminous, the streets lie dozing*

Beyond, great, empty blocks ... Up higher,
'Gainst sky, the Admiralty spire
Is clearly etched ...

Farther to the left one can see the gold cupola of St. Isaac's Cathedral set back into the block.

The Palace Embankment itself was one of the first to be build. The facing in granite of the Neva banks—the major building project in Petersburg during the 1760s to 1780s—required great inventiveness and truly titanic labour on the part of the builders.

> *Piles were driven into the river bed beyond the boundary between water and dry land. The space between the piles and the bank was strewn with large rocks and crushed stones. Finely-hewn granite blocks fastened together with metal ties were laid on this artificially created bank. The blocks were up to two metres or so long.*
>
> *The embankments changed the whole panorama of the central part of the city.*
>
> *They were built to last, for centuries. When comparatively recently one section of the embankment began to settle a little, it turned out that the fault lay in a shell which during the blockade fell into the Neva and exploded in the water. It had evidently damaged part of the embankment's underwater foundations and the Neva's strong current had then gradually eroded this place. Divers discovered an approximately ten-metre-deep underground cave and carefully filled it up.*
>
> *With time the embankments' granite turns grey. But with the help of sandblasting equipment they can be 'rejuvenated' so that the stone regains its natural rosy colour and the mica interspersed in it gets back its shine.*

The Neva's granite setting is one of the city's priceless ornaments. In your future walks around Leningrad, you will often come across various forms of descents to the Neva, which seem to have been mo-

The Spit of Vasilyevsky Island ▶

delled by the hands of a sculptor. They were designed by distinguished architects, whose projects were incarnated by skilful master stone-masons. One of these talented self-taught Russian masters was the shepherd's son Samson Sukhanov. He was one of the craftsmen who created the Kazan Cathedral and the Mining Institute's magnificent sculptural ornaments, and he directed the construction of the Spit Embankment. Near the Winter Palace the granite parapet is broken by an inclined plane, beautiful in its stern simplicity and paved with cobblestones, with cast-iron rings for mooring boats. On this same left bank of the Neva one can walk down to the water by means of narrow curving stone staircases. They begin at a semicircular platform with a granite bench and end below at another platform which is washed by the waves of the Neva. There are other, very wide, straight staircases which also lead down to the water. Two of them are located near the Admiralty. One is decorated with porphyry vases; the other, with sculptured bronze lions.

One very often comes across sculptured representations of lions in the city and its suburbs. There are hundreds of them — cast-iron, bronze and stone ones, winged and wingless, having the appearance of sphinxes and griffins. They guard the entrances to houses and decorate fountains, bridges and embankments.

The granite walls along the Spit's embankment are decorated on the Neva side with lion's masks holding rings in their mouths; these served to moor ships which had sailed into port.

At one time the Neva's waters splashed where the Spit's semicircular granite terrace now lies. To create a square here (previously called Exchange — Birzheváya — Square, it is now known as Pushkin Square), soil was dumped here to push back the river by 100 to 120 metres. The ramps which slope gently down to the river on both sides of the place originally had a utilitarian purpose: they were used for loading and unloading ships. Now these cobble-laid descents seem created expressly for walks. They end at the water's edge in massive granite blocks, which serve as the foundation for gigantic spheres, likewise carved out of granite. It seems as though the spheres are held in place by some miracle, since they touch their pedestals in only one point.

The Spit's terrace is the starting point of your detailed tour of the basic sights on the right bank of the Neva — that 'main architect' of the city, which still has new designs to offer it.

THE ARCHITECTURAL ENSEMBLE ON THE SPIT OF VASILYEVSKY ISLAND
The Exchange (Bírzha)

Built 1805-1810. Architect—Thomas de Thomon, with the assistance of A. Zakharov. The height of the building is 30 m. Its 44 columns are 11 m tall. The width of the exterior staircases is 40 m. The main hall has an area of 900 sq. m. and a height of 25 m. The group sculptures by S. Sukhanov. A commercial Exchange until 1885. Since 1940 the Central Navy Museum.

Architect Thomas de Thomon placed the Exchange strictly along the axis of the Spit. From a distance you can see the building's organising role in the ensemble as a whole. The Exchange was erected on a mighty granite foundation and reminds one of an antique temple. Columns rhythmically gird the building, forming a spacious open terrace.

On the attic of the main and the opposite façades stand allegorical sculptures. One of them depicts the Sea God Neptune rising out of the waves on his chariot, escorted by the Neva and Volkhov rivers; another represents the Goddess of Navigation, and Mercury, the God of Trade, surrounded by the two rivers.

There are two main staircases and ramps, one on each side, leading up to the Exchange's terrace. The staircases are so wide that in the Soviet period they have twice served as a stage for theatrical performances in which over two thousand persons took part.

Almost the whole interior of the building is taken up by the Central Hall, which is faced in marble and decorated with sculptures. Near the entrance are allegorical figures representing Time, Abundance and Justice, and on the opposite side, Commerce and Navigation.

The Central Naval Museum, which is located in the former Exchange and has been in existence since 1805, is one of the oldest and most interesting museums in the city. Its precursor was a depository created in 1709 by Peter the Great and called the Model-Chamber (Modél-kámera), which held a collection of models and blueprints of warships. There are now over half a million items in the museum's collection. Among them is a most valuable collection of about 1,500 model boats. On display are standards and banners, weapons, various documents linked with the history of the Russian and Soviet fleets, and a number of sea-scapes.

The former Exchange (to the right is part of the Rostral Column)

THE ROSTRAL COLUMNS (Rostrálnye colónny)

Built 1805—1810. Architect—Thomas de Thomon. The height of the sculptures, which are the work of S. Sukhanov, is 5 m.

When the plans for the Exchange had been approved by the Academy of Arts and the ceremony of laying the building's foundation took place, a gold medal with an engraved representation of then non-existent Exchange, embankment and Rostral Columns was placed under the first stone laid.

The Columns owe their name to the Latin word 'rostrum'—the prow of a ship. It was the custom in ancient Rome to decorate triumphal columns with war trophies, consisting of the sawed-off prows of defeated ships, in honour of victories at sea. The Columns on the Spit, conceived as imposing monuments to Russia's naval glory, are decorated with sculptured copper prows. These were badly damaged during the blocade, and the rostra you see today are new ones which were cast after the war.

The Columns are made of stone blocks and have a platform on top with metal brackets for lights. Inside the Columns are spiral staircases which were climbed to light the giant torches, since the Rostral Columns also served as beacons for ships. In 1957 gas was piped to the

The ring of moorings along the Spit Embankment

A Rostral Column

ops of the Columns and now seven-metre-high torches blaze here during festivities for purely decorative purposes.

From close up the Columns' finish seems rather rude, for the mighty allegorical figures at the base, representing the Russian Neva, Volkhov, Volga and Dnieper rivers, were executed without painstaking detail: he Rostral Columns were intended to impress from great distances.

The symmetrically standing Rostral Columns seem to emphasize the semicircular shape of the square in front of the Exchange. Their brownish brick colour contrasts with the Exchange columns' sparkling whiteness. The public garden which was laid out here in 1926—1927 successfully sets off this part of the ensemble. Each year several thousand tulips, whose bulbs are given to the city by Dutch growers, are planted here.

THE NORTHERN AND SOUTHERN WAREHOUSES
(Pakgáuzy Yúzhny i Séverny)

Built 1826-1832. Under supervision of the architect I. Luchini following the masterplan of A. Zakharov. The buildings were intended to store cargo. The Zoological Museum since 1900 in the Southern Warehouse. The Dokuchayev Central Museum of Soil Science since 1904 in the Northern Warehouse

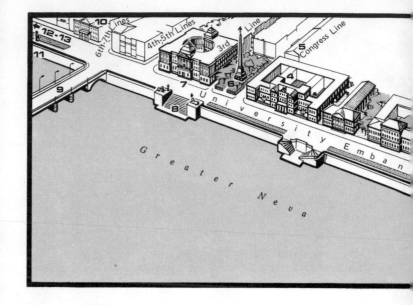

The two warehouses, both painted in the same light grey-green colour, are symmetrically placed alongside the Exchange, but being less voluminous and, in contour, more modest edifices, do not particularly attract one's attention. And this is what their architect planned. Three majestic buildings close together would have competed with each other, but in their existing form the warehouses serve as a neutral background for the monumental Exchange building.

On the opposite side of Pushkin Square the warehouses' two-storey semicircular façades follow a curve whose diametre is equal to that of the Spit's embankment.

After the Sea Port 'abandoned' the Spit, the warehouses were given a different function. The Southern Warehouse was remodelled inside to house the USSR Academy of Sciences' Zoological Institute and Zoological Museum. The museum's collections hold over 40 thousand specimens acquainting one with the animal world. Many of them are unique. In particular, the museum has a 'Hall of Mammoths', where the world's only stuffed mammoth is on display.

The Central Soil Science Museum in the Northern Warehouse was founded on the basis of the outstanding Russian scientist V. Dokuchayev's personal collections. The exhibits give one an idea of the composition of different soils and the ways of increasing their fertility.

1. Kunstkammer: Miklukho-Maklay Institute of Ethnography of the USSR Academy of Sciences; Peter the Great Museum of Anthropology and Ethnography of the USSR Academy of Sciences; Lomonosov Museum—3, University Emb. 2. Academy of Sciences (Main Building)—5, University Emb. 3. 'Twelve Colleges', Leningrad Zhdanov State University—7, University Emb. 4. Menshikov Palace—45, University Emb. 5. Cadet Corps—1-5, Congress Line 6. Obelisk (Rumyantsev Obelisk) in honour of Russian victories in 1768-1774 7. Academy of Arts—17, University Emb. 8. Sphinx Pier 9. Lieutenant Schmidt Bridge 10. House of the Academicians—2, Lieutenant Schmidt Emb. 11. Monument to Admiral I. Kruzenstern 12.—13. To the Naval Cadet Corps—17, Lieutenant Schmidt Emb. To the Mining Institute and Mining Museum—45, Lieutenant Schmidt Emb.

THE CUSTOMS HOUSE

Built 1829-1832. Architect—I. Luchini, with the presumed collaboration of V. Stasov. The building houses the USSR Academy of Sciences' Institute of Russian literature—Pushkin House (Pushkinsky dom)—and this institute's Museum of Literature

The Customs House is situated not far from the Northern Warehouse to the right of the Exchange. (One can see it from the Spit Embankment). The building's main façade looks out on the Little Neva. It is the last link in the history of the formation of the Spit's architectural ensemble. The building is adorned with an eight-columned portico topped by a pediment on which are mounted statues of Mercury, Neptune and Ceres cast in copper. The Customs House's cupola served as an observation point from which the arrival in port of trading ships was signalled.

The former Customs House now holds the Museum of Literature, the impulse for whose founding was the acquisition of Alexander Pushkin's personal library and manuscripts after the exhibition of 1899 which was dedicated to the hundredth anniversary of the great poet's birth. Today it is a major research centre, for the museum owns the largest collection in the USSR of artistic, documentary and pictorial

materials relating to the history of Russian literature. On display here
are memorial items linked with the work of Pushkin, Lermontov, Gogol, Turgenev, Lev Tolstoy, Dostoyevsky and other Russian writers
their manuscripts, first editions and portraits.

UNIVERSITY EMBANKMENT (Universitétskaya náberezhnaya)

After you have looked over the Spit's architectural ensemble, we
suggest you go back to the early history of Vasilyevsky Island.

To do so you need only cross Pushkin Square to University Embankment beyond the Palace Bridge.

> On your tours of Leningrad you will certainly visit Decem-
> brists' Square (Plóshchad Dekabrístov) and the 'Bronze Horseman
> (Médny vsádnik). (See chapter on 'The Central Squares'). From
> there, from the opposite bank of the Neva, we advise you to take
> a look at the University Embankment. At any time, whether in the
> morning or at dusk, in the middle of the day or late at night, an
> unforgettable sight will open before your eyes.

The University Embankment is the only district in Leningrad where
nearly every building is a monument of 18th-century architecture.

At the beginning of University Embankment you will come across
the Kunstkammer.

The University
Embankment

THE KUNSTKAMMER

1718-1734. Architects—G. Mattarnovi, G. Chiaveri, M. Zemtsov, N. Gerbel, S. Chevakinsky. The building is over 95 m long and its tower is 45 m high. At various times between 1728 and 1903 it housed a museum, a public library, an observatory and various institutions of the Russian Academy of Sciences. From 1903 on, it has held the Peter the Great Museum of Anthropology and Ethnography; here, too, is the Miklukho-Maklay Institute of Ethnography as well as the Lomonosov Museum

The façade of the Kunstkammer, which stretches along the embankment, consists of three parts: two wings joined by a three-tiered tower. The 'joyfully pagan' appearance of the Kunstkammer is so distinctive and picturesque that you can't confuse this building with any other.

It would perhaps be impossible to find another building in the city which has gone through as many changes in its history. The list of architects cited above is incomplete—it would be hard to enumerate all those who in some way or another took part in remodelling the building.

Its tower was erected three times. The first one soon collapsed, the second burnt down and the third was so unlike the original that it marred the building's appearance. Between 1947 and 1949 Soviet archi-

93

The Kunstkammer tower. The tower
of the Cabinet of Curiosities

The globe in the Kunstkammer towe

tects, going by old drawings and engravings which had been preserved
erected a graceful tower of a design close to the first and best variant

The vaults of the ground floor rooms were given baroque-style
mouldings in the 1760s. The allegorical bas-reliefs of 'Russia' and
'Europe Celebrating' date from the 1770s, as does the sculpture por-
traying the great mathematician L. Euler.

The Kunstkammer's grand appearance was determined not only by
the building's location but also by its purpose. This was the first building which was especially intended to house educational and scientific
institutions.

The first museum of natural science in Russia—the Kunstkammer—
gave its name the building as a whole (the Kunstkammer's collections
were originally on display in other premises). The astronomical instruments, maps, rare books, minerals and various unusual exhibits in the
museum were collected both on order of Peter the Great and by the
tsar himself, starting in 1714. In order to attract visitors, for whom
a museum was a novelty, not only was entry free at first, but guests
were also treated to a glass of vodka.

The old building and a newer one erected next to it at the end of
the 19th century now house the Peter the Great Museum of Anthropology and Ethnography, one of the biggest such museums in the world.

Petersburg in the 18th century. The Twelve Collegiums (engraving)

The museum's collection numbers over 400 thousand items having to do with the history, economy and art of the peoples of the world.

The Kunstkammer also contains a memorial museum of the eighteenth-century Russian scientist and encyclopaedist Mikhail Lomonosov, who worked here from 1741 to 1765. Apart from the scientist's books and personal effects, unique eighteenth-century scientific instruments are on display here. There is an interesting collection of recipes for stained glass concocted by Lomonosov, as well as samples of the finished product and mosaics made out of it.

On the fourth floor of the tower is a unique giant globe with a diametre of over 3 m. On its outer surface is a map of the earth, while its inner surface represents the night sky. Twelve persons can fit inside the globe, and a mechanism can be put into motion to create the effect of the motion of the night sky. This precursor of modern planetariums was manufactured between 1748 and 1754 with Lomonosov's participation in the workshops of the Petersburg Academy of Sciences.

During the Second World War the globe, which since 1901 had been kept in the town of Tsarskoye Selo (present-day town of Pushkin), was stolen by the fascist invaders and carried away to the town of Lübeck in Germany. In 1947 it was returned to Leningrad and after being restored was mounted in the Kunstkammer.

Zhdanov University, showing the Twelve Collegiums building

THE ACADEMY OF SCIENCES (main building)

1783-1789. Architect—G. Quarenghi. A rectangular plan. The façade is about 100 m long. At present the building houses the Leningrad division of the Institute of Linguistics and other institutions of the USSR Academy of Sciences

The building, with its eight-columned monumental portico and its main stairway which protrudes onto the sidewalk, belongs to the kind which produce a particularly striking effect when seen from a distance. It is one of Giacomo Quarenghi's first major works, and one of his most interesting.

The Academy of Sciences was founded by a decree of Peter the Great published in 1724 and was at first housed in the Kunstkammer. From the 1790s the Russian, and from 1925 the USSR, Academy of Sciences has been located in its own building. In 1934 the ruling organs of the USSR Academy of Sciences were transferred to Moscow. There are still 30 scientific institutions under the USSR Academy of Sciences in Leningrad, including, besides the previously mentioned Institute of Russian Literature, the Institute of Silicate Chemistry, the Pavlov Institute of Physiology and divisions of the Institute of the History of Natural Science and Technology, of the Institute of Oceanography and of the Institute of Theoretical Astronomy.

Plekhanov Mining Institute

THE ZHDANOV STATE UNIVERSITY ('The Twelve Collegiums')

1722-1742. Architect — D. Trezzini. The main façade, which is about 40 m long, is perpendicular to the Neva. The building was planned as the seat of the Senate and Collegiums — the highest administrative bodies, established by Peter the Great. From 1819 on, it was given over to Petersburg University. At present it belongs to the Order of Lenin and Order of the Red Banner of Labour Zhdanov State University

The University's main façade looks onto Mendeleyev Line and its side face is turned to University Embankment.

The building consists of 12 completely identical blocks which closely adjoin one another. In the 18th century it looked somewhat different. Each block had its architectural centre and its own entrance and open arcade. Peter's idea, embodied in D. Trezzini's design, was that separate premises for each of the twelve collegiums (the prototypes of the future ministries) would emphasize their independence, while their standing side by side would underline their mutual ties within the system of state administration.

The arcades were subsequently partially closed with bricks. A corridor running the whole length of the façade was built above them; its windows can be seen from the courtyard. In the wall spaces between the windows inside the corridor there are now paintings and sculpture representing the scientists who have brought fame to the University A panel showing the young Lenin addressing the professors of Peters burg University at his final examinations opens this original art gallery in 1891 the future leader of the Revolution passed the state examin ations on the material covered in the faculty of law as an externa student and received a first-degree diploma.

St. Petersburg University played a significant role in the Russia revolutionary movement. Within its walls studied revolutionary demo crats N. Chernyshevsky and D. Pisarev, M. Butashevich-Petrashe vsky—a Russian utopian socialist—and Lenin's older brother A. Ulyar ov, who was a participant in the Russian revolutionary movement.

The activities of many outstanding Russian scientists who mad great contributions to the development of Russian and world scienc are linked with this educational institution. Such world-famous scier tists as A. Butlerov, P. Chebyshev, V. Dokuchayev, E. Lentz, D. Mende leyev, I. Pavlov, A. Popov, I. Sechenov, K. Timiryazev and many other worked here.

Regardless of how spacious the premises housing Leningrad Un versity are (it also owns over twenty other buildings, as well as som neighbouring ones), it has become cramped for space: over 20 thous and students are now enrolled in it. The University has 15 facultie about 200 departments, 7 research institutes and over 100 education laboratories. This is why construction was begun in 1967 on a 'town o science' in the area of Petrodvorets, 29 km from Leningrad. The Un versity campus occupy a total area of 850 hectares in the greenery o a park on the shores of the Gulf of Finland. Some faculties have alrea dy moved to their new location.

THE MENSHIKOV PALACE

1710-1714. Architects—D. Fontana and G. Schädel. Built for A. Menshikov, th city's first governor and Peter the Great's closest associate. Turned over to th Hermitage and houses a permanent exhibition on 'The Culture of Russia in th First Third of the 18th Century'

The house of Alexander Menshikov was the first residential struc ure of Vasilyevsky Island and is the oldest building on University Embankment. The governor's residence was built at the same time as the Summer Palace intended for Peter I, but was much bigger and more luxurious in its appointments. Wooden sculptures stood along the cornice of the façade, which was decorated with pilasters on each floor. A ramp descended from the front of the palace to the Neva, for distinguished guests came by boat for receptions and audiences. At that time the building was often called the 'Embassadorial Palace'.

When after Peter the Great's death A. Menshikov fell into disfavour and was sent into exile, the building was turned over to a military educational establishment, the First Cadet Corps.

> *Both then and at other times in the future, the palace was remodelled. In those places where it is scientifically warranted and practically feasible, it is planned to restore the palace to its original exterior and interior appearance.*
>
> *Specialists in restoration and their volunteer helpers, members of the All-Union Society for the Protection of Monuments of History and Culture, are now conducting research here. They have, for example, brought to light two equally large, symmetrically placed halls with huge arches and columns down the middle, as well as twelve kinds of stone vaults. Interesting ornamented red brick floors were discovered underneath a layer of earth on the ground floor; and there turned out to be a gorgeous fresco beneath a rough coat of whitewash on the top floor's ceiling. Documents from Menshikov's archives were found. Since the 1720s the building has 'sunk' one and a half metres into the earth. It is planned to open the windows of the south façade's ground floor.*

THE FIRST CADET CORPS

1758-1760. Architect unknown (some have suggested V. Bazhenov). Other buildings later added. Received its present appearance 1938

A special building for the Cadet Corps was built alongside the Menshikov Palace. Its façade looks out on present-day Congress Line. (Syézdovskaya líniya) and is perpendicular to University Embankment.

The inscription on the commemorative plaque which has been affixed to the wall of the former Cadet Corps reads: 'In this house the first All-Russia Congress of Workers' and Soldiers' Deputies, which

Vladimir Ilyich Lenin twice addressed, was held between June 3 and 2
1917. On June 4, Lenin announced the Bolshevik Party's readiness t
take power into its own hands. On June 9, Lenin gave a speech abou
the war, in which he indicated the way to conclude a democratic peace
In memory of this event, Cadet Line was renamed Congress (Syézdov.
kaya) Line.

THE RUMYANTSEV OBELISK

1799. Architect—V. Brenna. In 1818 the composition was altered by archite
C. Rossi

In the garden behind the Menshikov Palace stands an obelisk whic
was erected in memory of the victories of the Russian forces led b
Field Marshal Pyotr Rumyantsev-Zadunaisky in the 1768-1774 wa
with Turkey. The obelisk was originally put up on the Field of Mar
Upon C. Rossi's suggestion, the monument was moved to Vasilyevsk
Island and put up near the Cadet Corps, where Rumyantsev ha
studied.

THE ACADEMY OF ARTS

Built 1764-1788. Architects—A. Kokorinov and J.-B. Vallin de la Mothe. A nea
ly square-shaped building with a large round courtyard of forty-metre diametr
inside. The building houses the world's largest higher educational institutic
specialising in the arts—the Leningrad Repin Institute of Painting, Sculptur
and Architecture—and the research museum of the USSR Academy of Art
And since 1964 Shevchenko museum-flat has been opened here

The majestic building of the Academy of Arts rises at the end c
University Embankment. As in other large structures of the 1760s an
1770s, the first floor of the Academy serves as ground floor, while th
two upper ones are joined by columns and pilasters. Sculptures c
Hercules and Flora are placed between the portico's four columns.
'The academy of the three greatest arts' (painting, sculpture an
architecture) has formed a large number of talented painters, sculptor
and architects, such as D. Levitsky, K. Bryullov, I. Repin and V. Serov
F. Shubin, P. Clodt and M. Antokolsky; V. Bazhenov, A. Voronikhi
and A. Zakharov.
A. Kokorinov, one of the building's designers, was subsequentl

a professor and director of the Academy of Arts. Quite a few masters of fine arts who have later become famous throughout the country and brought glory to their native culture have left these walls during the years of Soviet power.

The building also holds one of the oldest art museums in the country, which was established at the same time as the Academy. In it are exhibited the thesis works of the Academy of Arts' students from the day the institute was founded. There is an interesting collection of copies of outstanding antique and West European sculptures. Displays describe the development of Russian architecture from the 11th century to our day. Here one can also find original designs and drawings made by architects, and unique models of buildings such as, for example, St. Isaac's Cathedral, the Smolny Monastery, the Academy of Arts itself, and so on.

The studio of Taras Shevchenko, in which he lived and worked until the end of his life after his return from exile (from 1858 to 1861), is one more museum that is housed in the building, as a memorial to this great Ukrainian poet and painter, a graduate of the Academy of Arts.

> Between 1832 and 1834 a pier designed by the architect K. Ton was built in front of the Academy's main façade. On its upper terrace are two bronze torch-holders, while on its lower one are winged lions, or griffins. Above, on both sides of the wide staircase, two stone sculptures (each over 3.6 metres high and 5 metres long) rest on high granite pedestals, inscribed as follows: 'This sphinx from ancient Thebes in Egypt was brought to the city of Saint Peter in 1832.' The hieroglyphic inscriptions on the stone sculptures glorify the Egyptian Pharaoh Amenhotep III, who lived from 1455 to 1419 B.C. It follows from them that the artist gave his sculptures the traits of this ruler. The sphinxes were submerged during a flood of the Nile, covered with silt and only brought to light in 1820. The Russian government bought them from Egypt. The ship which transported the sphinxes, each of which weighs more than 23 tons, took almost a year to reach the banks of the Neva.

THE LIEUTENANT SCHMIDT EMBANKMENT (Náberezhnaya Leitenánta Shmídta)

The Lieutenant Schmidt Bridge separates University Embankment from Lieutenant Schmidt Embankment.

LIEUTENANT SCHMIDT BRIDGE

Built 1842-1850. The first permanent bridge across the Neva. (Originally called Annunciation Bridge, then Nikolaevsky Bridge.) Rebuilt and made 4 metres wider 1937-1938. In 1975-1976 the surfacing of the raisable part of the bridge was modernized

The bridge's beauty enraptured people and in particular those who witnessed its inauguration. In the memoirs of one of them one reads

'My favourite walk is now along Annunciation Bridge, a marvellous necklace for the fair Neva and the summit of art in all respects! By day it seems transparent, but in the light of midnight it appears to you as an enormous mass...' Eighty years later when the bridge was reconstructed, its cast iron arches were replaced by a welded steel structure. And once again this bridge was first—the first all-welded bridge in the country. Its gorgeous cast-iron grating, whose design symbolizes the sea, has been preserved.

In 1918 both the embankment and the bridge were renamed in honour of a hero of the first Russian revolution of 1905, Pyotr Schmidt who led the uprising of the cruiser 'Ochakov'. P. Schmidt was a graduate of the Petersburg naval college.

'THE HOUSE OF THE ACADEMICIANS'

The 1750s. Architect—S. Chevakinsky. Remodelled 1808-1809 by the architects A. Zakharov and A. Bezhanov. The museum-flat of Academician Ivan Pavlov is open to visitors

This old three-storey building on the corner of the embankment and Seventh Line (Sedmáya líniya), adorned with columns and elegant casings, is a special kind of sight. Twenty-six commemorative plaques are affixed to the house's façade. Over the past hundred and fifty-odd years, leading lights of Russian and world science have lived and worked in this house, including the inventor of the electric arc V. Petrov, the outstanding mathematician and founder of the Russian school of number theory, function theory and theory of mechanisms P. Chebyshev, the reformer of Russian orthography J. Grot, and the great physiologist I. Pavlov.

The apartment in which I. Pavlov lived from 1918 to 1936 has been made into a memorial museum.

THE NAVAL CADET CORPS

Built 1796-1798. Architect—F. Volkov. Now the Frunze Higher Naval School

At the beginning of the 18th century the section of the embankment where this building stands was built up with residential houses. Architect F. Volkov joined the old structures behind a single façade. This was the first attempt to reconstruct a city block.

The building houses the oldest naval school in the country, where a pleiade of outstanding commanders of the fleet, navigators and scientists received their education. Its graduates include Admiral F. Ushakov, the founder of Russian naval tactics for sailing fleets; Admiral P. Nakhimov, a hero of the defence of Sevastopol during the Crimean War of 1853-1856; Admiral M. Lazarev, a member of the Russian navigator F. Bellingshausen's expedition which in 1820 discovered the Antarctic; and a number of other distinguished naval commanders.

In this building on May 8 (21), 1917, Lenin gave a report to a city-wide meeting of the Petrograd Bolshevik Party Organisation on the results of the 7th (April) All-Russia Conference of Bolsheviks, which mapped out the ways of transition from the bourgeois-democratic revolution to a socialist revolution.

MONUMENT TO ADMIRAL I. KRUZENSTERN

1873. Architect—I. Monighetti, sculptor—I. Schröder

In front of the naval college on the bank of the Neva is a monument 'To Admiral Ivan Fyodorovich Kruzenstern' the first Russian circumnavigator of the world, as the inscription on it reads. The monument was put up in honour of the first Russian circumnavigatory expedition of 1803-1806. I. Kruzenstern was a student in the Naval Corps, and later became its director.

THE MINING INSTITUTE

1806-1811. Architect—A. Voronikhin. Group sculptures: 'The fight between Hercules and Antaeus' by S. Pimenov, and 'The Abduction of Proserpine by Pluto' by V. Demut-Malinovsky. The building also houses the Mining Museum, founded at the same time as the institute. In 1956 the Mining Institute was conferred the name of G. Plekhanov

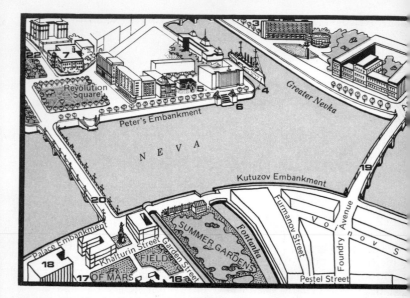

1. Statue of Lenin—Lenin Sq. 2. Finland Railway Station 3. Leningrad Hotel—7, Pirogov Emb. 4. Cruiser *Aurora*. Branch of Central Naval Museum—Petrograd Emb. 5. Peter the Great's Cottage—3, Petrovskaya Emb. 6. Shih Tze Stone Figures—Petrovskaya Emb. 7. Museum of the Great October Socialist Revolution (Kshesinskaya Mansion)—4, Kuibyshev Str. 8. Taurida Palace—4, Voinov Str. 9. Kikin Mansion—Voinov Str. 10. Smolny Convent—Rastrelli Sq. 11. Smolny (Smolny Institute)—Proletarian Dictatorship Sq. 12. Propy-

> *The majestic portico, crowned by a mighty pediment, is made up of twelve columns. Its sculptural decorations harmonise with the building's architectural peculiarities and symbolically disclose its purpose. One of the sculptures, set up near the entrance shows the abduction of the young goddess Proserpine by Pluto, the God of the Underworld. The other depicts the encounter between Hercules, the son of Zeus, and Antaeus, the son of Earth, who was invincible as long as he touched his mother Earth. The bas-relief frieze on the façade is also saturated with symbolism. It represents scenes connected with Venus and Apollo's visit to Vulcan, the god of fire and patron of blacksmithing.*

A Mining College founded in 1773, on the basis of which arose the Mining Cadet Corps, has been an institute since 1866. Now the Leningrad Mining Institute bears the name of G. Plekhanov, the distinguished Russian revolutionary and outstanding populariser of Marxism in Russia, who studied here from 1874 to 1876. The remarkable 19th-century Russian writers V. Garshin and V. Korolenko also studied here.

Affiliated with the Mining Institute is a Mining Museum, where one finds materials connected with the history of mining technology (prospecting for and exploitation of minerals, ore-dressing processes, metallurgy, etc.). Among the exhibits are such unique objects as a meteorite weighing over 300 kg, a block of Ural malachite weighing 1,504 kg,

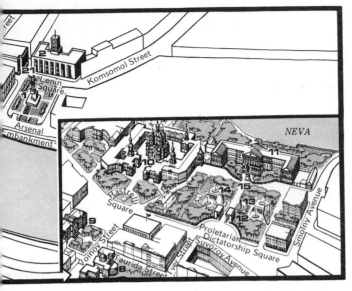

laea **13.** Statue of Marx **14.** Statue of Engels **15.** Statue of Lenin **16.** Monument to the Heroes of the Revolution—Field of Mars **17.** Barracks of the Pavlovsky Regiment—Field of Mars **18.** Leningrad Branch of the Central Lenin Museum (Marble Palace)—5, Khalturin St. **19.** Liteiny Bridge **20.** Kirov Bridge **21.** Ploshchad Lenina Metro Station **22.** Gorkovskaya Metro Station

a copper nugget from Kazakhstan weighing 842 kg and marvellous specimens of diamonds from Yakutia. The exhibition gives one a graphic idea of the mineral wealth in the Soviet Union.

The building of the Mining Institute, which stands almost at the very mouth of the Neva, is a most fitting conclusion to our tour of the Vasilyevsky Island embankments.

Lenin Memorial Places. Relics of the Revolution

As we describe places of interest in the city on the River Neva, we shall be telling the reader about various revolutionary events and about V. I. Lenin's life and work. There are more than 250 addresses associated with Lenin alone in the city. In this chapter, we recommend a route which, while not covering all the city's relics of the revolution and places associated with Lenin, makes it possible to view monuments of interest connected with the history of the 1917 Revolution.

The objects of the excursion are situated in different parts of Leningrad, many of them some distance apart, so you will certainly need some form of transport if you follow our suggestions. The sequence of the tour is shown on the maps and is indicated in numerical order (addresses are given in the explanatory notes). The map gives places of historical and cultural interest which you will notice on the way, though they have no direct bearing on the subject of this excursion.

We suggest beginning the excursion at Lenin Square (Plóshchad Lénina) in front of the Finland Railway Station.

Our route is dictated by the development of the historical events which we shall be describing further on. It will take you to Kuibyshev Street, (Úlitsa Kúibysheva) to former mansion of Kshesinskaya, which now houses the Museum of the Great October Socialist Revolution.

On your way from Lenin Square to Kuibyshev Street, you can look round the legendary cruiser *Aurora,* permanently anchored at the Petrograd Embankment (Petrográdskaya náberezhnaya) (for visitors' rules, see the section 'Museums').

From the Museum of the Revolution, you proceed to the left bank of the Neva and to Voinov Street (Úlitsa Voinóva), where the Taurida Palace (Tavríchesky dvoréts) stands. Voinov Street will lead you to Rastrelli Square (Plóshchad Rastrélli). On the right are Proletarian Dictatorship Square (Plóshchad Proletárskoi diktatúry) and the Smolny.

From the Smolny, you head towards the Field of Mars (Mársovo pólye), the ensemble of which includes the Field of Mars itself, the Memorial to the Fighters for the Revolution, the former Barracks of the Pavlovsky Regiment and the former Marble Palace (Mrámorny dvoréts), which now houses the Leningrad Branch of the central Lenin Museum.

Your route ends with the museum exhibition, which will give you a complete and stage-by-stage account of Lenin's life and work.

Public transport: Lenin Square: Trolleybuses—3, 8, 12, 13, 18, 19, 21, 23, 25, 30; Buses—2, 3, 7, 47, 49, 53, 57, 75, 78, 104, 106, 107, 262; Metro station—Plóshchad Lénina. Museum of the Great October Socialist Revolution: Buses—1, 23, 25, 46, 65; Trams—3, 6, 12, 25, 26, 30, 34, 51; Metro station—Gorkovskaya, Cruiser *Aurora:* Bus—49; Trams—2, 6, 22, 25, 26, 30. Taurida Palace: Buses—6, 14, 26, 43. Smolny: Trolleybuses—5, 15, 16, 25; Buses—1, 6, 14, 23. The Field of Mars: Trolleybuses—2, 3, 12, 22, 34, 51; Buses—1, 2, 23, 25, 46, 65, 100.

The city excursion bureau organises tours of Lenin memorial and historical revolutionary places in Leningrad on foot and by bus. If you wish to go on the excursion 'Leningrad Is the City of Great Lenin', you can avail yourself of the services of Intourist. As you go round the historical and revolutionary museums, guides will tell you about revolutionary events and about episodes in Lenin's life which were associated with Leningrad. For information concerning the work of the historical and revolutionary museums, see the section 'Museums'.

> *... The great events of October 1917, which decided the destiny of our country, took place in Petrograd. Hundreds of Petrograd workers were the first to follow Comrade Lenin ... Lenin's revolutionary activity was at its most intensive in Petrograd. The first-ever workers' and peasants' government was formed in this city.*
>
> *In view of all this, the 2nd Congress of Soviets of the Union of Soviet Socialist Republics considers it quite justifiable to meet the request of the Petrograd Soviet of Workers', Peasants' and Soldiers' Deputies and, supported by resolutions of the workers from all Petrograd factories and plants, to give the city of Petrograd the name Leningrad.*
>
> *May this major centre of the proletarian revolution be associated henceforth with the name of Vladimir Ilyich Ulyanov-Lenin, the greatest leader of the proletariat.*
>
> *From the Resolution of the 2nd Congress of Soviets of the USSR, January 26, 1924.*

Let us remind the reader of some of the stages in Lenin's life and work associated with the city on the Neva.

Lenin first arrived in St. Petersburg (later Petrograd) late in August 1890 to obtain permission to take examinations for the full extra-mural course at the Law Faculty of the University. In April and September-November 1891, he passed his examinations, being the only one of the students taking exams (87 in spring and 134 in autumn) to receive top marks for all subjects. The examination commission awarded him a 1st Degree Diploma.

Not counting several short stays in the city, historians single out three periods in Lenin's life and revolutionary activity in St. Petersburg-Petrograd which were to play a historic role in the country's destiny.

1893-1897. Establishment of contacts with St. Petersburg Marxists. Lenin's ideological struggle against Narodism and 'legal Marxism'—ideological and political trends that became obstacles to the development of the Social-Democratic movement and the dissemination of Marxism in Russia. Marxist propaganda in workers' study groups. Theoretical substantiation of the necessity to create an independent political Marxist party, the nucleus of which became the League of Struggle for the Emancipation of the Working Class, a St. Petersburg Social-Democratic organisation founded by Lenin in the autumn of 1895. Arrested on December 9 (22), 1895; three years' exile in Siberia (1897-1900) and subsequent emigration.

1905-1907. Return from emigration on November 8 (21), 1905. Leadership of the Central and St. Petersburg Committees of Bolsheviks, and of Party organisations in other towns which headed the revolutionary movement of the masses during the first Russian bourgeois-democratic revolution. Lenin's struggle for unity of the working class and its party, and for the purity of Marxist theory. Illegal revolutionary activity. Bolshevik centre's decision that Lenin should go abroad after the defeat of the first Russian revolution.

1917-1918. Lenin's return from emigration on April 3 (16), 1917. The struggle for the 1917 February bourgeois-democratic revolution to develop into a socialist revolution. Work in hiding after July 1917 events. Illegal return to Petrograd. Leadership in preparing and carrying out the October armed uprising on October 25 (November 7), 1917. The Resolution of the 2nd Congress of Soviets concerning the formation of the first-ever government of workers and peasants—the Council of People's Commissars, headed by V. I. Lenin.

July 1920, when he attended the ceremonial opening of the Second Congress of the Communist International was Lenin's last visit to Petrograd after the government moved to Moscow in March 1918.

LENIN SQUARE

The Square was reconstructed and trees and bushes were planted in Soviet times—in the 1920s. Its architectural ensemble took its present form under the General Plan for the Development of Leningrad after the Great Patriotic War (1941-1945)

Events that followed the 1917 February bourgeois-democratic revolution are associated with the square in front of the Finland Railway Station.

The February revolution radically changed the situation in Russia. The tsarist autocracy was overthrown, that is, the immediate task was accomplished, which the Leninist party had set from the very first days of its emergence. Lenin lost no time in defining the new tasks that faced the proletariat and the Bolshevik Party. He made every effort to return to his homeland and revolutionary Petrograd as soon as possible.

... It was daytime, April 3, when the news swept through Petrograd that Lenin was due to arrive that evening. Although it was Easter and newspapers were not on sale and the factories were closed, the joyful news reached every corner of the city. Military units, workers, soldiers and sailors began preparing to give Lenin a hearty welcome. Finland Railway Station ... The guard of honour was drawn up on the platform. Great excitement ... Vladimir Ilyich stepped out of the train.

Lenin made a brief speech and went to the car with his wife, Nadezhda Krupskaya. But it turned out that the car could not move off since it was surrounded by a dense ring of people. Many thousands of workers and soldiers filled the then narrow square and adjacent streets. Willing hands lifted Lenin over the crowd on to the turret of one of the armoured cars guarding the square. Lenin used it as a rostrum for his speech. (This armoured car now stands in front of the Leningrad Branch of the Central Lenin Museum). Lenin's speech lasted no longer than ten minutes, but it decided the destiny of Russia. His first address to revolutionary Petrograd's workers and soldiers concluded with an ardent call:'Long live the socialist revolution!'

'That characteristic gesture of Lenin's, when he thrust his right hand forward, has remained forever in the memory of all who heard and saw Lenin on the armoured car in front of Finland Station,' wrote one of those present at the historic meeting in April 1917.

MONUMENT TO LENIN

1924-1926. Sculptor—S. Yevseyev; architects—V. Gelfriekh and V. Shchuko. Bronze figure 4.35 metres high. Total height of monument—10.7 metres. Unveiled on November 7, 1926, on the 9th anniversary of the Great October Socialist Revolution

Originally, the monument was erected on the exact spot from which Lenin, standing on the armoured car addressed the masses that had come to meet him on his return from emigration. During the reconstruction of the square, the monument was moved some 180 metres nearer the Neva embankment. It is now surrounded by beds of flowers and stands on a 1.5-metre mound to conform with the new proportions of the square.

The foundation stone was laid on April 16, 1924 after a competition with more than sixty designs being submitted by the best sculptors and architects in the Soviet Union. The erection of the monument became a nationwide affair; workers raised funds and contributed their own labour. Some 10 tons of bronze were needed which, after the civil war was in very short supply. The metal was resmelted from used shell-cases...

Lenin is portrayed standing in full height. Everything is very simple with no external effects. However its emotive power comes from 'that characteristic gesture of Lenin's: the leader has thrust out his right hand in a movement both assertive and challenging.

During the 900-day defence of Leningrad, the monument was care-fully covered with sandbags. Every day in that frosty and hungry block-ade winter of 1942, Sergei Yevseyev, one of the sculptors, trudged all the way from Theatre Square (Teatrálnaya plóshchad) to Finland Sta-tion (there was no transport) to make sure that monument was safe and sound...

The monument to Lenin at Finland Railway Station remains as a consummate masterpiece of Soviet monumental sculpture. It is one of the symbols of Lenin's city.

FINLAND RAILWAY STATION

The old building dates back to 1870. Only a small part of it has been preserved in the west section. The new building was erected in 1955-1960. The central hall (35 m × 35 m) is covered with a ferro-concrete vaultshell without supports. A cast-iron high-relief frieze depicts scenes from the revolution

On the east part of Finland Railway Station, a glass pavilion was built by the platform (1964). It protects a small, old-fashioned steam locomotive No.293 from the weather.

> *Lenin left secretly for Finland aboard this locomotive in Au-gust 1917, compelled to go into hiding again after the counter-rev-olutionary events of July 1917. On board the same locomotive driven by the same engine driver, H. Jalava, he returned to Petro-grad in the autumn of 1917 to head the October armed uprising. Later on, this engine was handed over to Finland together with other Finnish locomotives. In 1957, on the 40th anniversary of the October Revolution, the locomotive was returned to Leningrad. On*

April 22, 1961, Lenin's 91st birthday, Locomotive No. 293 was put on display as another relic of the Revolution.

A brass plate on the locomotive bears inscriptions in Russian and Finnish: 'June 13, 1957. The Government of Finland presented this locomotive to the Government of the Union of Soviet Socialist Republics in commemoration of journeys over Finnish territory made by Lenin in troubled times.'

THE CRUISER AURORA, A BRANCH OF THE CENTRAL NAVAL MUSEUM

Built 1900. Listed among the Russian Navy in 1903. Displacement—6,731 tons, length—123.7 m, width—16.8 m. Draught—6.4 m, speed—about 20 knots. Carried a crew of 570. In 1948, the *Aurora* brought to permanent moorings anchorage and a branch of the Central Naval Museum was opened on board in 1956

The combat history of the ship began during the Russo-Japanese war of 1904-1905. The *Aurora* took part on May 27, 1905, in the battle of Tsusima, which ended in the total defeat of the tsarist navy squadron.

Early in 1906, on their return to St. Petersburg, the crew was disbanded as disloyal because of frequent unrest on board ship caused by the intolerable conditions of service.

The freedom-loving traditions, high sense of political awareness and revolutionary spirit of her crew found reflection in the fact that the *Aurora* was the first in the Baltic Fleet to raise the Red Banner, on the second day of the 1917 February revolution. The sailors took over command. The *Aurora* did not succumb to the counter-revolutionary Provisional Government and became a reliable bulwark for the Bolsheviks.

Lenin regarded the participation of sailors in the revolution to be of utmost importance. When the October armed uprising began, the ship's crew, on the instructions of the Military Revolutionary Committee, prevented the former Nikolayevsky Bridge (now Lieutenant Schmidt Bridge) across the Neva from being raised. Had they failed, workers in different parts of Petrograd would have been isolated from each other and from the uprising's centre.

On the night of October 25 (November 7), the cruiser entered the Neva, anchored by the central span of the Nikolayevsky Bridge and

The Museum of the Great October Socialist Revolution (former Kshesinskaya house)

trained her guns on the Winter Palace, residence of the Provisional Government.

At 9.45 p.m., the *Aurora*'s bow gun fired a blank round as a signal to begin the final storming of the Winter Palace. Men from her crew were among the attackers.

Since 1923, the *Aurora* has served as a training ship for Soviet naval officers. During the Great Patriotic War of the Soviet people against fascism, sailors from the *Aurora* bombarded the enemy with heavy guns taken from the cruiser, which became part of the anti-aircraft defence system of the Leningrad Front. Even in those trying days, the gun that had signalled the beginning of the October onslaught was preserved as a historic relic.

In 1927, the *Aurora* was awarded the Order of the Red Banner, and in 1968, in the eve of the 50th anniversary of the Soviet Armed Forces, the Order of the October Revolution (with a representation of the legendary cruiser in the centre).

Seven million people, including visitors from 127 countries, have visited the memorial historical-revolutionary museum on board the cruiser in the last fifteen years. A collection of articles presented to the *Aurora* is exhibited there; among them is a memorial medal, minted in France in honour of the Normandie-Niemen Regiment, which fought courageously against nazi Germany in Soviet skies; a medal represent-

The Taurida Palace

ing the destroyer *Vikhr* (Whirlwind), a gift from the sailors of the Polish People's Republic; banners of Italian Resistance fighters who fought against fascism during World War II; and a model schooner *Granma*, '*Aurora*'s younger sister' as the Cubans call her.

MUSEUM OF THE GREAT OCTOBER SOCIALIST REVOLUTION
(Kshesinskaya Mansion)

1902. Architect—A. Gauguin. Built for a ballerina of the Mariinsky Theatre. Since 1957 houses the Museum of the Great October Socialist Revolution

Let us return to the events of April 1917. After the rally in front of Finland Railway Station, Lenin, surrounded by a crowd of people, moved in the armoured car towards Kshesinskaya mansion, which then housed the Central and Petrograd Committees of the Bolshevik Party. There he met his comrades-in-arms and city Party organisation activists and set forth his viewpoint concerning the tasks of the revolution and its prospects.

'It was not a report. Nor was it a speech', recalls N. Podvoisky, who was present at the meeting. 'It was a heart-to-heart talk between Lenin

113

and the members of the old Party guard, his friends in battle who had missed their leader badly and who were now listening to every word of his'.

During that night, Lenin, on the request of the people, several times broke off the conversation which lasted well into the morning to address thousands of people who had gathered there, from the balcony of the mansion.

Later on, until July 1917, when the counter-revolutionary forces took the offensive and began persecuting the Bolshevik Party, Lenin was at the mansion practically every day. Hundreds of people went there at the headquarters of the Bolshevik Party to receive advice and instructions directly from Lenin and his comrades-in-arms on how to explain the Bolshevik programme to the masses and how to carry it out; how to put an end to war and achieve peace; how and in what direction would the revolution develop; what were the Soviets of Workers', Soldiers' and Peasants' Deputies, what was their class content and what role were they to play in the revolution. All those questions by the revolutionary people needed clear and concise answers. Lenin was at the centre of the Party's political and organisational work among the masses. In the 90-day period between his return to Russia and his last journey into hiding, he had written more than 170 articles, pamphlets, draft resolutions, appeals, and so on. He worked ardently, inspiring everyone with his extraordinary energy and his faith in the victory of the socialist revolution. Several workers who participated in the meetings of those days recorded their impressions.

Worker Vassili Yemelyanov recalls: '...I was present at many meetings in 1917 and I heard speakers from ... goodness knows how many different parties, but I've never heard anyone to match Lenin. His words brought people together and showed them the way, how and what every worker should do...' And here is Pyotr Danilov from the former Putilov (now Kirov) Works: 'What Lenin said really gripped you and fired your imagination. Fear and tiredness just seemed to vanish. And you got the impression that it wasn't just Lenin speaking: it was all forty thousand workers talking, sitting, standing or not even finding room to put their feet down on the ground, and they were expressing their most cherished thoughts. It was as if Lenin was voicing all that the workers wanted to say...'

July 4 (17) was the last time that Lenin addressed the people from the balcony of Kshesinskaya mansion. On July 6, the building was seized by the troops of the Provisional Government and the premises were smashed up.

The mansion and adjacent building now house the Museum of the Great October Socialist Revolution, with an exhibition which gives a detailed account of the 1917 revolution.

The Museum was set up in late 1919, when Anatoly Lunacharsky, Maxim Gorky and other public figures, cultural workers and scientists launched a campaign to collect historical and revolutionary relics, material and documents. In the early days, the Museum collection was kept in the Winter Palace. The Museum was opened at its new premises during the celebrations of the 40th anniversary of the October Revolution.

The Museum displays a variety of documents, photographs and works of art associated with the revolution, as well as many different relics. The exhibits tell the visitor about the history of the people's struggle against the Russian autocracy and how the October Revolution was prepared and accomplished. Evenings dedicated to revolutionary events and in honour of the veterans of the revolution are often held in the mansion's biggest hall, where Lenin used to make his speeches.

Historical documentary films about Leningrad, the October Revolution and Lenin are shown in the Museum cinema, and visitors can hear sound recordings of Lenin's speeches.

THE TAURIDA PALACE (TAVRÍCHESKY DVORÉTS)

1783-1789. Designed by the architect I. Starov with F. Volkov. Main façade—260 metres long. Area—65,000 sq. m. Restored 1802-1804, architect—L. Ruska. Partially reconstructed in 1906 for State Duma. Now used for municipal conferences, congresses and meetings; houses the Leningrad Higher Party School

The Taurida Palace is situated in Voinov Street (formerly Shpalernaya). The street was renamed in honour of Ivan Voinov, a Petrograd railway worker and workers' correspondent of the Bolshevik newspaper *Pravda* who was killed by counter-revolutionary Cossacks and military cadets in Shpalernaya Street on July 6, 1917.

The palace exterior looks as the architect conceived it in the 18th century.

The Smolny

The monument to V. I. Lenin near the Smolny

Early in the 20th century, the palace became the seat of the State Duma, a legislative institution with limited rights which the tsarist autocracy had been compelled to set up under the pressure of the first Russian revolution.

During the 1917 February revolution, the State Duma building became an arena of stormy political events.

On February 27 (March 12), at 9 p.m. in the left wing of the Taurida Palace, the first session of the Petrograd Soviet of Workers' and Soldiers' Deputies was opened as an expression of the revolutionary people's interests. The right wing of the palace housed the reactionary Provisional Committee of the State Duma and, later, the bourgeois Provisional Government formed by it.

On April 4 (17), the day after his arrival in Petrograd, Lenin took the floor here three times. In his report on war and the tasks of the revolution, he substantiated his famous *April Theses*, which armed the Party with a scientifically-based programme for going over from the bourgeois-democratic to the socialist revolution.

After the victory of the October Revolution, Lenin spoke from the

The Smolny's Assembly Hall

rostrum of the Taurida Palace on several occasions. His speech at the opening of the 2nd Congress of the Communist International on July 19, 1920, was the last. It was devoted to the international situation and the tasks of the Comintern.

Since the October Revolution, the Taurida Palace has been the traditional venue for major public gatherings in Leningrad.

THE SMOLNY ENSEMBLE

THE SMOLNY CONVENT

Founded 1748. Finished in the rough 1764.
Architect—B. Rastrelli. Completed by architect V. Stasov 1832-1835. The Convent's Cathedral now houses a permanent exhibiton 'Leningrad Today and Tomorrow'

> *When in Voinov Street, you can see the Smolny Convent in the distance. It stands out among Rastrelli's greatest works. He designed it as a palace-convent with the cathedral as the compositional centre. Its graceful five domed towers are reminiscent of the ancient Russian churches.*

In 1764, some of the convent buildings were put at the disposal of

Russia's first women's educational establishment — the Imperial Educational Society for Young Noble Ladies. But the Convent buildings proved inconvenient for classroom work and therefore a special building was erected which came to be known as the Smolny institute and later housed the famous October Revolution headquarters.

SMOLNY (Smolny Institute)

1806-1808. Architect — G. Quarenghi. The façade is 220 m long. The two protruding wings of the main building, each 40 m long, form the main court. I now houses the Leningrad Regional and City Committees of the CPSU

The Smolny Institute is situated in Proletarian Dictatorship Square (Plóshchad Proletárskoi diktatúry), which adjoins Rastrelli Square on the right.

The name 'Smolny' comes from the Russian word 'smola' (tar). In the time of Peter the Great, the land on which the Smolny Convent was later built belonged to the Tar Yard (Smolyanói dvór) place where tar was distilled and stored for the needs of the rapidly growing Russian fleet.

Quarenghi erected his building, simple and austere in form, beside Rastrelli's exuberant baroque creation, with no fear of the styles clashing. Indeed, the two buildings have 'hit it off' well together, making a unique ensemble based on violent contrast.

The Institute for Young Noble Ladies existed till the summer of 1917. After the overthrow of the autocracy, its pupils were transferred to other educational establishments. The premises were taken over by the Petrograd Soviet, which moved from the Taurida Palace, and by the All-Russia Central Executive Committee of the Soviet of Workers and Soldiers' Deputies.

The most glorious pages in the history of the Smolny Institute are associated with the time when it housed the headquarters of the October Revolution. The Military Revolutionary Committee of the Bolshevik Party, which headed the armed uprising, was accommodated in three rooms in the second floor.

Lenin arrived there on the evening of October 24 (November 6), 1917.

... Lenin had left his last hiding place. During this whole period, which was among the busiest in his life and work, the workers, the rank-and-file Party members, took great care of him, guarding him against counter-revolutionaries, often at the risk of their lives. Vladimir Ilyich Lenin was deeply appreciative of the concern shown for him by the ordinary working people.

Now that he had arrived at the revolution's headquarters, Lenin took over the direct leadership of the whole armed uprising.

The Smolny was a majestic spectacle on that historic night. It was brightly lit and crowded with people. From all parts of the city, the Red Guards and representatives of military units and factories streamed into the building for instructions. The Military Revolutionary Committee on the second floor conferred practically without intermission. Delegates of the 2nd All-Russia Congress of Soviets—workers and peasants, sailors and soldiers—gathered in the Smolny's Assembly Hall.

By the morning of October 25 (November 7), 1917, the city was practically in the hands of the insurgent people, with the exception of the Winter Palace, the refuge of the Provisional Government, and the building of the Military District headquarters. The power of the counter-revolutionary Provisional Government was overthrown. In the Smolny, Lenin wrote his historic appeal, 'To the Citizens of Russia!' announcing that the power had been taken over by the Soviets. At 2.30 p.m., at a special meeting of the Petrograd Soviet, Lenin's historic words rang out, accompanied by an enthusiastic ovation from all those present in the Assembly Hall: 'The workers' and peasants' revolution, about the necessity of which the Bolsheviks have always spoken, has been accomplished'.

Some minutes after 3 o'clock in the morning of October 26 (November 8), 1917, the 2nd All-Russia Congress of Soviets heard the announcement that the Winter Palace, that last bastion of the counter-revolutionary forces, had been taken.

That evening, the most memorable meeting of the 2nd All-Russia Congress of Soviets was opened in the Assembly Hall of the Smolny.

> *John Reed, an American journalist, author of the book "Ten Days That Shook the World", has left us this description of Lenin in those historic days:*
> *'It was just 8.40 when a thundering wave of cheers announced the entrance of the presidium, with Lenin—Great Lenin—among*

> *them. A short, stocky figure, with a big head set down in his shoul-
> ders, bald and bulging. Little eyes, a snubbish nose, wide, genero-
> mouth, and heavy chin, clean-shaven now, but already beginnir
> to bristle with the well-known beard of his past and futur
> Dressed in shabby clothes, his trousers much too long for hir
> Unimpressive, to be the idol for a mob, loved and revered as pe
> haps few leaders in history have been. A strange popular lea
> er—a leader purely by virtue of intellect; colourless, humourle.
> uncompromising and detached, without picturesque idiosyncr
> sies—but with the power of explaining profound ideas in simp
> terms, of analysing a concrete situation. And combined wi
> shrewdness, the greatest intellectual audacity.'*

The very first words of the newly-born state were those of peac
The Congress adopted its first historic acts—the Decree on Peace an
the Decree on Land—and formed the world's first government c
workers and peasants, the Council of People's Commissars headed b
Vladimir Ilyich Lenin.

The *Assembly Hall,* where Soviet power was proclaimed, is one c
the three memorial places of the Smolny.

Decorated with white marble, a moulded ceiling, a friez
(sculptor—I. Terebenev) and two rows of windows, it creates an im
pression of solemnity and grandeur. The Assembly Hall is one of Qua
renghi's finest works.

Lenin's first study in the Smolny. At the entrance to the small roor
on the second floor of the Smolny's south wing there is a memoria
plate bearing the inscription: 'This room served as the first study fo
Vladimir Ilyich Lenin, Chairman of the Council of People's Commis
sars, after the Soviet Government had been formed at the 2nd Con
gress of Soviets.'

It was in this room that Lenin signed the first decrees and instruc
tions of the Soviet Government. It was visited by an endless stream o
workers, peasants and soldiers. The furniture is commonplace in th
extreme: a desk, chairs, nothing superfluous. At that time, Lenin wa
living at No.5, Khersonskaya Street (see section 'Museums'). Fre
quently, however, he could not afford the time to go home, and so a
iron camp bed stood behind the partition in the study. The distinctiv
feature of any of the flats, studies and rooms in which Lenin lived and
worked is their ordinariness, the complete disregard for ostentatio
and even the minimal comforts.

Lenin's living room in Smolny. In the middle of November, a room as prepared for Lenin and his wife, Nadezhda Krupskaya, on the first oor of the Smolny. 'Vladimir Ilyich and I went to live in the Smolny. Ve were given a room which had previously belonged to a schoolmis-'ess. There was a partition behind which the bed stood. We had to go rough the washing-room,' recalled Nadezhda Krupskaya.

It is now a flat-museum. The former washing-room is now used for display of documents and material associated with the time when enin lived in the Smolny. Visitors can hear Lenin's speech from tape-recording of an old gramophone record.

Lenin lived and worked in the Smolny for only 124 days, during hich time he wrote more than 200 articles, speeches, resolutions and ppeals, not to mention rough copies, essays and sketches to various aterial and, on top of that, urgent work related to the practical guid-nce of new type of state being created for the first time in history.

ROLETARIAN DICTATORSHIP SQUARE
lóshchad Proletárskoi diktatúry)

The pre-revolutionary appearance of the square in front of the molny has changed radically. Two symmetrical five-columned portico avilions serve as an entrance to a shady garden laid out on what was nce a badly paved open space. These pavilions form the *Propylaea,* or ain entrances (1923-1924. Architects — V. Shchuko and V. Gelfreikh). ne of the pavilions bears an inscription: 'The first Soviet of Prolet-rian Dictatorship', the second — the immortal appeal of the Commu-ist Party Manifesto: 'Workers of all countries, unite!'

A wide, straight avenue leads from the Propylaea to the Smolny. ronze *busts* to *Karl Marx* and *Frederick Engels,* the founders of scien-fic communism, stand on either side of the avenue (1934. Sculptor — . Yevseyev). In front of the entrance to the Smolny towers a bronze *onument to Lenin,* unveiled on the occasion of the 10th anniversary f the October Revolution (1927. Sculptor — V. Kozlov, architects — . Shchuko and V. Gelfreikh. The monument is 6 metres high and the ronze figure 2.15 metres high). Like the sculpture in front of the Fin-and Railway Station, this statue of the leader is one of the symbols of eningrad.

THE FIELD OF MARS (Mársovo pólye)

Area of about 12 hectares. Borders on the Swan Canal (Lebyázhya kanávka the Summer Gardens (Létny sád), the river Moika and the Mikhailovsky Ga dens

After city had been laid out this territory was never used for build ing purposes. The marshland had been drained when the Summer Ga dens were laid in 1710. The Field of Mars owes its name to the fact tha from the end of the 18th century it served for a long time as a militar drill and parade ground.

When you see the green splendour of the Field of Mars today, it hard to believe that the former drill ground was once called 'the Pe tersburg Sahara' before the revolution, since not a blade of grass a single little shrub grew on the dusty surface. Trees and shrubs wer planted and the square was modernised in the 1920s.

The uniqueness of the modern Field of Mars is due to the gree garden in the centre of the square and the adjacent parks and garden which together create an impression of compositional unity, althoug the architectural styles of the surrounding buildings are somewhat d verse.

MEMORIAL TO THE FIGHTERS FOR THE REVOLUTION

Foundation stone laid on March 24 (April 5), 1917. Unveiled in the summer 1920. Architect—L. Rudnev. It is an open rectangle formed by staggered wall of pink granite with epitaphs carved on the butt-ends

'Not knowing the names
Of all the Heroes in struggle
For Freedom
Who shed their blood
The human race
Honours the nameless
In memory
And in honour of them all
This stone has been placed
To stand here
Throughout the ages.'

ANATOLY LUNACHARSKY

In the days of the February revolution, 1917, hundreds of workers and soldiers were killed or wounded in the streets and squares of Petrograd by the defenders of tsarism. On March 23 (April 4), 1917, crowds of people thronged towards the Field of Mars along the city's main streets to the strains of funeral marches. 180 salvoes were fired by the guns in memory of the 180 fallen heroes who were buried with due honours in the square. The foundation stone for the monument was laid on the following day.

Several years later, lines of inspired solemnity were to be carved on the marble slabs of the memorial. They were composed by Anatoly Lunacharsky, the first People's Commissar of Public Education and an outstanding journalist and author:

'Not victims but heroes lie beneath these stones. Not grief but envy is aroused by your fate in the hearts of all your grateful descendants.'

Between February and October 1917, the old square was a scene of endless mass rallies and demonstrations. Many of the episodes of the October Revolution are associated with the Field of Mars. It has gone down in the annals of the city as a significant revolutionary memorial place in Leningrad.

On May 1, 1920, more than 11,000 citizens took part in the communist *subbotnik*, voluntary and non-paid work on a day off, to plant shrubs and trees and modernise the Field of Mars under the guidance of I. Fomin, Petrograd's chief architect. The historic square was reconstructed, in the main, according to his design by the day of the opening of the 2nd Congress of the Communist Third International on July 19, 1920.

On the evening of July 19, together with Lenin, delegates to the Congress from all corners of the world came to the Field of Mars and laid a wreath of red roses and oak leaves on the common grave. The ribbon bore an inscription: '... To the Fallen Fighters for Communism from Proletarians of All Countries ...' This was the last time Lenin visited the city on the Neva. On the same day he addressed a rally of working people in Palace Square for the last time.

During the days of mourning in January 1924, when the whole country took its leave of Lenin, 53 giant bonfires blazed on the Field of Mars, symbolising the years of his life. On the day of Lenin's funeral, the city on the Neva was renamed Leningrad.

In 1957, on the occasion of the 40th anniversary of the October Revolution, an Eternal Flame was lit in the centre of a granite rec-

The Field of Mars

tangle to the memory of the fallen Fighters for the Revolution. The eternal flames at the graves of the heroic defenders of Leningrad in the Piskaryovskoye Memorial Cemetery, at the grave to the Unknown Soldier near the Kremlin Wall in Moscow and at other memorials throughout the country, were all lit from the sacred flame in the Field of Mars.

BARRACKS OF THE PAVLOVSKY REGIMENT

1817-1821. Architect—V. Stasov. The façade is 140 m long. Now the premises of the Leningrad Energy System Board (Lenenérgo)

The building occupies almost all of the west side of the Field of Mars. The enormously long façade has three porticos on raised granite bases. The middle portico is decorated with sculptured panels depicting weapons and suits of armour. The austere lines of the building give a solemn and majestic appearance.

> *The Pavlovsky Grenadier Regiment became famous during the Patriotic War of 1812 and was awarded the title of 'Guards'. The edifice in the grand style was built specially for the regiment. In February 1917, the soldiers of the regiment were the first among the tsarist army to go over to the side of the insurgent people. When they had been ordered by Tsar Nicholas II to shoot*

The Leningrad branch of the Central V. I. Lenin Museum (The Marble Palace)

the workers, the indignant soldiers of the Pavlovsky Guards Regiment took up their arms, left their barracks and engaged in armed conflict with the mounted police. Nineteen of the 'instigators of the rebellion' were imprisoned in the Peter and Paul Fortress, awaiting execution. But the autocracy was overthrown two days later and they were released by the insurgents.

During the October Revolution in 1917, the regimental barracks housed a field headquarters of the uprising. Together with the soldiers from the guard of the Peter and Paul Fortress, soldiers of the Pavlovsky Regiment defended the Kirov (the Troitsky) Bridge. They also took part in the storming in the Winter Palace, holding the streets lying between the Field of Mars and Palace Square.

Opposite the former barracks of the Pavlovsky Regiment on the Neva side stands the Marble Palace (Mrámorny dvórets).

LENINGRAD BRANCH OF THE CENTRAL LENIN MUSEUM (Marble Palace)

1768-1785. Architect—A. Rinaldi. Sculptures and decorations by F. Shubin and M. Kozlovsky. Thirty-two different kinds of marble were used. Since 1937, the premises of the Central Lenin Museum

'All that is truly great and heroic in the proletariat—a fearless mind, a will of iron, unbending, persistent and able to surmount all obstacles, a burning, undying hatred of slavery and oppression, a revolutionary passion that moves mountains, boundless faith in the creative energies of the masses, vast organisational genius—all this found splendid embodiment in Lenin, whose name has become the symbol of the new world from East to West, from North to South ...'

From an appeal by the Plenum
of the CPSU Central Committee
February 22, 1924

10.30 a.m. The doors of the Museum open. The first visitors are greeted by the guide with the words: 'Vladimir Ilyich Lenin was born on April 22, 1870, in the town of Simbirsk ...' And so the story of Lenin begins.

The twenty-five rooms in the Museum containing 7,000 exhibits provide a documentary narrative about a thinker and fighter who dedicated his life to the revolutionary renewal of the world, about a man who, in the words of the poet Vladimir Mayakovsky, 'even now is more alive than all the living'.

First editions of Lenin's books and pamphlets, photo-reproductions of his manuscripts, newspapers and magazines, his personal belongings, rare photographs, paintings, drawings and sculptures devoted to Lenin and collected in the first eighteen Museum rooms all give a detailed stage-by-stage, strict and expressive picture of Lenin's life, boundless as history itself. Many pages from this life will already be familiar to you, for Leningrad has already told you about them.

Room No.19 is the Hall of Mourning. Photographs, drawings and paintings tell of the country's last farewell to its great leader.

Beginning with Room No.20, the museum exhibition is laid out on a thematic as well as a chronological basis and illustrates how Lenin's plans to industrialise the country and reconstruct its agriculture were implemented, and how national and cultural developments were achieved. The story of the Soviet Union today is yet another chapter telling us about the immortality of Lenin's ideas and plans.

Room No.25 is Leniniana devoted to 'Lenin is the most widely read writer in the world', 'Lenin memorial places in the USSR and abroad'—these subjects are illustrated with numerous exhibits and provide a fitting conclusion to the exhibition.

'Lenin readings' (reading of Lenin's works) are conducted regularly, nd documentary films are shown in the Museum, such as 'The Living enin', 'Lenin's Last Hiding Place','Lenin's Manuscripts' and others. Phi-atelists and other collectors are attracted to the Museum by the wide ange of stamps and badges connected with Lenin's image.

This museum is the biggest branch of the Central Lenin Museum in Moscow and has its own branches elsewhere in Leningrad and its sub-rbs. You can read about them in section 'Museums' and in other chap-ers of this book.

The Peter
and Paul Fortress.
The Summer Gardens

The Peter and Paul Fortress (Petropávlovs-kaya krépost) and the Summer Gardens (Létny sád) are situated on the opposite banks of the Neva. Nevertheless, on a histori-al basis, as the coevals of the city — the Summer Gardens, it is true, are a year ounger — they are included in the same sightseeing tour.

Public transport from Revolution Square: Buses — 1, 23, 25, 46, 65, 80; rams — 2, 3, 6, 12, 22, 25, 26, 30, 34, 51, 53; Metro station — Gorkovskaya.

From the Peter and Paul Fortress it is a ten-fifteen minutes' walk to the eter Embankment (Petróvskaya náberezhnaya) which is to the left of Revo-ation Square, if you are facing the Neva. On the embankment, you will find nother monument — Peter the Great's Cottage, which dates back to the times of ounding the city.

From the Cottage you go back to Revolution Square and cross the Kirov Bridge (Kírovsky móst) to the left bank of the Neva where the Summer Gar-ens are. It is best to begin its sightseeing from the side facing the Neva.

Public transport: Buses — 1, 23, 25, 46, 65, 80; Trams — 2, 3, 12, 22, 34, 51, 53.

You can go over the gardens in any order you like — you will certainly find t pleasant just to walk in them. But you can also follow the route shown in the nap.

In getting acquainted with the places of interest described in this chapter, ou will both see them from the outside and visit museums.

127

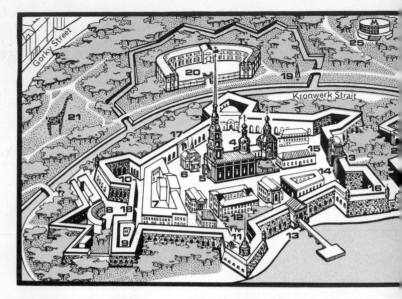

1. St. John's Bridge **2.** St. John's Gate. Main Entrance to the Fortress **3.** St. Peter's Ga▮ **4.** St. Peter and St. Paul Cathedral **5.** Belfry of the St. Peter and St. Paul Cathedral **6.** 'Boฺ House' **7.** Mint **8.** Alexeyevsky Ravelin **9.** Trubetskoi Bastion. Prison of Trubetskoi Baฺ tion **10.** Zotov Bastion **11.** Naryshkin Bastion and Signal Cannon **12.** Commandant's Housฺ **13.** Neva Gate. Commandant's Pier **14.** Engineers' House **15.** Artillery Arsenal **16.** H▮

REVOLUTION SQUARE
(formerly Trinity or Tróitskaya Square)

from which your excursion begins is the city's oldest. In 1917, it was th▮ place in which mass rallies and demonstrations were held. Today it i▮ one of the most beautiful squares in Leningrad.

From the square, crossing the Kronwerk Strait, you get to the Pete▮ and Paul Fortress.

JOHN'S BRIDGE (Ioánnovsky móst)

1703, a wooden bridge. Architect—D. Trezzini. Partly rebuilt in stone in 173▮ Length—74.5 m, width—10.5 m. Rebuilt several times afterwards. Decorate▮ with iron railings and lamp-holders in 1953

Initially a floating bridge, it was later replaced by a timber pil▮ bridge. By the date of its construction, it is the first permanent bridge i▮ the city. Whenever it was rebuilt, the architects and builders manage▮ successfully to preserve its appearance breathing a spirit of antiquity.

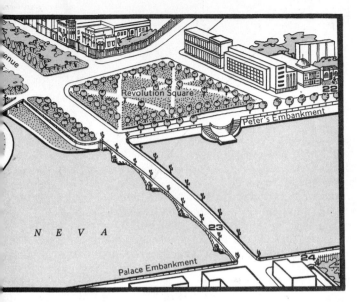

Majesty's Bastion **17.** Nikolsky Gate **18.** Vasilyevsky Gate **19.** Monument to Decembrists **20.** Kronwerk. Artillery, Engineers and Signals Museum—7, Lenin Park **21.** Zoo **22.** Peter the Great's Cottage. Shih Tze Stone Figures—3, Peter's Emb. **23.** Kirov Bridge **24.** Summer Gardens **25.** Gorkovskaya Metro Station

THE PETER AND PAUL FORTRESS
(Petropávlovskaya krépost)

Foundation laid 1703. 1706-1725 and 1779-1787, original dirt ramparts replaced by brick ones subsequently faced with granite slabs. Maximum height—12 m, average thickness—2.5 to 4 m, stretched along the Neva for 700 m. 1717-1918, served for the incarceration of political prisoners. Since 1922, it has been under the protection of the state as a historical and architectural monument

May 16, 1703, the day on which the fortress started being built has gone down in history as the date of the foundation of St. Petersburg. Hare's Island (Záyachy óstrov), chosen by Peter the Great as the site of the fortress is somewhat stretched between the Neva and the strait which was subsequently named Kronwerk Strait (Krónverksky prolív). Viewed from above, the fortress looks like a slightly flattened hexahedron, repeating the outlines of the island. Three protruding parts of the rampart—bastions—face the Neva, the other three, the Kronwerk Strait.

The bastions are named after the courtiers who superintended the construction (Naryshkin, Trubetskoi, Zotov, Golovkin, Menshikov). The bastion overlooking the present Kirov Bridge was named His Majesty's (Gosudárev). Later two ravelins—fortifications which were to protect the fortress from the rear and on the sides—were added to the main structure. And in 1790, small granite bays for sentries, resting on stone cantilevers, were added.

The construction of the fortress on the deserted little island proceeded at an unusually rapid pace. The Great Northern War was on. The Swedish ships in the Gulf of Finland and infantry camped at the northern approaches of the city threatened invasion. Roughly 20,000 labourers worked simultaneously. They lived in huts built of branches or just in the open and worked from dawn to dawn. The mortality was high. The construction of the fortress is believed to have cost about 100,000 lives. The earthworks started in May were completed in the autumn of the same year, 1703. Three hundred guns were installed in the bastions together with the necessary supply of shells, gunpowder and provisions.

During the Great Northern War the enemy could not approach the fortress, let alone attack it. The enemy ground forces were kept at a large distance while from the sea the entrance into the Neva was reliably guarded by the fort built on an island in the Gulf of Finland.

As it was, however, the fortress built of earth did not provide sufficient protection for the city. The dirt ramparts were replaced by brick ones. At the end of the 18th century these brick walls were 'clothed in stone', i.e. faced on the side overlooking the Neva with granite slabs which have survived to this day.

The fortress was not destined to fire its guns in earnest ever in its 200-odd years' existence.

One who finds himself in the fortress at noon will be able to see how from the Naryshkin Bastion (it is situated on the Neva side) a blank shot is fired from a howitzer at 12.00 sharp. This tradition sprang up in the 18th century. The shot allowed the inhabitants to know exactly what time it was.

Before ten years had elapsed since the construction of the fortress, the most formidable structure in the new city began to be used as a prison for political offenders. One of the first to be incarcerated in it was the son of Peter the Great, Tsarevich Alexei, who had been involved in a plot against his father. Historians suppose that it was in the fortress that Alexei was strangled to death.

The history of the Peter and Paul Fortress is closely connected with the history of the revolutionary movement in Russia.

As early as the first decades of the 18th century it became a place where the best sons of the people were imprisoned. Here are just a few episodes taken from the 200-year-old tragic history of the Peter and Paul Fortress.

Alexander Radishchev, the first revolutionary nobleman, writer and thinker, imprisoned in the Peter and Paul Fortress by the order of Catherine II, spent six weeks there, awaiting the execution of his death sentence, subsequently commuted to penal servitude.

The leaders of the Dekabrist (December) Insurrection of 1825 were incarcerated in the 'Secret House' of the Alexeyevsky Ravelin (a prison for especially important prisoners). One of them, Sergei Muravyov-Apostol, wrote that the 'fortress stands there like a vile monument to the autocracy against the background of the Imperial palace, as a portentous warning that they cannot exist one without the other'.

Forty years later, the casemates of the fortress became the prison of the most prominent of the Russian revolutionaries of another generation. In 1862, the prison doors of the Alexeyevsky Ravelin closed behind Nikolai Chernyshevsky, a revolutionary democrat, author, literary critic and philosopher.

Imprisoned in the 'Secret House' of the Alexeyevsky Ravelin thirteen years before had been Fyodor Dostoyevsky who had taken part in the meetings of the revolutionary circle of M. Butashevich-Petrashevsky. In 1884 the prison in the Alexeyevsky Ravelin was closed, but not before a new prison in the Trubetskoi Bastion had taken in its first inmates.

Kept in solitary confinement in the Trubetskoi Bastion were most of the members of the revolutionary party the People's Will (Naródnaya Vólya), sentenced in the 1880s: A. Zhelyabov, N. Morozov, M. Frolenko, V. Figner, and others.

In 1887, the elder brother of Lenin, Alexander Ulyanov, imprisoned in the fortress for his part in the attempt on the life of Alexander III, had his last meeting with his mother. Ten days later, five prisoners condemned in connection with the attempt were executed. Alexander Ulyanov was then 21 years old.

A third generation of revolutionaries, with Lenin and his comrades-in-arms at the head, entered the struggle against the government of the bourgeoisie and landlords.

At the entrance of the solitary cells of the Trubetskoi Bastion yo can see the photographs of those who were imprisoned in them an read the biographies of N. Bauman (No. 561), P. Lepeshinsky (Nos. 2 and 54), M. Olminsky (No. 53) and other comrades-in-arms of Leni

In January 1905, Maxim Gorky was incarcerated in the prison c the Trubetskoi Bastion for having written a revolutionary leaflet. Her in the casemate, in spite of an acute form of tuberculosis and rheumati fever, he wrote his play 'Children of the Sun'.

The events of the revolutionary year of 1917 opened the doors c the prison which for two centuries had been the living grave of thous ands of fighters against tsarist tyranny. When in February 1917, th monarchy fell, the political prisoners were carried out of the Peter an Paul Fortress on the shoulders of the jubilant throng. On the very firs day of the Great October Socialist Revolution, the garrison of th fortress took the insurgent proletariat's side. The weapons and ammu nition were handed out to workers. The Field Headquarters of th uprising were established in the fortress. In accordance with Lenin' plan of the assault on the Winter Palace, the last stronghold of the bourgeois government, a lantern was lit on the flagstaff of one of the bastions—a signal to the cruiser *Aurora*. It was then that she fired th historic volley which was itself the signal to begin the storming of the Winter Palace in which the counter-revolutionary Provisional Govern ment had taken cover. The ministers of the Provisional Governmen were the last prisoners the fortress has seen.

Today 30 buildings and structures of the Peter and Paul Fortres are under the protection of the state. They may not be altered o moved from their places; no new buildings may be erected in the for tress.

ST. PETER'S GATE (Petróvskiye voróta)

1707-1718. Architect—D. Trezzini. Sculptors—N. Pineau and K. Osner. Shapec like a triumphal arch. Rebuilt in stone in 1717-1718

St. Peter's Gate was first built of timber and later rebuilt in stone. I was the main entrance to the fortress, and the architect aimed to give i a festive look. Of the initial decorations, nothing but the wooden bas-reliefs have survived.

The St. Peter's Gate to the Peter and Paul Fortress

The belltower of the cathedral in Peter and Paul Fortress

It is worth mentioning one of the wooden bas-reliefs, *The Defeat of the Simon the Fortune-Teller*, whose allegorical meaning is of some interest. As Peter the Apostle by force of his prayer threw down to the earth the heathen sorcerer, so does Peter I vanquish, and so shall he vanquish, his foes. The carver gave the Apostle the features of the tsar.

In the niches of St. Peter's Gate are statues of Roman goddesses: Bellona, the goddess of war, and Minerva, the patroness of handicrafts and arts, represented holding a snake and a mirror in her hands. The statues symbolised the military and political genius of Peter the Great.

St. Peter's Gate is the only practically unaltered structure dating back to the early 18th century, which has survived on the premises of the fortress.

THE ST. PETER AND ST. PAUL CATHEDRAL
(Petropávlovsky sobór)

1712-1732. Architect—D. Trezzini. The length and height of the interior are 61 and about 16 metres, respectively. The iconostasis dates back to 1722-1726. The burial place of the Russian tsars is in the building of the cathedral. A museum since 1924

A straight alley leads from St. Peter's Gate to the St. Peter and St.

Paul Cathedral, the most important architectural monument in the fort ress. In its composition and furnishings the cathedral is rather differen from the traditional Russian churches of the period. Its exterior is im posing and majestic. Its interior is light and has a festive look. The cathedral is lighted by chandeliers of crystal, gilt bronze and stained glass (the late 18th century).

The iconostasis with 43 icons is a unique specimen of wood carving produced by over forty skilled joiners, carvers and gilders who worked after the designs of the architect and artist Ivan Zarudny.

Peter the Great himself chose his resting place to the right of the southern entrance of the cathedral, not far from the altar. Most of the othery thirty tombs of tsars and Great Princes buried there are marked by similar white marble tombstones.

Thanks to the work carried out in recent years, it has been possible to restore not only the original colouring of the walls, but also the 18th-century paintings above the windows.

THE BELFRY OF THE ST. PETER AND ST. PAUL CATHEDRAL

1712-1733. Architect—D. Trezzini. Height—122.5 m. The figure of the angel topping the spire has a height of 3.2 m and wing span of 3.8 m. The height of the cross is 6.4 m

This belfry, the tallest in the city, often suffered from the elemental calamities. Before 1778, when a lightning rod was installed, lightning had often caused fires. During a fire in the middle of the 18th century the spire collapsed, the chime with 35 bells was ruined, and the mason-ry of the walls impaired. The belfry was dismantled down to the win-dows of the first tier and was practically erected anew. The work took twenty years. A new chime was installed as well.

> The figure of an angel on the top of the spire caused a great deal of trouble. The fixed figure broken by the wind was replaced by one which could turn about like a giant weathercock. But a strong gust of wind made it and the cross lean over to one side. The story of how the top of the structure was finally fixed seems incredible. The job was undertaken by a Russian artisan, Pyotr Telushkin, a roofer, known for his great strength and extraordi-nary aptitude. He climbed up the spire in a spiral way holding on

the vertical edges of the copper plates with which the spire was faced, coiling a rope round. When he reached the smooth sphere—the base of the weathercock 3 metres in diameter—Telushkin managed to tie himself to the spire and, hanging in the air, flung the rope round the foot of the cross just above the sphere. Then he let down from the height a rope ladder which he used for the six weeks it took him to do the repairs. It happened in 1830.

In the middle of the 19th century it was decided to replace the timber framework of the spire by a metal one. The spire was made at a plant in the Urals and brought to the city in sections. Then it was assembled in the square in front of the cathedral and covered with gilt copper plates. Stairs were provided inside the spire, measuring two-thirds of its height. The stairs lead to a hatch from which starts an external staircase reaching the foot of the cross.

In 1941, mountain-climbers went up these stairs in order to camouflage the glittering spire which would otherwise have provided a reference point for the fascist aircraft and artillery. Still, one of the bombs that hit the fortress made a hole in the spire with a splinter. The famous clock was badly damaged by a detonation wave.

In 1957, shortly before the celebration of yet another of the city's anniversaries, it was decided to restore the original colouring of the spire of the Peter and Paul Fortress. With the help of 36,000 thin gold plates glued on by hand, the surface of the facing was restored, and the spire now has an appearance which you have a chance to appreciate.

After the war, too, the mechanism of the chime was restored. To do it, the bells were lowered down to the ground. Two experts—an engineer and a musician—tuned the 11 bells, the smallest of them weighing 16 kg and the biggest, five tons. The chime is not wound by hand as previously but automatically, with the aid of an electric motor.

Since 1950, the chime plays four times a day the tune of the Anthem of the Soviet Union: at 6 a.m. and p.m., at noon, and at midnight. Visitors can listen to the chimes every quarter of an hour.

At present, the stress in the metal part of the framework is measured every five years with the help of sensing units. The results of a recent examination showed that the spire is as reliable as ever.

An elegant pavilion beside the cathedral, decorated by columns and a statue of the goddess of navigation, and quite unlike the other buildings in the fortress, catches the attention. It is the *Boat House* (Bótny dómik), built in 1761 specially for storing the little ship on which Peter had navigated the river Yauza in Moscow. The little boat of Peter the Great is considered to be the 'grandfather of the Russian fleet' and is displayed at present at the Central Naval Museum.

THE MINT (Monétny dvór)

1798-1806. Architect—A. Porto (supposedly). One of the best samples of 18th century Russian industrial architecture

As you come out of the St. Peter and St. Paul Cathedral you can see opposite the original, beautifully proportioned, yellow-white building of the Mint, decorated by a pediment. Before this building was erected silver coins were minted in one of the bastions of the fortress. The emergence of the Mint is usually referred to 1724, i.e. the production of coins was started in the Peter and Paul Fortress even in the lifetime of Peter the Great.

Here, at the Mint, in 1811, the first lever press in the world for coining money was built. The principle of this invention is still used at mints throughout the world. The capacity of the Leningrad Mint makes it a major enterprise by international standards.

It marked its 250th anniversary in 1974.

The Mint currently produces small change and makes orders, medals and badges of all kinds. The Mint's workers take particular pride in having made the streamers taken by Soviet space rockets to the Moon, Venus and Mars.

Beyond the Mint building are the *Trubetskoi* and *Zotov Bastions* where visitors are shown the casemates in which many prisoners of the Peter and Paul Fortress were incarcerated.

THE COMMANDANT'S HOUSE (Oberkomendántski dóm)

1743-1746. Built as living quarters for the Commandant of the fortress. It also housed the office of the fortress and the courtroom in which prisoners' cases were heard. Since 1975, a section of the History of Leningrad Museum

The two-storey white-and-pink building with a high roof is opposite the cathedral on the side facing the Neva. It houses the exhibition, History of St. Petersburg-Petrograd, 1703-1917'.

Its exhibits—from the finds excavated by archaeologists in the territory of the city to relics of the Revolution—tell of the social, political, economic and cultural life of the former capital starting from its founding till the February bourgeois-democratic revolution.

Prisoners incarcerated in the Peter and Paul Fortress were brought to the Commandant's House for questioning. Of particular interest is the so-called 'memorial hall', restored in every detail, where in July 1826 sentence was pronounced on the participants in the Decembrist Insurrection. At the place where they heard the sentence one can now see a marble slab. Standing next to it is a marble stela with the names of the condemned and those sentenced to penal servitude carved on it.

THE ENGINEERS' HOUSE (Inzhenérny dóm)

1748-1749. Built for the engineer force of the fortress and their workshops. Since 1971, part of the History of Leningrad Museum

A little farther on, also on the right, you can see an oblong one-floor building painted sandy-pink and white. The original timber structure was eventually dismantled and the stone Engineers' House erected in its place. Its appearance was altered several times in the process of repairs. The original exterior of the stone building was restored in 1957. Today it houses the permanent exhibition 'Architecture of St. Petersburg-Petrograd from the Early 18th Century up to the Early 20th Century.' Displayed at the exhibition are the authentic drawings after which many of the city's remarkable buildings were constructed. There are many prints, water-colours and pictures with the views of the capital as it was in the 18th, 19th and early 20th centuries, as well as models of its monuments. In a special room, models of the Leningrad bridges are displayed.

OTHER HISTORICAL AND ARCHITECTURAL MONUMENTS IN THE PETER AND PAUL FORTRESS

The *Artillery Arsenal* is opposite the Engineers' House, on the other side of the alley leading from the cathedral to St. Peter's Gate. It was built in the early 19th century.

The *Neva Gate* (Névskiye voróta) in the south part of the fortress wall, decorated by a four-column portico with a pediment, is one of the best architectural structures in the fortress. It was built as a gate with architectural decorations, opening onto the water side of the fortress (1787, architect—N. Lvov).

A three-span granite bridge joins the Neva Gate with the recessed grounds of the *Commandant's Pier* (Komendántskaya prístan).

Through the Neva Gate prisoners were led out from the casemates at night to the granite Commandant's Pier to be taken to the Schlüsselburg Fortress or to Fox's Nose (Lícii Nos) on the shore of the Gulf of Finland—the place of execution of Russian revolutionaries down the ages.

Beyond the Neva Gate is *His Majesty's Bastion* (Gosudárev bastión) in whose dungeons languished prisoners of the Peter and Paul Fortress.

THE MONUMENT TO DECEMBRISTS

1975. Architect—A. Lelyakov. Artists—A. Petrov and A. Ignatyev. The height of the obelisk—9 m

You leave the fortress through St. Peter's Gate. Standing in the middle of John's Bridge on the other side of the strait, on the Kronwerk rampart, you get a good view of the obelisk.

The place where it now stands saw one of the most dramatic episodes in the history of the revolutionary movement in Russia. Tsar Nicholas I pointed it out as the place of execution of the five leaders of the 1825 uprising.

> *The construction of the gallows was being completed in the presence of the condemned men. They were calm and self-composed. One of the condemned, Kondrati Ryleyev, said to the prison priest: 'Put your hand on my heart and see if it is beating faster.'*

> *Before the execution the Decembrists embraced and kissed each other. The hangmen made them stand on a bench and put white canvas hoods covering their faces on their heads and nooses round their necks. Then the bench was knocked from under their feet. Three men whose ropes had broken fell on the rough boards of the scaffold badly bruising themselves. It is on record that one of them broke a leg. According to custom, in such circumstances the execution had to be cancelled. But in an hour new ropes were brought at the order of the Governor-General, and the execution was carried through.*

On the front side of the obelisk you can see a bas-relief representing the five executed Decembrists and their names. On the other side is a poem by Alexander Pushkin, who was a contemporary and close friend of many Decembrists. They end with the prophetic words:

And despotism, impatient, crushing,
Upon its ruins our names incise!

On the granite pedestal of the obelisk there is a composition in hammered copper—a sword, epaulettes and broken chains.

PETER THE GREAT'S COTTAGE, A MUSEUM (Dómik Petrá)

1703. Length—12 m. Height from floor to ceiling—2.5 m. A log structure painted on the outside in imitation of brickwork. In 1844 a stone pavilion with glazed windows was erected over it. Since 1930, a memorial museum. The bust of Peter the Great in the garden in front of the cottage was put up in 1835, sculptor—P. Zabello

Coming out on the quiet Peter's Embankment (Petróvskaya náberezhnaya) you will find yourself before the very first dwelling built in the city—Peter the Great's Cottage.

From this place it was convenient for Peter I to watch the progress of the work on the Peter and Paul Fortress and the adjacent buildings.

The cottage was built within the space of a few days in May 1703, as soon as the foundations of the Peter and Paul Fortress had been laid. The carpenters made it after the fashion traditional in Northern villages. It differs from an ordinary cottage only by its broad windows with leaden frames. The cottage had a wooden model of a mortar fixed

141

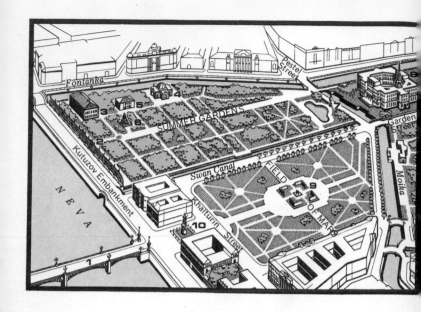

to its roof to show that it was the quarters of the commander of the bombardier company, as Peter the Great would be addressed.

The cottage is very small with no provision for foundation. It has just two rooms: a dining room and a sleeping room, the latter also serving as a study, separated by an antechamber. To save the cottage from crumbling, it was covered with tent-shaped pavilions, a wooden one in the 18th century, and a stone one in the 19th century, which has survived to this day. The cottage was repaired several times, and its original look was unfortunatelly altered as a result.

It was completely restored in 1974, when the restorers managed to make it look again exactly as it did in the days of Peter the Great.

Displayed at the museum is the furniture and utensils of the times of Peter I. Inside the pavilion is an exhibition devoted to the initial period of the city's construction. Also to be seen there is a boat supposedly built by Peter I himself.

On the embankment opposite the cottage you can see granite stairs descending to the Neva. They are decorated by unusually-looking statues of lions. The pedestals bear this inscription: 'Shih Tze from Kirin, Manchuria. Brought to St. Petersburg in 1907.' *Shih Tze* (the Chinese for lion) are fantastic creatures whose statues were erected at the gates of palaces and temples and in graveyards in China. The sculptures have a height of 4.5 m and weigh 2.4 tons each. They supplement the spectacular collection of sphinxes, gryphons and lions exhibited by Leningrad.

1. Kirov Bridge **2.** Railing of the Summer Gardens **3.** Peter the Great's Summer Palace **4.** Coffee House **5.** Tea House **6.** Statue of Ivan Krylov **7.** Porphyry vase **8.** Engineers' Castle **9.** Monument to the Heroes of the Revolution **10.** Statue of Field Marshal Suvorov

Part of the Summer Gardens grille

THE SUMMER GARDENS (Létny sád)

Laid in 1704. Area—11 hectares. Layout geometrical. 2700 trees—mostly limes—and 82 marble sculptures. Public gardens with free admission

> *Give me roses, the gardens that are second to none,*
> *the finest park railings the world ever known.*
>
> . . . .
>
> *I dream in the sweet-scented shade of the limes*
> *Of mainmasts a-creak as in earlier times.*
> *And the swan slowly sails through the centuries,*
> *Admiring the grace of the double he sees.*
>
> *ANNA AKHMATOVA*

The railing of the Summer Gardens (1784. Architects—Y. Felten and P. Yegorov) has given rise to the story that a foreign traveller once came to the city solely to admire the beautiful railing. He never went ashore but stayed the whole day on the deck of his ship which had cast anchor not far from the Peter and Paul Fortress. Having scrutinised the railing minutely through his spyglass, the traveller gave the order to sail for home. As a matter of

143

Peter the Great's Summer Palace

fact, he missed quite a lot, if only for the reason that the railing is seen to the best advantage from the gardens, outlined against the sky, not from the river at all.

The massive base and pillars of ash-pink granite make the slender black spears pointed at the sky look amazingly light and delicate. The spears are connected by gilt ornamental work of noble design. The tall gates match the railing in elegance. It is worth noting that the railing suggested the motive for other fences in the city. The best of them are to be seen at the building of the former Bank of Issue (30-32 Griboedov Canal, close to Nevsky Prospekt) and round the cathedral in the Peter and Paul Fortress.

Soon after the Revolution, when the young Soviet republic suffered terrible economic hardships, some Western businessmen offered locomotives in exchange for the Summer Gardens railing. But, badly as the locomotives were needed to help restore the transport, the offer was declined.

The gardens got their name from the fact that in summer they were the centre of social and court life in the new capital, where all sorts of festivities were arranged.

On the day of an official reception the imperial standard was hoisted over the Peter and Paul Fortress. A gun was fired to announce that he assembly was about to begin. The guests were to arrive in boats or yachts. There was at that time a special canal in the gardens and some mooring places with oaken galleries in which tables were set and dances held.

Fireworks were in great favour at the Summer Gardens.

In the times of Peter the Great the Summer Gardens were much larger than they are now. They covered what now is the Field of Mars (Mársovo póle) and stretched almost to Nevsky Prospekt. The fountains of the Summer Gardens were the prototypes, as it were, of the fabulous Petrodvorets fountains. They drew water from a river which came to be known as the River Fountain (Fontánka). An ensemble of palaces was built in the Summer Gardens but they did not survive. Two disastrous floods, in 1777 and 1824, destroyed the fountains, pavilions, many trees and marble statues. In the lifetime of Peter I the gardens had 250 marble statues by Italian sculptors.

After the floods, the gardens were not restored to their former glory, and balls and receptions were now given at other, more sumptuous royal residences out of town.

In the mid-18th century some of the nobility were allowed to use the gardens for walks, and twice a week they were open to the public.

In the mid-19th century Nicholas I issued an edict by which the Summer Gardens were 'open to all military officers and decently dressed persons. Common people, to wit *muzhiks*, must altogether be prohibited from entering the gardens'. The edict had not been repealed until 1917.

Toward the end of the 18th century the Summer Gardens began to resemble landscape parks which were coming into fashion then. In the 19th century the gardens looked very much like they do today.

The Summer Gardens, framed by water, with their venerable trees forming shady alleys, and statues artfully arranged against the greenery is one of the adornments of the city. In the cold seasons the sculptures have cases put over them for protection from rain and snow. The trees too are carefully preserved. Not a single tree was cut during the years of the blockade when trenches were dug, and antiaircraft guns installed in the Summer Gardens and when the people of Leningrad had nothing at all to warm their homes with. The sculptures were also carefully preserved.

Many of the sculptures adorning the Summer Gardens now were put there as long ago as under Peter the Great. They are: The allegori-

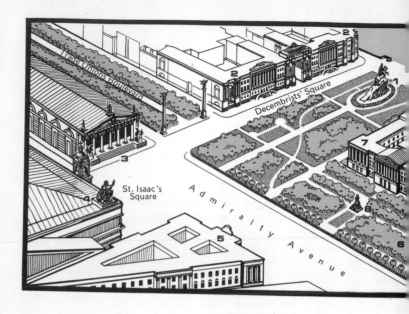

St. Isaac's Square

cal group 'Peace and Abundance', the busts of John Sobieski, the king of Poland, and Christina, Queen of Sweden, 'Cupid and Psyche', statues of Nemesis, Ceres, Night, etc. The antique Venus—also an original—that used to be in the Summer Gardens, can now be seen at the Hermitage.

PETER THE GREAT'S SUMMER PALACE (Létny dvoréts)

1710-1714. Architect—D. Trezzini. Since 1934, a historical museum (of mode of life)

Not far from the entrance to the Summer Gardens on the side facing the Neva stands Peter the Great's Summer Palace. The building typifies the architecture of early St. Petersburg with its simple and austere form, clean-cut layout and modest façades.

Peter I moved into the palace when its interior decoration was not yet finished and stayed there every summer until his death.

The ground floor was occupied by Peter himself and the first floor by his wife Catherine. The upper floor is furnished with great splendour. The spaces between the columns in the dancing room are decorated with Venetian mirrors which were in fashion at the time, and the throne-room has a decorated ceiling representing Catherine in a char-

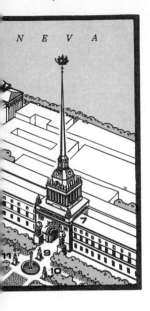

1. Statue of Peter the Great (Bronze Horseman) 2. Buildings of former Senate and Synod 3. Manege of the Horse Guards. Show-room of the Union of Artists 4. St. Isaac's Cathedral 5. Lobanov-Rostovsky Mansion 6. Gorky Gardens 7. Admiralty 8. Statue of Przhevalsky 9. Statue of Glinka 10. Statue of Lermontov 11. Statue of Gogol

iot drawn by eagles. The walls are hung with tapestries representing exotic landscapes and genre scenes. On the ground floor are displayed the personal belongings of Peter the Great.

In 1961-1964 the palace was thoroughly restored. The painstaking study of old documents and the architecture of the palace itself and similar 18th-century structures undertaken by the scholars and restorers concerned enabled them to bring the exterior and the interior of the palace to their original condition.

THE COFFEE HOUSE OR ROSSI'S PAVILION (Koféiny dómik)

1826. Architect—C. Rossi. Stucco bas-reliefs by sculptor V. Demut-Malinovsky. At present houses a library and a show-room

Not far from the central alley one can see a small pavilion—a valuable relic of 19th-century park architecture. It was put up by Carlo Rossi on the site of the grotto created under Peter I by the most celebrated architects of the period. The grotto was considered an outstanding St. Petersburg structure, and was referred to as a 'marvel'. The layout and size of the pavilion were determined by the composition of the old grotto.

At the Coffee House today one can attend concerts of chamber music, recitals by poets and composers, and lectures.

THE TEA HOUSE (Cháiny dómik)

1827. Architect—L. Charlemagne

The Tea House is the only wooden structure in the Summer Gardens which has survived since the 19th century.

THE STATUE OF I. KRYLOV

1855. Sculptor—P. Clodt. Bronze

In a flower garden by the main alley stands a statue of Ivan Krylov, the great national fabulist of Russia. It was erected in the mid-19th century with the donations of the public.

There is a children's playground by the monument to 'Grandfather Krylov. Children like to pick out the subjects of their favourite fables among Krylov's characters going in a ring round the pedestal of the monument.

On the side facing the River Moika, the Summer Gardens are fenced by a low railing (1826, designed by L. Charlemagne). Near the railing in the gardens there is a five-metre-high porphyry vase presented by the king of Sweden to the Russian tsar. It was put there in 1839.

The history of the Summer Gardens is associated with many illustrious Russian names. Pushkin often visited them. Tchaikovsky opened his favourite opera, *The Queen of Spades,* with a scene in the Summer Gardens. The old limes and maples have seen Krylov, Zhukovsky, Blok, taking their walks there.

The people of Leningrad love their Summer Gardens—the museum gardens—as one of the most celebrated sights of their city.

The Central Squares

The plan of observing the three central squares of Leningrad is simple. Decembrists' Square (Plóshchad Dekabrístov) and St. Isaac's Square (Isaákievskaya plóshchad) adjoin. Going a short distance (you had better walk it) past the Admiralty building you will emerge onto Palace Square (Dvortsóvaya plóshchad).

The succession in which the historical and architectural monuments in the squares should be seen is indicated by ordinal numbering on our maps.

Public transport to Decembrists' Square: Trolleybuses—5, 14; Trams—21, 26, 31;

    to St. Isaac's Square: Trolleybuses—2, 5, 9, 10, 14;
    Buses—2, 3, 10, 22, 27, 60, 100; Trams—8, 21, 26, 31;
    to Palace Square: Trolleybuses—1, 2, 5, 7, 9, 10, 14, 22;
    Buses—2, 3, 6, 7, 14, 22, 26, 27, 47, 100;
    Trams—8, 21, 22, 26, 31, 51.

For all that the observation of the places of interest to be found in the central squares takes no more time than usual, the present chapter is the longest in the book. This is due to the fact that the squares on the left bank of the Neva are saturated with monuments most of which are immortal masterpieces of world architecture closely associated with the major events in Russian history.

The idea of laying three main squares in the city centre emerged in the mid-18th century when it was put forward by the Commission for the Stone Construction of St. Petersburg, launched in 1762. The Commission believed that by carrying out this design the city would be invested with a 'magnificence due to it as the capital of so vast a country'. The idea could not be realised right away. The square ensemble was shaped over more than a century by the efforts of several generations of architects and thousands upon thousands of Russian craftsmen.

DECEMBRISTS' SQUARE (Plóshchad Dekabrístov)

Decembrists' Square radiates out onto the Neva, and it makes it look particularly spacious and picturesque.

It took final shape in 1874 when a garden was laid at its far side. In the hundred-odd years that have elapsed since, the young saplings grew into giants standing guard over a large and beautiful rose-garden. In winter, thousands of rose-bushes growing in Decembrists' Square are covered with fir-branches and timber cases.

During its existence the square changed both its aspect and name several times. At the beginning it was called Senate Square (Senátskaya plóshchad) as in 1763 the Senate (the highest government institution) was moved from the 'Twelve Colleges' to one of the buildings in the square. After the erection of the statue of Peter the Great in 1782, it

Decembrists' Square

was renamed Peter's Square (Petróvskaya plóshchad). But the name did not stick and after a new building for the Senate had been constructed, the old name existed for a long time. In 1925, on the occasion of the centenary of the Decembrist uprising the square, which was a major arena of the celebrations, was renamed Decembrists' Square.

A hundred and fifty years ago, in 1825, there were not so many buildings in the square. The new Senate and Synod building did not exist yet. The St. Isaac's Cathedral which now towers in front of you was under construction at that time.

On an overcast winter morning, December 14, 1825, those who are known in Russian history as Decembrists came to the square at the head of their regiments, with flying colours.

Decembrists were already mentioned in the introductory part of the book dealing with the history of Leningrad, and in the chapter on the Peter and Paul Fortress. Now, in Decembrists' Square, it is time to describe them in more detail. What kind of men were they, then? Lenin called them 'the best of the nobility'. Alexander Herzen, thinker and revolutionary who belonged to the generation which succeeded the Decembrists, wrote that to all intents and purposes they were knights forged from pure steel. The Decembrists were highly-educated, gifted men, and some of them were extremely talented, high-minded, noble and courageous. The majority of the first Russian revolutionaries were heroes of the Patriotic War of 1812.

The Bronze Horseman statue of Peter the Great

There was unrest among Russian peasants. During the first quarter of the 19th century, there were 280 peasant revolts. The Patriotic War had a rousing effect on the people. Young army officers who had brushed shoulders with soldiers and went into battle side by side with them had witnessed the heroism, grit and dedication of those Russian peasants in uniform. After the victorious ending of the 1812 war, the future Decembrists could not reconcile themselves to the situation in which the peasants who had won for the tsar's army the fame of the liberator of Europe remained the landlords' chattels. 'The best of the nobility' were influenced by the ideas of the French Revolution and the Encyclopaedists. They were influenced by the revolutionary ferment in Italy, Spain, Portugal and Greece. Secret societies appeared in Russia. The more radical of their members wanted to abolish the monarchy and serfdom and establish a republican government and equality of all citizens. 'We ... had a word which shakes the hearts of all orders of men without distinction. It is Freedom,' wrote to his judges P. Kakhovsky from his cell in the Peter and Paul Fortress.

On November 19, 1825, Alexander I died suddenly. The revolutionary-inclined officers considered it an opportune moment for carrying out their plan which had been preparing for several years. After heated debates, it was finally decided to stage an open rising. The leaders' plan was to force the Senate to issue in its own name a 'Manifesto to the Russian People' proclaiming a constitutional form of government.

For that purpose, the guard regiments were brought to Senate Square. The insurgents, however, did not know that Nicholas I, th future tsar, had already been informed about the proposed uprising an that earlier in the day the Senators had already sworn allegiance to hir and left for their respective homes. It was an empty Senate buildin that the Moscow Regiment, the first to have arrived at the square, wa facing. Apart from that, Prince S. Trubetskoi, who had been elected to lead the uprising, did not turn up at the square.

The Moscow Regiment formed square near the statue of Peter th Great. It was joined by the Naval Guards and grenadiers of the life guards. The number of the insurgents increased to 3,000 men, but the were undecided. By then it was already one o'clock and the tsar ha managed to summon the loyal regiments, outnumbering the insurgent three to one.

'Workers at St. Isaac's Cathedral began to throw billets at us from behind the fences,' Nicholas wrote later in his memoirs. '... The revol could well spread to the rabble.' The tsar was not far wrong. Th throng—according to contemporary reports, there were tens of thou sands present—was seething, the people was on the side of the insur gents, but the latter did not venture to summon it to their aid.

Seizing the initiative, the tsar several times sent into attack the cavalry squadrons ranged by the Neva and at the back of the square but they were forced to retreat not so much by the insurgents who fired overhead to avoid bloodshed, as because of the stones and billets with which the crowd pelted the attackers.

Then at the tsar's order guns were brought to the square and opened fire. The insurgents wavered. Many ran for their lives, hoping to find shelter in adjacent streets, others tried to get to the other bank of the Neva across the ice already pierced by shells. At 6 p.m. all was finished and police raids and arrests began. On the night preceding December 15 the first prisoners were brought to the Peter and Paul Fortress. A hundred and twenty-one of those involved in the events that took place on December 14 in Senate Square were to spend thirty years in prison, penal servitude and exile. Five leaders of the uprising— Pavel Pestel, Kondrati Ryleyev, Sergei Muravyov-Apostol, Mikhail Bestuzhev-Ryumin and Pyotr Kakhovsky were hanged on the crown-work of the Peter and Paul Fortress. Hundreds of officers were de-graded to the ranks and exiled without trial. Severe punishment was meted out to private soldiers who had taken part in the uprising. To the five executed Decembrists one must add the privates flogged to death, some of them having been sentenced to run the gauntlet of a thousand men twelve times, which amounted to 12,000 blows by rods.

Lenin wrote that the Decembrist uprising was a supreme patriotic feat arousing the pride and admiration of posterity.

Such are the main historical events that the square has seen.

And now let us turn to the architectural and cultural monuments to be found here.

THE STATUE OF PETER THE GREAT OR THE BRONZE HORSEMAN
(Médny vsádnik)

Cast 1768-1770. Unveiled 1782. Sculptor—E. Falconet. The head of the horseman is by the sculptor's pupil M. Collot and the snake under the horse's feet, by F. Gordeyev. Height 13.6 m

The horseman in bronze by the glorious river,
Old friend to much true inspiration in Russia.

PAVEL ANTOKOLSKY

This magnificent work of monumental art, majestic and full of expression, may be observed from different spots. It produces a strong impression wherever you look at it from.

After Pushkin wrote his *The Bronze Horseman,* the monument commonly went under this name in literature and everyday life.

E. Falconet worked at the Bronze Horseman for twelve years. A sand hill with a plank ramp were built under the windows of his studio. Expert riders took the best horses in the royal stables, Brilliante and Caprice, up the ramp at full gallop and held them in a rearing position while the sculptor was making sketches.

When the statue was being cast, the mould cracked and the molten metal began to pour out. The workshop caught fire. Falconet ran out of the foundry, certain that the results of so many years of work were lost irretrievably. The work was, however, saved by the foundryman Yemelian Khailov, who managed to close up the crack with clay. He was badly burned, but the casting was saved.

Falconet decided to put the Bronze Horseman on a natural stone instead of a common pedestal.

> They looked for a suitable rock for a long time. It was found by a peasant, Semyon Vishnyakov, in the forest, at a distance of more than ten kilometres from the city. At one time, it had been split by lightning and was known among the people as the 'Thunder-stone'.
>
> The rock was about 13 metres long and more than 6 metres high. It weighed approximately 1,600 tons. With the help of levers and windlasses, it was hoisted on a platform and hauled along chutes lined with sheets of copper, on thirty cooper balls—prototypes of the ball-bearing—to the Gulf of Finland, and from there, on a barge constructed specially for the purpose by Russian shipbuilders, to St. Petersburg. The journey took more than a year. To commemorate this titanic effort, a medal was issued bearing the inscription 'Epitomy of Enterprise' and the date, 'January 20, 1770'.

The monument is kept under constant observation by restorers. During the blockade the Bronze Horseman was covered by sacks filled with sand, lagged with boards, and remained intact.

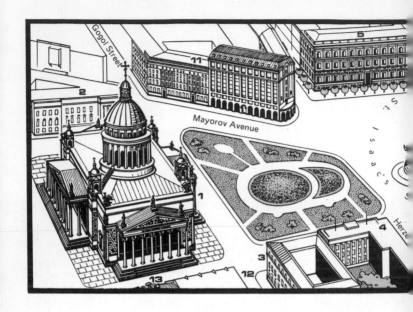

The Bronze Horseman—the hero of Pushkin's poem—was sung by Mickiewicz, Bryusov and many contemporary poets. Its picture is engraved on medals. It has provided the subject for a ballet of the same name by the Soviet composer Glier. It is represented in the stamp issued for the 30th anniversary of the rout of fascist troops at Leningrad. And, last but not least, it is the subject of numerous treatises on the history of art.

THE SENATE AND THE SYNOD

1829-1834. Architect—C. Rossi. The height of the buildings joined by an arch exceeds 18 m. The building on the left was meant for the Synod—the supreme body for the administration of the orthodox church, the one on the right, for the Senate. Since 1955 houses the Central Historical Archives

Attracting the attention on the right-hand side of the square (with your back to the Neva), are two imposing yellow-white buildings joined by a resplendent arch across the street.

It is the last major work by Carlo Rossi. The construction was superintended by the architect A. Staubert. The appearance of the buildings reveals the influence of the tastes of the tsar and the Synod. The baroque arch is decorated with sculptured figures. The attic is

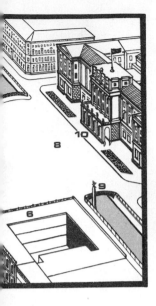

1. St. Isaac's Cathedral 2. Lobanov-Rostovsky Mansion 3. 'Myatlevs' House' 4. Leningrad Intourist Amalgamation 5. Institute of Plant Protection of the USSR Academy of Sciences. Ministry of State Property 6. Vavilov All-Union Institute of Plant Breeding of the USSR Academy of Sciences. Ministry of Agriculture 7. Statue of Nicholas I 8. Blue Bridge 9. An Obelisk with five bronze bands marking the height to which the water rose during the worst floods in the city's history 10. Executive Committee of the City Soviet of People's Deputies (Mariinsky Palace) 11. Astoria Hotel 12. To the Central Post Office and the Popov Central Communications Museum 13. Museum of Musical Instruments

opped by a group representing Justice and Piety, which was to symbolise the unity of temporal and church authority.

The length, height, colonnades and colour of the Senate and Synod buildings make them go well with the side façade of the Admiralty just opposite.

Abutting on Decembrists' Square is St. Isaac's Square. On the side where the Senate and Synod buildings are, but already in St. Isaac's Square is situated

THE MANEGE OF THE HORSE GUARDS
(Konnogvardéisky manézh)

1804-1807. Architect— G. Quarenghi. The statues of Dioscuri by sculptor P. Triscorni (brought to St. Petersburg in 1817). Since 1977, the show-room of the Union of Artists

The Horse-Guard Manege is one of the last and most remarkable productions of Giacomo Quarenghi. The architect took it into account that the side façade of the Manege would be well open to view from

Senate (now Decembrists') Square. He decorated this side of the building with an eight-column portico resembling one of an antique temple.
In front of the portico are placed the marble figures of Dioscuri—twin
sons of Zeus in Greek mythology—reining in ramping horses. The artistic value of the building consists in the perfection of its architectural
forms and proportions.

The manege, which was built for the Horse Guards, was not used
exclusively for training horsemen and for horse racing. In the middle of
the past century, for instance, an exhibition of farm machinery was
arranged here and subsequently Johann Strauss gave concerts in this
building.

Currently the building houses an exhibition hall of Union of Artists.

ST. ISAAC'S SQUARE (Isaákievskaya plóshchad)

St. Isaac's Square emerged between the 1830s and 1840s as Market-
place. It took final shape at the end of the 19th century and beginning
of the 20th century. It was renamed after the St. Isaac's Cathedral
which was built in the middle of it. In front of the cathedral's main
entrance, on the side facing the Neva, there is a public garden whose
lawns and walks form a picturesque design. The garden unites, as it
were, the buildings of different periods round this part of the square
concealing the discrepancy in their architectural styles. The other side

the square, beyond the public garden, is more uniform in style which reminiscent of the architecture of the late Italian Renaissance.

St. Isaac's Cathedral dominates the square. In clear weather, its gilt ome is visible from a distance of 30-40 km.

HE ST. ISAAC'S CATHEDRAL (Isaákievsky sobór)

18-1858. Architect—A. Montferrand. Cruciform in plan. Total height—101.52 m; ngth—111.2 m; width—97.6 m. Wall thickness up to 5 m. Weight of the ucture estimated at 300,000 t. 112 polished granite columns. The 48 lower terior columns have a height of 17 m, and weight 114 t each; the 24 upper lumns, 13 m and 67 t, respectively.

e central dome is 22 m in diameter. The area of the interior exceeds 4,000 m., has plenty of room for up to 14,000 persons. Since 1931, a museum

St. Isaac's should be observed from a distance, e.g. from the centre the south half of the square.

In this architectural monument, everything strikes the eye—its stu-ndous size, the grand colonnade, an abundance of sculptured deco-tions of great beauty, reliefs, gilt-work, marble. Specialists even con-der the decoration somewhat excessive, making the cathedral appear en more massive than it actually is.

The story of its construction goes back to the period of Peter the reat.

The first wooden church dedicated to St. Isaac emerged as long ago 1710, in the drawing shop—re-equipped for the purpose—of the dmiralty which was under construction at that time. The church soon came dilapidated and was dismantled.

In 1719, Peter the Great personally laid the first stone of the new urch of St. Isaac. Very close to the Neva, almost in the site where the ronze Horseman was later set up, a building was erected, with a ta-ering spire somewhat like the cathedral of the Peter and Paul Fortress. ut the Neva bank was not shored up yet and the structure began to ollapse. In 1768, the construction of another cathedral of St. Isaac arted, this time on the site of the present St. Isaac's. The cathedral as opened in 1802. But even towards its completion it was clearly either big nor imposing enough for the capital which had grown quite lot by that time. So after the victorious termination of the Patriotic Var of 1812 it was decided to construct yet another, a fourth, St. aac's. A competition for the best design was announced, in which the st architects took part. The winner was August Montferrand, quite known at that time. The tsar, Alexander I, was greatly impressed by s album of architectural renderings, excellently executed, which con-ined as many as twenty-four designs of the cathedral in every imagi-able style. Although these were merely pretty pictures and not real ans after which something could be built, Montferrand was chosen to uild the cathedral. Montferrand was a gifted architect but had no

experience in building. For this reason the noted architects and ci
enginee s of the time who were members of a committee set up sp
cially to superintend the construction and rectify Montferrand's erro
may be regarded as co-authors. They were V. Stasov, the brothe
Mikhailov, G. Rossi, A. Melnikov, and some others.

The construction was made still more difficult by the fact that t
tsar made it an absolute condition that the walls of the old building
preserved as they had been consecrated by the church. This and th
further interference by the tsars led to further mistakes. The uneve
settling of the building due to its enormous weight could not
avoided. Three years later, they had to stop building and dismantle,
fact, what still remained of the old structure. Construction was resume
only after the Committee had prepared new, feasible plans.

During the construction of St. Isaac's Cathedral, the columns of t
portico, each hewn out of a solid piece of rock (monolithic columns
such size are not known in world building practice) were put in pla
with the help of ingenious devices which allowed this staggering ta
to be performed by hand. The huge columns were raised to an uprig
position in a matter of 40-45 minutes, thanks to the cleverness of th
mechanics and skilled craftsmen. One can get a visual idea of how
was done from the engravings and models displayed at the museum
the cathedral.

The construction of the central dome was yet another sign
achievement of engineering thought. The dome consists of three hem
spherical shells mounted with relation to each other something li
a Russian 'matryoshka'. Between the beams of the intermediate dom
and the sheets of the top dome are fixed about 100,000 hollow cla
pots which form a light-weight vault as well as provide for an excelle
acoustic effect in the cathedral.

St. Isaac's Cathedral produces a striking effect by the splendour

The Bronze Horseman
Atlases at the entrance to the Hermitage
Inside the Hermitage
Foundry Bridge
Lomonosov Bridge
The Kirov Theatre of Opera and Ballet
View of the Peter and Paul Fortress
The Marine Canal at Petrodvorets
The Grand Palace at Petrodvorets
The Chess Hill cascade at Petrodvorets
The Grand Cascade at Petrodvorets
Catherine Palace in the town of Pushkin
The park surrounding Catherine Palace in the town of Pushkin
The Cameron Gallery in the town of Pushkin
The monument to A. Pushkin in the town of Pushkin
Pavlovsk Park

PETRO PRIMO
CATHARINA SECUNDA
MDCCLXXXII.

АЛЕКСАНДРУ СЕРГѢЕВИЧУ
ПУШКИНУ.

ts decorations. It is not for nothing that the cathedral went on painting and decorating seventeen years after it was built. The state did not spare the expense. The total cost of the cathedral was nearly ten times the expenditure on the royal residence, the Winter Palace.

The exterior and interior are faced with fourteen different kinds of marble. You can see in the museum a multi-coloured bust of Montferrand made from samples of every kind of marble used in the interior decoration.

> Besides marble and granite of a great variety of hues and colours, so many kinds of minerals were used for the decoration of the cathedral that it is justly called a 'museum of minerals'.
>
> More than 400 sculptures and bas-reliefs by the best masters embellish the cathedral on the outside and inside. Each of the four bronze haut-reliefs on the pediments of the porticoes weigh up to 600 t. There are two scenes on biblical subjects, executed in bronze. It is interesting that one of the haut-reliefs, on the west side, has in its bottom left-hand corner a semi-recumbent figure of a man in a Roman toga. In his hands he holds a model of St. Isaac. The identity of his features with those of the author of the project leaves one in no doubt that it is just yet another peculiar memorial of Montferrand. Most of the sculptures were executed by I. Vitali, a well-known Moscow sculptor of the 19th century.

Approximately 200 canvases, frescoes and mosaics, executed altogether by 22 artists, adorn the iconostasis and the ceilings, walls, niches and pillars in the interior of the cathedral. In the altar part there is a huge stained glass window with a crucifix. The ceiling of the main dome was decorated by Bryullov, a major painter of the Russian academic school.

A St. Petersburg newspaper wrote that the cathedral 'will be a pantheon of Russian art as first-rate artists have left monuments to their genius in it'. Yet, the conception of its architects was realised through the back-breaking toil of tens of thousands of unknown craftsmen over forty long years. St. Isaac's was one of the last major structures erected by serf labour.

The builders, driven here from all over Russia, lived in appalling conditions. Many died. Sixty workers died, to quote but one instance, of exposure to poisonous mercury fumes when gilding the main dome. They worked fifteen hours a day, including holidays and Sundays. Concerning it, we have the following pharisaical 'explanation' written by Nicholas I with his own hand: 'Under the present circumstances, idleness among work-people can only do them harm.' The tsar had not forgotten how shortly before his accession to throne, on the day of the Decembrist uprising, the workers of St. Isaac's threw stones, planks, bricks and billets from the scaffolding at the loyal troops, the retinue and the tsar himself, to help the insurgent regiments.

St. Isaac's Cathedral was inaugurated with great pomp as the main cathedral church of the capital.

After the victorious Great October Socialist Revolution, the cathedral was placed under the control of the congregation and clergy. But the latter cared nothing for the preservation, maintenance and restoration of the outstanding architectural monument. In 1928, the government came to a decision to comply with the request of working people that the cathedral be closed and turned into a museum. The building was thoroughly restored and in 1931 the museum was opened. Today it is one of the city's museums most frequented by tourists and townspeople.

St. Isaac's Cathedral served as a repository for numerous art treasures evacuated from the palace-museums in the environs of Leningrad during the Great Patriotic War of 1941-45. It was not, of course, an objective of any military significance. Nevertheless, the skyline of St. Isaac's was marked on enemy operation maps as 'reference point No. 1'.

Some columns, the roof and exterior sculptures were damaged by fragments of enemy bombs while the windows and the unique stained-glass arrangement in the altar were also badly damaged by air-blasts. Restoration was started as soon as the war was over. Today both the exterior and interior of St. Isaac's Cathedral are in an excellent state of preservation.

> *Besides objects of art and exhibits telling the story of the construction of the cathedral, the museum also displays the largest Foucault pendulum in the world—weighing 54 kg and 93 m long—which visually demonstrates the rotation of the earth about its polar axis. There is an observation platform situated at the level of the upper colonnade, which is highly popular with sightseers.*

LOBANOV-ROSTOVSKY'S MANSION
(Osobnyák Lobánova-Rostóvskovo)

1817-1820. Architect—A. Montferrand, sculptor—P. Triscorni

St. Isaac's Cathedral is not the only project to have been designed by Montferrand. He also built the mansion of Prince Lobanov-Rostovsky, a noted Russian diplomat. The front façade of the house, which faces St. Isaac's Cathedral, partly repeats the composition of the main façade of the latter. At the entrance of the house, looking from Admiralty Avenue, one can see marble lions on granite pedestals. Pushkin mentioned the lions in his *The Bronze Horseman*, for on one of them the hero of his poem found refuge during the flood. This house is sometimes referred to as the 'House with the lions'.

THE MYATLEVS' HOUSE (Dom Myátlevykh)

The 1760s. Architect—A. Rinaldi (supposedly)

On the other side of the square, on the corner of Communications Union Street, you can see the oldest and artistically the most valuable house in St. Isaac's Square, known as the Myatlevs' House. Its façades are decorated by excellently executed round medallions and busts, long reliefs and armour compositions. D. Diderot, the French Enlightener, stayed in this house in 1773-1774. Pushkin, who was on friendly terms with the poet Ivan Myatlev, often visited the house.

THE LENINGRAD INTOURIST AMALGAMATION (formerly the German Embassy)

1910-1912. Architect—P. Behrens. Now the premises of Intourist

Next to the Myatlevs' House is situated a building faced with rough red granite. It was built for the German Embassy and was used as such for a short time, until the beginning of World War I in 1914.

This 20th-century building looks somewhat out of line with the older architecture of the square.

THE HOUSES OF THE MINISTRY OF AGRICULTURE AND MINISTRY OF STATE PROPERTY

1844-1853. Architect—N. Yefimov. Now institutes of the Lenin Academy of Agricultural Sciences. The western building houses the Vavilov All-Union Institute of Plant Breeding; the eastern, the Institute of Plant Protection

The two buildings of the same type situated in the square opposite each other bear witness to the fact that initially the intention was to develop the square in a uniform style.

The scientific centres housed in the buildings at present are internationally known for their contributions in the fields of plant breeding and pest control. Even before the war, a unique collection of seeds of useful plants of all continents had been amassed at the Plant Breeding Research Institute. It contained over 13,000 specimens of different strains of maize, and more than 43,000 specimens of wheat. During the years of the blockade, when enemy troops were within a stone's throw from the city, the Institute's experimental fields out of town were temporarily occupied while some of the plots were in the front area. Risking their lives, the workers of the Institute got in the precious harvest under enemy fire. The collection—so eminently edible—was preserved without the loss of a single tuber or seed by the Institute staff, 29 of whose members died of undernourishment during the famine that ravaged the city during the blockade.

They performed a truly heroic deed both as citizens and scientists.

In the south part of the square, opposite the St. Isaac's Cathedral, there is

The Admiralty Spire

The Admiralty, details of the decorative sculptures

THE STATUE OF NICHOLAS I

1856-1859. Sculptor—P. Clodt. Architect—A. Montferrand. Bronze, on a pedestal of granite, porphyry and marble of different colours. Height—16.25 m Bas-reliefs and allegorical figures by sculptors N. Ramazanov and R. Salemann. The lamp-holders made after designs by P. Clodt

In ordering the monument, the wife and daughters of Nicholas I certainly had in mind the glorification of the deceased monarch. But the pompous splendour of the monument merely emphasises the haughty coldness, harshness and proclivity for attitudinising typical of Nicholas I, a gendarme at heart. The truthful artist that he was, Clodt could hardly have been inspired by the personality of the tsar whom the people aptly nicknamed Nicholas the Stick. The bas-reliefs on the base commemorate the events of his sorry rule. One of them, for example, shows the tsar addressing the courtiers after the suppression of the Decembrist Insurrection. The four allegorical figures at the corners of the pedestal, whom the sculptor Salemann gave the features of the wife and three daughters of the deceased emperor, were to represent Faith, Wisdom, Justice and Might, which was treated with irony already at the time.

Frieze on the Admiralty building

For all that, the sculptor managed successfully to relate the separate parts of the monument in scale to give it an effective general outline and find a unique solution to an engineering task in making the heavy equestrian statue rest merely on two points.

THE BLUE BRIDGE (Síny móst)

1818. Rebuilt and broadened 1842. Width — 99.95 m

It is usual for urban bridges across rivers and canals to be a continuation of the streets. The Blue Bridge is a continuation of the spacious square so that one does not immediately become aware that it is a bridge and that a river, the Moika, is flowing under it. The Blue Bridge is the broadest of all Leningrad bridges. It derives its name from the colour it is painted on the side facing the water. Up the river there are also Green and Red Bridges.

Associated with this bridge are tragic and infamous chapters in the history of tsarist Russia as it was here — before serfdom was abolished in 1861 — that a slave market (for what else could it be called?) took place where serfs were bought and sold.

> Near the Blue Bridge, at the River Moika Embankment, look
> ing from the side of Intourist building, one can see a tetrahedra
> obelisk of light pinkish-and-gray granite, topped by a trident, th
> attribute of Neptune.
>
>> Here in the city, on Rastrelli's marble
>> Or on plain brick, we see from time to time
>> A mark: 'The water-level reached this line'—
>> And we can only look at it and marvel.
>>
>> VERA INBER
>
> Five bronze bands encircle the obelisk, marking the height t
> which the water rose during the worst floods in the city's history
> During three such floods the water even overflowed the parapet o
> the embankment.

To the back of the square, beyond the bridge, rises, closing th
perspective, the former Mariinsky Palace (Mariínsky dvoréts).

THE EXECUTIVE COMMITTEE OF THE LENINGRAD
CITY SOVIET OF PEOPLE'S DEPUTIES
(Mariínsky Palace)

1839-1844. Architect—A. Stakenschneider. Since 1948 the Executive Committe
of the Leningrad City Soviet of People's Deputies

The front of the palace is adorned with columns and pilasters anc
crowned with a massive attic. The palace was built for Maria, a daugh
ter of Nicholas I, and was sold to the state by her heirs in 1894. It wa:
subsequently given over to the State Council, the supreme legislative
consultative body of the Russian Empire.

>> The centenary of the Council was celebrated with great pomp
>> on May 7, 1901. The jubilee meeting of the dignitaries in the white
>> column gala rotunda of the Mariinsky Palace was commemorat
>> ed on canvas by Repin. It is an enormous picture. The artist paint
>> ed about a hundred portraits of those attending the meeting. Its
>> profound realism and psychological penetration have made
>> Repin's picture 'The Solemn Meeting of the State Council'—now ai
>> the Russian Museum—a scathing satirical condemnation of the
>> highest dignitaries of the Russian monarchy.

After the victorious Great October Socialist Revolution the palace
housed different institutions of the young Soviet republic. Here, in De
cember 1917, Lenin addressed a meeting of the Bureau of the Supreme
Economic Council on the nationalisation of the private banks. This
event is commemorated by a plaque you can see on the façade of the
building.

Today, the flag of the RSFSR—red, with a vertical blue stripe along
the staff—flies over the building which now houses the Executive Com
mittee of the Leningrad City Soviet of People's Deputies. The attic and
side pediments bear the Emblem of the Russian Soviet Federative So-

:ialist Republic and representations of the orders and medals the city of
Lenin has been awarded for its revolutionary, labour and military contributions.

THE ASTORIA HOTEL

1910-1912. Architect — F. Lidval

The building of the *Astoria* Hotel is a graphic example of the search
for new ideas in architecture early in the 20th century. Taller, than the
other buildings surrounding the square, the hotel is somewhat distinct
from them both in size and exterior.

Hitler intended, presumptuously enough, to celebrate the taking of
the city in the autumn of 1941 in the banquet hall of the *Astoria*. The
month and hour of the proposed festivities (the exact date alone was
omitted) were indicated in the invitation cards prepared in advance. Of
course the banquet at the *Astoria* did not take place, and the invitation
cards remained a historical absurdity.

One of the smartest hotels in the city, the *Astoria* accommodates
a large number of tourists.

OTHER SIGHTS IN ST. ISAAC'S SQUARE
AND ADJACENT STREETS

No. 72, River Moika Embankment, used to be the meeting place of
members of the secret society who prepared and took part in the uprising in Senate Square on December 14, 1825.

No. 66, River Moika Embankment, used to house the Department of
the State Economy and Public Buildings to which Nikolai Gogol, the
'King of Russian Laughter', belonged for some time.

At *23 Gogol Street,* Fyodor Dostoyevsky lived before his arrest and
incarceration in the Peter and Paul Fortress (April 1849). Here he
wrote *The White Nights* and *Netochka Nezvanova.*

At *9 Communications Union Street,* you can see the Central Post
Office (1789. Architect — N. Lvov). In 1859, a gallery designed like an
arch (Architect — A. Cavos) was added. It linked the Post Office buildings on the opposite sides of the street. In 1962, a 'World Clock' was
mounted on the arch, by which one can tell the time in the cities of all
continents. At *4 Podbelski Street,* near the Central Post Office and Telegraph buildings, is the *Popov Central Communications Museum.* At *5 St.
Isaac's Square* is the *Museum of Musical Instruments* (See chapter 'Museums').

The best way to reach Palace Square from St. Isaac's Square is by
walking along the Admiralty Embankment or Admiralty Avenue,
which will allow you to observe one of the most remarkable architectural monuments in the city on the Neva.

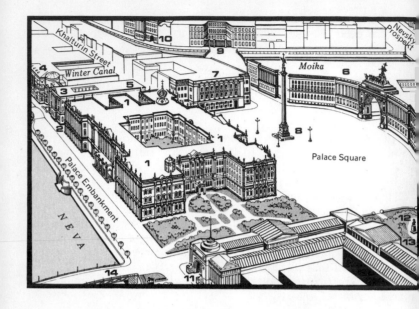

THE ADMIRALTY

1806-1823, Architect — A. Zakharov. Shaped like a double Π in plan. The main façade, length — 407 m; the sides, 163 m in length. The height of the central tower, with spire and weather-vane — 72.5 m. Statues and reliefs by F. Shchedrin, I. Terebenev, V. Demut-Malinovsky, S. Pimenov. Since 1925 the Dzerzhinsky Higher Naval School

The Admiralty was considered, even by the contemporaries, to be one of the chief adornments of the city. In the century and a half that have passed since, this opinion never changed. The Admiralty is among the best works of world architecture in the UNESCO register.

The spire of the Admiralty, capped by a gold weather-vane shaped like a frigate has firmly established itself as the emblem of Leningrad. Its picture is stamped on the Medal 'For the Defence of Leningrad'. It is a common decoration of Leningrad streets, shops and exhibitions.

There is unfortunately no spot from which one could get a comprehensive view of this majestic building and appreciate its composition as a whole. The architect conceived the building to look onto the Neva, so that there would be an excellent view of it from the river and the opposite bank. Towards the end of the 19th century, however, the Naval Minister, 'with criminal unforethoughtfulness, to say nothing more', as the newspapers wrote at the time, sold the site between the side wings of the Admiralty indiscriminately to private contractors, and

View of the Admiralty Embankment from Palace Bridge

the view of its north façade was eventually blocked by apartment houses. On the south side, the building is screened by the trees of a garden laid in the 1870s, which has rather spread out over the years.

There is a good view, however, of the central part of the building, the arch of the main gate, and the tower with its gilt spire.

The history of the Admiralty starts in the earliest days of the city, when, in 1704, Peter the Great, ordered an 'admiralty house' or a shipyard with all its related facilities to be built after his own drawings in that particular site.

In the first ten years of its existence the shipyard became the largest industrial concern in the city, employing as many as 10,000 workers. The central body for superintending the Navy—the Admiralty College—also had its seat there.

Like the present, the first Admiralty was П-shaped, with its front façade looking onto the Neva. In 1711, a wooden spire topped by a gold apple and boat was added to the central part for decoration.

In the 1730s, the Admiralty was rebuilt after the design of I. Korobov, who retained the old shape, only making the spired tower taller and more slender.

The national significance of the Admiralty, its important disposition in the centre of the city, and the nearness of the Winter Palace—all

Palace Square ▶

The archway of the General Staff   A fragment of the archway

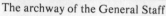

required that the modest Admiralty buildings be replaced by a more imposing structure.

The man entrusted with rebuilding the Admiralty this time was Zakharov, then a professor of the St. Petersburg Academy of Arts, in the heyday of his life and talent.

Zakharov submitted the plan in 1806.

He planned the building so as to retain as much as possible of Korobov's design. But he had to do something to prevent the façade, almost half a kilometre in length, from looking monotonous. Zakharov divided it into three parts. There was a massive cube in the centre, capped by a light tower (Korobov's timber tower remained enclosed in it) with a gilt spire, and two symmetrical wings with three porticoes. The building is both graceful and majestic in aspect, thanks to the happily found proportions and the rhythmical alternation of the parts. The tiered tower makes one think of the towers of old Russian churches and kremlins.

Another remarkable thing about the Admiralty is that the meaning and purpose of the building as the symbol of the country's naval might is graphically emphasised by sculptures. It is enough to look at the decorations of the central tower to see that it is so indeed.

On both sides of the arch there are sculptured groups on granite pedestals, representing 'sea nymphs carrying the terrestrial

172

The Winter Palace

and celestial spheres'. Over the arch, winged Nicas soar with banners in their hands. Higher still, the cubic base of the tower is crowned by a frieze in haut-relief on the subject of 'Russia starting a fleet for herself'. Placed in the centre of the composition is Peter I receiving from Neptune the trident as a symbol of mastery over the sea.

A little higher up you can see four military leaders, heroes of the ancient world, Achilles, Ajax, Pyrrhus and Alexander the Great. There are 28 slender columns round the middle part of the tower, with 28 figures on the cornice above, symbolising the elements, Fire, Air, Water and Earth, seasons of the year, and winds of different directions.

Unfortunately, the sculptures one can view today are but a part of the decorations with which the building was adorned originally. The rest was mercilessly destroyed in 1860 when the clergy insisted on having the 'pagan' statues removed. And, with the permission of tsar Alexander II, twenty-two figures which had adorned the porticoes were lost irretrievably.

The Admiralty sustained grave damage during the blockade of Leningrad. It had 26 high-explosive and hundreds of incendiary bombs dropped on it and was bombarded by long-range artillery, scoring 56 direct hits. The people of Leningrad conducted themselves heroically, doing everything possible to save the Admiralty. Here are a few instances: Ya. Troupyansky, a sixty-year-old sculptor, fixed the bas-reliefs on the porticoes in any weather, disregarding enemy fire; V. Shcherbakov, an artist, copied on tracing-cloth the unique paintings on the walls and ceilings. He did it with hands numb with cold for it was winter and it was freezing cold in the vast unheated halls of the Admiralty. Leningrad mountain-climbers successfully camouflaged the celebrated Admiralty spire thus saving it from scoring direct hits. Full restoration of the Admiralty after the war took more than ten years.

As you walk toward Palace Square, it is worth dropping in at the Gorky Gardens abutting on the Admiralty building on the side farthest from the Neva. The gardens were made open to the public in 1874. Here one can see busts of Gogol, Lermontov, Glinka, the poet Zhukovsky and other Russian cultural figures. Ever since 1958, exhibitions of garden flowers in their beds, used in decorating Leningrad streets, gardens and parks, have been arranged in these gardens.

PALACE SQUARE (Dvortsóvaya plóshchad)

Palace Square is one of the most perfect architectural ensembles in the world, even though the buildings round it were put up at various periods and in various styles.

It is impossible to talk about this square without mentioning its historic role in the country's destiny.

Palace Square became a symbol of the revolutionary struggle against the autocracy. The first Russian revolution (1905-1907) began here. On Sunday, January 9 (22), 1905, over a hundred and forty thousand workers with their wives and children moved off towards the Winter Palace, intending to present Nicholas II with a petition describing their intolerable living conditions. It was a peaceful march with icons, banners and portraits of the tsar. In a leaflet issued specially for the occasion, the Bolshevik Party warned the workers about the pointlessness of this action.

The tsarist government was ready to meet the demonstrators. Their route was barred by troops who fired point blank at the unarmed crowd. Over a thousand were killed and more than five thousand gravely injured. January 9, 1905, went down in history as 'Bloody Sunday', when the last remnants of the people's faith in the autocracy were destroyed. The very next day, Petersburg was in the grip of a general strike supported by the whole country. As the revolutionary fervour steadily mounted, there came into being a hitherto unprecedented form of mass political organisation of the working people—the Soviets of Workers' Deputies which were the forerunners of Soviet power. The Petersburg Soviet of Workers' Deputies was formed on October 13 (26), 1905.

The year 1905 has rightly been called the prologue to October 1917. The inglorious end of the 300-year-old Romanov dynasty, so hateful to the people, was to be delayed for some twelve years.

The February bourgeois-democratic revolution of 1917 put an end to the Russian monarchy. The tsar's standard was taken down forever from the flagstaff on the Winter Palace.

However, only the third, proletarian revolution led by the Bolshevik Party ended in the final victory of the working people in October 1917. This was the most glorious page in the history of Palace Square.

It was here on October 25 (November 7) that there began the storming of the last bulwark of the counter-revolution, the former residence of the tsars, then occupied by the bourgeois Provisional Government.

The Winter Palace was spared by the Military Revolutionary Committee (an organ for the direction of the uprising, set up by suggestion of the Central Committee of the Bolshevik Party in the Petrograd Soviet), which delayed military operations. However, the Provisional Government was disinclined to capitulate and at 7.45 p.m. rejected the final ultimatum of the Military Revolutionary Committee, stating that it did not recognise the authority of the Bolsheviks and would not voluntarily lay down arms. Only then did regiments of the workers' Red Guard and of the revolutionary soldiers and sailors launch an attack on the Winter Palace at a signal from the cruiser *Aurora*.

As soon as it had been taken, the Winter Palace and the Hermitage treasures belonging to it were placed under the protection of Red Guard detachments.

One of the first appeals by Soveit power reads:

'Citizens, the old owners have gone, leaving a vast heritage behind them. It now belongs to the people.

'Citizens, look after this heritage, look after the pictures, the statues and the buildings—they are the embodiment of your spiritual strength and that of your ancestors. Art is the beauty that gifted people succeeded in creating even under the yoke of despotism, and it testifies to the beauty and strength of the human spirit.

'Citizens, do not touch a single stone, preserve the monuments, the buildings, the antiquities, the documents—all these are your history and your pride... Remember, all these are the ground for your national art.'

The practical answer to this appeal was that the Winter Palace became part of the State Hermitage Museum, and the architectural ensemble of Palace Square and the other monuments of history and culture were taken under state protection. It can be said with confidence that neither the separate buildings nor the squares and streets of Leningrad were ever maintained in such an excellent state of order and preservation as now, exactly as their creators had intended.

After the victory of the October Revolution, Palace Square became a scene of festive processions, parades, public celebrations and mass meetings of the working people. Palace Square was presented to the citizens of Leningrad and its visitors in new array for the 60th Anniversary of the October Revolution.

The square was once paved with cobblestones and wooden blocks so that the carriages should not rattle over the stones. Then asphalt was put down. This has now been replaced with a new surface — mosaic. The stone blocks are exactly like the ones depicted on old etchings and lithographs of Palace Square. The plinths of the Alexander Column and of the Winter Palace columns will no longer be covered with layers of asphalt. A unique system of underground communications (gas, water, sewage, etc.) has been laid down.

There is a never-ending 'pilgrimage' to this square of visitors who love history and appreciate beauty.

THE WINTER PALACE (Zímny dvoréts).
THE HERMITAGE

1754-1762. Architect — V. Rastrelli. Restored 1838-1839 after the fire of 1837 by architects V. Stasov and A. Bryullov. Plan — an enclosed rectangle. Length — about 230 m, width — 140 m, height — 22 m.

At the present time, one of the State Hermitage Museum buildings. Other buildings: *The Little Hermitage*, 1775. Architect — J.-B. Vallin de la Mothe. *The Hermitage Theatre*, 1787. Architect — G. Quarenghi. Now the Hermitage Lecture Hall. *The Old Hermitage*, 1775-1787. Architect — Yu. Felten. *The New Hermitage*, 1852. Architect — L. Klenze, with V. Stasov and N. Yefimov. Sculptor — A. Terebenev. All the buildings are interconnected by passages in the form of arches, covered bridges and a hanging garden

The Winter Palace is sixty years younger than the city on the Neva. The palace you see now is the sixth of that name in Petersburg and was built by Rastrelli to replace the former tsar's residences during the reign of Elizabeth, daughter of Peter I.

In dimensions, architectural style and sumptuousness of interior decoration, it had to be worthy of the Russian state's growing authority. V. Rastrelli, the designer, wrote that the palace had been built 'solely for the glory of all Russia'.

The gigantic proportions of the building impress us no less than they did its contemporaries. It covers a site of 9 hectares; the length of the cornice is over 2 km and the floor area (decorated parquet of valuable woods) is over 46,000 sq.m. There are 1057 rooms, 1886 doors, 1945 windows and 117 staircases . . .

Everything built after the Winter Palace had to be on the same scale. And, of course, the palace influenced the future dimensions of the square.

Under a special law passed in the mid-19th century and in force until 1905, all the buildings in Leningrad, except churches, had to be lower than the Winter Palace by at least one *sazhen* (an old Russian unit of length equal to 2.134 m).

Each of the palace's façades is different, but within the limits of a unified design and style. The side façades, with their projecting wings nd the entrances in the centre, form parade-grounds opening out to-wards the city. The northern façade extends from the Palace Embank-ment for almost a quarter of a kilometre. The smooth stretch of the wall and the stately rhythm of the columns harmonise beautifully with the wide, low-banked and calmly flowing River Neva.

The main façade looks south on to Palace Square. Emphasis is giv-en to the façade's centre by its being slightly set forward and interrup-ed by the three arches of the wrought iron gates.

The two-tiered colonnade is decorative in function and gives the building an impression of the grace and airiness so typical of baroque architecture. A festive note is lent to the palace by the whimsical curves of the intricate cornices, the ornamental window-frames and the use of three colours: the white of the columns against the pistachio-green of the wall, and the dark gilt of the mouldings. One hundred and seven-ty-six vases and sculptured figures alternating along the upper cornice over the white balustrade stand clearly silhouetted against the sky.

The rich exterior of the palace is echoed by the beauty and sumptu-ousness of the interiors. The former chambers of the tsars are finished with great luxury: polished marble of various colours and shades, mala-chite, azurite, porphyry, jasper and other semiprecious stones; gilt, bronze, crystal; sculptures, mouldings, wall and ceiling paintings, carved wood, incrustation, chased metal and tapestries are all impres-sive in their brilliance of colour, the intricacy of the form and the mastery of execution. The enormous halls and suites of the ceremonial rooms, the parquet, the staircases, the fireplaces and the lamps display an infinite wealth of fantasy—there are over a thousand rooms, and not one of them repeats any of the others. As you walk round the palace, you become more and more bewildered. What should you concentrate on? Everything is worth studying here, from the jewelled handle on the magically encrusted door to the painted ceiling and the mosaic of the floor.

While marvelling at the infinite resources of Rastrelli's artistic fan-tasy, you cannot help being delighted by the perfection with which his designs were followed by the thousands of craftsmen.

The era of classicism had begun, and Rastrelli, a master of the baroque, fell into disfavour. For several more decades, his work was completed by Russia's finest architects—S. Chevakinsky, Yu. Felten, J.-B. Vallin de la Mothe, A. Rinaldi, I. Starov, G. Quarenghi, C. Rossi and others.

After the fire of December 1837, which destroyed all the decorative work of the 18th century and beginning of the 19th, the Winter Palace was completely restored by Russian craftsmen in an incredibly short space of time—by the spring of 1839. The façades were rebuilt from Rastrelli's designs almost without any changes, the interior planning and decoration were done by architects of the new generation V. Sta-sov and A. Bryullov, being partly done in the style of Russian classicism and partly restored.

The Great Throne, or St. George's Hall used for solemn official ceremonies, was restored with especial splendour. At the back of the hall, where the throne once stood, there is now a unique geographical map of the Soviet Union. It was skilfully assembled from 45 thousand tesserae of various Russian semiprecious stones by skilled craftsmen from the Urals and from the Petrodvorets Diamond-Cutting Factory for the 1937 International Exposition in Paris. In 1939, it was admired by visitors to an exhibition in New York. This map is now one of the Hermitage treasures.

The collections at the Hermitage, one of the biggest museums in the world, contain two million seven hundred thousand exhibits. The museum is assumed to have been founded in 1764. At the beginning of the 20th century, the Hermitage contained 600,000 works of art and monuments of antiquity. After the October Revolution, the museum's collection was increased four-and-a-half times.

Even the most general facts about the distribution of the main exhibitions will give some idea of the wealth and variety of the art collections in the Hermitage. The section of Russian culture is on the first floor of the museum, while the sections dealing with the history of primitive culture and the history of the culture and art of the Soviet Eastern peoples are on the ground floor. The exhibition illustrating the history of the culture and art of the Eastern foreign countries is housed mainly on the second floor, and also on the ground. The ground floor also accommodates section covering the history of the culture and art of the ancient world. The collections illustrating the history of West European art take up most of the rooms of the first and part of the second floor (in the Winter Palace building that looks out on to Palace Square). Also on the second floor (facing the Palace Embankment) are the collections of the numismatics department.

> *Details of the museum treasures are given in a guide-book,*
> The Hermitage, *brought out in 1976 by Progress Publishers in English, French, German, Spanish, Polish, Czech and Slovak.*

At the beginning of the Great Patriotic War, before the ring of the fascist blockade had closed in, the most valuable transportable works of art were sent from the Hermitage to the city of Sverdlovsk in the Urals. Part of the collection survived the blockade in the Palace cellars.

On the enemy's map of city with the artillery targets indicated on it, the Hermitage was marked as 'Objective No. 9'. Aerial bombs and 32 artillery shells did serious damage to the museum buildings. They were rebuilt and restored in the post-war years. Priceless art treasures were saved from destruction for the benefit of future generations.

THE GENERAL STAFF

1819-1829. Architect—C. Rossi. Total length of all the façades—2 km. Length of the concave semicircle of the façade—580 m. In the centre, a triumphal arch;

width of span—17 m, height (without sculptures)—28 m. Surmounted by a figure of Glory in a triumphal chariot. Height of sculptural group—10 m, length—5 m. Sculptors—I. Pimenov and V. Demut-Malinovsky. The building is now the premises of administrative and design organisations

C. Rossi, a master of the big architectural ensemble, was commissioned to lay out the square in front of the Palace as a parade centre. He rebuilt the residences of the court dignitaries, which stood on the south side of the square, converting them into buildings for the Ministries of Foreign Affairs and Finance and for the General Staff. The blocks are arranged in a curve and linked by a triumphal arch, forming together the longest façade of the time in European architecture.

The austere and majestic classical style of the architecture balances and emphasises the brilliant and sumptuous baroque of Rastrelli's Winter Palace. The triumphal arch was erected to commemorate the victories of the Russian troops over Napoleon in the Patriotic War of 1812. The design of the arch is dedicated to this theme: soldiers, winged geniuses of Glory and suits of armour.

Consisting, in fact, of two arches, it is an inspired combination of sculpture, architecture and engineering.

> At the time, many said that the arch would surely collapse under its own weight, all the more so because of the copper sculptures surmounting it. Confident of his calculations, the architect told the tsar: 'If it should fall, I am ready to fall with it.' It is said that on opening day, when the scaffolding was removed, Rossi climbed up on to the arch in person to demonstrate his confidence in its safety.

As you come out of Herzen Street and walk under the arch into Palace Square, you get an unforgettably beautiful panoramic view of the Winter Palace. This effect was undoubtedly 'programmed' by Rossi, who was a master of perspective.

The other façades of the General Staff overlook the Nevsky Prospekt and the River Moika Embankment. The way across this river from the square lies through Choristers' Passage (Pévchesky proyézd) and a wide bridge also called the Pevchesky, since it ends before the building of the former Imperial Choristers' Capelle, now the Glinka Academic Capelle.

The Pushkin Museum-Flat is situated at No. 12, River Moika Embankment several houses further along to the left of the Capelle. It was here that the great poet lived from October 1836 until the day of his death on January 29, 1837. One of the memorial rooms, the study, contains almost all those of the poet's personal belongings that have been preserved. The setting of the apartment has been reproduced from the documentary archives, and numerous items tell us about Pushkin's life and work during the last months of his life.

On the other side of Choristers' Passage, opposite the General Staff in the east part of Palace Square, is situated

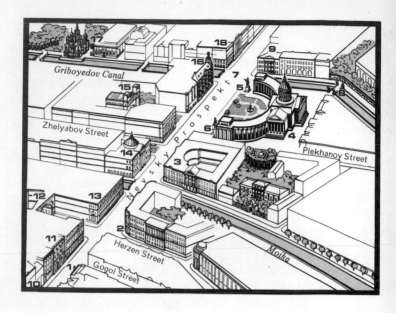

GUARDS HEADQUARTERS

1837-1843. Architect — A. Bryullov. Now an administrative building

This building, the last erected on the Square, successfully round off the ensemble. Undoubtedly of great architectural merit, it links up the work of Rastrelli and Rossi with great tact and without distracting the eye from the two main architectural masterpieces, the Winter Palace and the General Staff.

A memorial plaque states that the Staff for the defence of Red Petrograd from the counter-revolutionary forces was stationed in this building, and that it was from here that their rout was directed from October 27 to 31 (November 9 to 13) by V. I. Lenin in person.

THE ALEXANDER COLUMN (Alexándrovskaya kolónna)

1830-34. Architect — A. Montferrand. Total height — 47.5 m. A monolithic pillar of polished granite, 25.58 m in height and weighing over 650 t. Statue of an angel with a cross by sculptor B. Orlovsky. Bas-reliefs on pedestal by sculptors P. Svintsov and I. Leppe

Nevsky Prospekt

In the centre of the square, as if unifying the surrounding buildings of several periods, stands another monument raised in honour of the victorious end to the Patriotic War of 1812 against the Napoleonic invasion. Victory is symbolised in the spirit of the Roman tradition by a mighty Doric column higher than the Vendome column in Paris (46 m) and Trajan's column in Rome (44.5 m).

The monument is a unique example of civil engineering. It took three years for the granite monolith, weighing over 700 t, to be hewn from a crag on the Karelian Isthmus before it could be transported to the Winter Palace by water on a specially built craft. The enormous weight of the memorial bearing down on the marshy ground called for the construction of a specially firm foundation. The gigantic granite pillar was stood on a cubic socle without any form of fixture, like a glass tumbler standing on a table. All the work of setting the column up was done by the craftsmen who built St. Isaac's Cathedral. Working with the aid of a system of block and tackle, they finished the job in 100 minutes. The column was given its finishing touches and polished *in situ.*

A. Montferrand, the architect, wrote with enthusiasm about the achievements of the hewers, polishers and other rank-and-file craftsmen thanks to whose efforts the monument was erected.

The Main Thoroughfare— Nevsky Prospekt

It is best to go by foot along the Nevsky Prospekt, especially since the most interesting part of the street, from the Admiralty to the Anichkov Bridge, is only about two kilometres long. The Nevsky Prospekt runs past Ostrovsky Square, Arts Square, Manege Square—all well worthy of attention. Their location is shown on our maps.

Public transport (along the Nevsky Prospekt), main routes: Trolleybuses—1, 5, 7, 10, 14, 22; Buses—3, 4, 6, 7, 22, 43, 44, 45; Metro stations—Nevsky Prospekt, Gostiny Dvor.

To assist you in identifying the more noteworthy sights, reference is made to the odd-numbered houses on the right and even-numbered on the left as you go down the Nevsky Prospekt from the Admiralty.

NEVSKY PROSPEKT

From 1709 to 1710, a 'Big Perspective Road' (the route of the future Prospekt) was cut through the forest. In 1738, plans were drawn up and buildings went up

Nevsky Prospekt

along the 'Nevsky Perspective'. In 1766, there was an order for the demolition of the wooden structures and the erection of houses, all to be of the same height and with a unified frontage. It became the Nevsky Prospekt in 1783. Length—4.5 km, width—varying between 25 and 60 m. Crossed by three waterways: the River Moika, the Griboyedov Canal and the River Fontanka.

> *There is nothing finer than the Nevsky Prospekt, at least in Petersburg, for which it is everything. In what does it not shine, this street that is the beauty of our capital?'*
>
> *NIKOLAI GOGOL*

Although the city's main thoroughfare took over a period of more than 250 years to build, it creates a general impression of grace and harmony. Architects believe that the most successful possible balance was found between the height of the buildings and the width of the street. Its picturesque originality is due to the fact that on several stretches the general line of the frontage is interrupted and a row of buildings is set back into that particular quarter and fronted with squares, gardens and avenues of ancient lime trees. Moreover, the many short wide streets crossing the Prospekt end in architecturally remarkable buildings which can be seen from the Nevsky. This gives it a second dimension, as it were, considerably extending it in visual terms.

All the buildings along the central part of the Prospekt, from the

183

Admiralty to the Insurrection Square (Plóshchad Vosstániya), were put up before the Revolution. The sole exception is House No. 14, a school built in 1939. It was fitted into the setting with much taste and has become a successful part of the view of this stretch of the Nevsky.

The Nevsky Prospekt is the business and cultural centre of Leningrad. The intense rhythm of the great city can be felt here more than anywhere else.

The Right Odd-Numbered Side

'VAVELBERG'S HOUSE', No. 9

1911-1912. Architect—M. Peretyatkovich. Originally a bank. Now the premises of the Aeroflot City Booking Hall and shops

Before the Revolution, the Nevsky Prospekt and the adjacent streets were called 'Petersburg's City': there were several dozen houses here belonging to banks and insurance societies. Anxious to give the building as imposing an aspect as possible, the architect faced the walls to their full height with rough-hewn stone brought from Sweden. The same material was used for the columns of the lower storey and also for the sculptured details of the façade. The building creates a some-

Kazan Cathedral

vhat gloomy but majestic impression and is slightly reminiscent of the
Doge's Palace in Venice. There is no building like it anywhere else in
he city.

THE HOUSE WITH COLUMNS' ('Dom s kolónnami'), No. 15

he 1760s. Architect unknown. Originally a palace-type dwelling house. Now
ccommodates the Barricade (Barrikáda) Cinema, a cafe and shops in the lower
toreys

This was formerly the site of a temporary wooden palace to which
vas adjoined the building of the palace theatre where public perform-
ences of the first Russian professional theatre began in 1757. Later, the
tudio in which E. Falkonet made 'The Bronze Horseman' was built on
o the theatre.

In spite of frequent rebuilding, the 'House with Columns' has re-
ained its original character. The two-tiered colonnades are highly ex-
ressive—at the time when this house went up, the Winter Palace had
lready been built and the decorative motifs on its façades influenced
he work of many architects. That influence is detectable here too. This
ouse is one of the few surviving monuments of municipal architecture
lating back to the second half of the 18th century.

THE STROGANOV PALACE, No. 17

1752-1754. Architect—V. Rastrelli. Until 1917, the private property of the Counts Stroganov. In the near future will be handed over to the Russian Museum to house an exhibition of Russian applied art

The palace stands at the intersection of the Nevsky Prospekt and the River Moika Embankment. It is an outstanding work by the famous V. Rastrelli.

The Stroganov Palace is over 200 years old, but its exterior has been preserved in the form conceived by the architect. The interior decorations were destroyed by fire at the end of the 18th century. Restoration of the palace was entrusted to A. Voronikhin, a famous architect who, as a young man, had been a serf of Count Stroganov and lived in the palace himself.

In spite of some upsetting of the proportions—a third of the building's base is covered with earth as a result of the repeated paving of the Prospekt and the Embankment, the green-and-white façades of the palace look as imposing as ever. In the centre of the Nevsky façade stands an arched gateway, the window over which is decorated with ornate mouldings. The windows of the first story, where the ceremonial rooms were situated, are decorated with carved borders bearing lion masks and medallions and, below, with wrought iron grilles.

The statuary that once graced the palace garden has been preserved in the front courtyard.

THE KAZAN CATHEDRAL (Kazánsky sobór)

1801-1811. Architect—A. Voronikhin. Plan—an elongated cross. 96 columns each 13 metres high. The diameter of the semicircle which forms Kazan Square in front of the cathedral, is about 70 m. The height of the building with its dome is over 71 m. The bas-reliefs, sculptors—I. Martos and I. Prokofiev. The statues in the wall niches are by S. Pimenov, I. Martos, and V. Demut-Malinovsky. In 1837, the memorials to M. Kutuzov and Barclay de Tolly were sculptured by B. Orlovsky, with pedestals by architect V. Stasov. Since 1939, a Museum of the History of Religion and Atheism

The line of houses breaks off at the Kazan Cathedral— and the small square on the Nevsky Prospekt is formed by the wings of the light and graceful cathedral colonnade. It is the side of the cathedral and not the front which faces the Nevsky Propekt, owing to the rules for positioning the altar in the Orthodox Church.

The difficult task of designing the side façade was brilliantly dealt with by A. Voronikhin, the architect. A colonnade of 96 pillars of classical height (one quarter of the diameter of the square), which he made equal in height to the portico, seems to grow out of the building itself. This effect is enhanced by sculptures having been placed at the back of

he colonnade in niches between the great windows. The sculptors skilfully adapted their work to the architect's designs. The reliefs on the
attics over the wings of the colonnade are meant to be viewed from
some distance away.

The cathedral is entered from the Nevsky Prospekt through bronze
doors which are replicas of the 15th-century Baptistery doors in Flo-
rence — the doors into paradise, as Michelangelo called them. Voronikhin, however, designed different surrounds for them and the skilful
metal-worker Vassily Yekimov, who cast and hammered these works
of art, rearranged the patterns to some extent.

It is interesting to study the colonnade while strolling under the
domes of the portico amid the forest of columns, hewn — like the capi-
tals, balustrades and bas-reliefs — out of 'Pudostsky stone', a limestone
named after the village in the outskirts of the town where it was
quarried. Immediately after being taken from the ground, 'Pudostsky
stone' is so soft that it can be cut with an ordinary saw. Exposed to the
air, however, it becomes as hard as kiln-baked brick.

The interior of the Kazan Cathedral bears little resemblance to that
of ordinary churches and is more like the majestic hall of a palace.
There are two rows of columns — fifty-six altogether — in polished pink
granite. The mosaic floor, done in black, grey and pink Karelian marble
and in red stone, repeats the structural outline of the dome.

The decoration of the interiors was contributed to by V. Borovi-
kovsky, O. Kiprensky and K. Bryullov, the most outstanding painters at
the end of the 18th century and the beginning of the 19th.

The collections housed in the cathedral, now a Museum of the History of Religion and Atheism, illustrate the characteristics of various
religious cults and there is also a display of pictures, sculptures, photographs, documents and manuscripts. There are various sections: 'The
Origin of Religion', 'Religion in the East', 'Religion and Atheism in the
Ancient World', 'The Origin of Christianity', 'Religion and Atheism in
the West', and 'The History of Russian Orthodoxy and Atheism'.

After the Patriotic War of 1812, the cathedral became a special
monument to the glory of Russia. The remains of Field Marshal
Mikhail Kutuzov, who commanded the Russian Army during the war,
are interred in the North Chapel. Many trophies of those times were
kept here: enemy banners and standards, and the keys to fortresses
captured by the Russian army.

During the celebrations of the 25th anniversary of Napoleon's flight
from Russia, monuments to two field marshals were put up in front of
the cathedral: one to Mikhail Kutuzov and the other to Mikhail Barclay de Tolly, the military leader and hero of the war with Napoleon.
The sculptor has caught their likenesses with great skill. Thanks to the
choice of site, the final effect of the monuments is majestic in the
extreme: the gaps in the wings of the colonnade serve as frames for the
statues.

On the right-hand side, if you stand facing the cathedral, you can see a semicircular railing, one of the most beautiful in the city. Called 'the Voronikhin railing' after its designer, it was put up in 1811-1812. The lacy sections of intricately wrought iron are supported by massive granite sphere-topped pillars.

The main square in front of the cathedral was frequently the scene of revolutionary disturbances. It was here in 1876 that the first revolutionary demonstration in Russia took place with the participation of the workers and it was here that the red flag fluttered for the first time as a symbol of liberty. An impassioned speech was made by Georg Plekhanov, then a student at the Mining Institute, who was subsequently to become a distinguished philosopher and the first propagandist of Marxism in Russia. This event is commemorated by a marble plaque on the cathedral front.

Mentioning the violent measures taken against the participants at one of the later political meetings on the square, Maxim Gorky wrote to Anton Chekhov in 1901: 'I shall never forget that battle! They fought savagely, brutally . . .'

At the beginning of the century, to prevent political demonstrations in front of the cathedral, the authorities laid out a garden with a fountain in front of the cathedral, but this did not help: the square continued to be a traditional place for revolutionary meetings and demonstrations against tsarism.

Immediately after the Kazan Cathedral, the Nevsky Prospekt is crossed by the Griboyedov Canal (dug at the end of the 18th century) spanned by one of the first stone arch bridges in St. Petersburg, the Kazan Bridge.

THE KAZAN BRIDGE (Kazánsky móst)

1738, a wooden bridge. Replaced by stone one in 1766. In 1805, widened to its present dimensions. Length — 17.5 m, width — 90.6 m

The second widest bridge in the city. And here is a remarkable coincidence: I. Golenishchev-Kutuzov, an engineer who took part in building the bridge, was the father of the great military leader whose monument we saw by the cathedral on the square.

Owing to the building of the Kazan Cathedral, the bridge was widened considerably and the iron balustrade was replaced with granite parapets. The arches, as seen from the canal, have preserved their original graceful appearance. A small and unusually light and beautiful bridge over the canal can be seen from the Kazan Bridge beyond the cathedral.

BANK BRIDGE (Bánkovsky móst)

1825-1826. Length — 20.1 m, width — 1.85 m

This is one of six hanging (chain) bridges built in the first quarter of the 19th century. The metal chains supporting the bridge are fixed to our abutments which serve as pedestals for gryphons with gilt wings. Taken down at the end of the 19th century, the barrier grille and the street lamps were reproduced from the original drawings in 1952 when the bridge was being restored. This was carried out in the workshops of the V. Mukhina School of Industrial Art.

HOUSE NO. 27

During a comparatively recent investigation of the house, which was built in the last century, it was found that the frame of the building was deformed beyond repair. The house was virtually rebuilt in conformity with its original appearance.

The treatment of this ordinary residence is another example of the care taken to preserve the city's exterior in the form in which it developed over the centuries.

'THE SILVER ROWS' ('Serébryaniye ryadý')
and the CITY DUMA BUILDING (Gorodskáya dúma), Nos. 31-33

The Silver Rows', 1784-1787. Architect — G. Quarenghi. The City Duma (ratusa) Building with its multi-tier tower, 1799-1804. Architect — D. Ferrari

This three-story building with its adjoining tower is a remarkable architectural monument. At first, shopping 'silver rows' were built with an open arcade along the Nevsky Prospekt. This was the site for the wooden booths of the silver merchants. Next to the booths was the so-called Guild House, where the merchants used to foregather. In 1799, a project was confirmed for the reconstruction of Guild House as a town hall, and provision was made for the erection of a tower typical of the West European Rathaus. The tower also had to serve a more functional purpose. Since it was visible from a distance, it was used to send out alarms in case of fire, floods and exceptionally severe frosts. Later, the tower served as one of the relay stations for the 'mirror telegraph' that linked the town and suburban residences of the tsar: a beam of light announced the departure or arrival of the monarch with his suite.

On the third tier of the tower there is an ancient clock which strikes the quarters and can be seen from all directions.

In December 1917, one of the halls of the City Duma was the scene of a speech by Lenin at a session of the 2nd All-Russia Congress of Soviets of Peasants' Deputies.

The tower of the former City Duma serves as an eye-catcher in the central part of the Nevsky Prospekt with its level rows of houses.

After the planned capital repairs have been carried out, it is prop
osed to house a children's music philharmonic in the tower and in th
five-storey building adjoining it on the Perinnaya Line, a side street.

THE PORTICO OF PERINNAYA LINE (Perínnaya líniya), No. 33a

1802-1806. Architect—L. Ruska. A decorative structure. Now the Central Ci
Theatre Booking Office

The portico was built to decorate the end façade of a long shoppin
gallery built at right angles to the Prospekt at the end of the 18t
century. The gallery was of no artistic value and was demolished du
ing the building of the Metro. The portico, however, was reproduced i
1972 from the old drawings.

THE 'GOSTINY DVOR' DEPARTMENT STORE
(Bolshói Gostíny dvór), No. 35

1761-1785. Architect—J.-B. Vallin de la Mothe. Plan—a rectangle. Total leng
of façades overlooking 4 streets—above a kilometre. Now the biggest depar
ment store in Leningrad

In old Russia, merchants visiting the city used to put up at th
'gostiniye dvory', or guest houses, which also served for business.

Vallin de la Mothe designed a series of open two-tiered arcad
which formed very convenient galleries: they protect the shops fro
the damp, and also from the heat in sunny weather. This Gostiny Dvo
was used as a model for shopping centres in Petersburg itself and i
other cities.

During the blockade, it was seriously damaged by shellfire. Th
façade of the Gostiny Dvor overlooking the Nevsky Prospekt wa
restored in its original form and the interior was completely rebuilt.
is now rows of spacious shopping premises incorporating a Metro er
trance hall.

THE SALTYKOV-SHCHEDRIN STATE PUBLIC LIBRARY, No. 37

1796-1801. Architect—Ye. Sokolov. The block on the Ostrovsky Square sid
was added in 1828-1832; architect—C. Rossi. Length of façade—90 m. On th
attic there is a statue of Minerva by V. Demut-Malinovsky. Between the co
lumns of the façade are the sculptures of ancient scholars and poets b
S. Pimenov, N. Tokarev and others. Opened in 1814. Since 1932, has borne th
name of the Russian 19th-century author, M. Saltykov-Shchedrin

The library building, which was put up first, overlooked the corne
of Sadovaya Street and the Nevsky Prospekt, and only a small projec

on, three windows wide, encroached on Ostrovsky Square. The prem-
es soon became overcrowded. Architect Rossi made such a success
f augmenting the first structure with a second running along the
quare that they seem to be part of a whole. The majestic colonnade of
e portico—its 18 columns alternating with large windows and statues
f ancient philosophers, orators and poets—is admirably suited to the
nction of the building.

In the Soviet Union, the Saltykov-Shchedrin Public Library, with its
ook collection of over 20 million items, comes only second to the
enin Library in Moscow.

The Public Library's reading rooms are housed in other buildings in
e city. Up to five thousand visitors can work in them at a time. The
çade of the main building bears a memorial plaque:

> 'V. I. Lenin was a regular reader at the Public Library,
> 1893-1895'.

The Public Library has a priceless store of hand-written documents,
cluding manuscripts of antiquity and others that were written by Pe-
r I and great personalities in the history of Russian culture; it also has
e of the world's biggest collections of incunabula (books published
efore 1500) and the 'Rossica' collection which includes writings on
ussia in foreign languages. Voltaire's library of some 7 thousand vol-
mes is kept here. The library stocks include books in 89 languages of
e peoples of the USSR and im 156 foreign languages.

STROVSKY SQUARE (Plóshchad Ostróvskovo)

Ostrovsky Square is part of an ensemble conceived and executed by
arlo Rossi. An unprepossessing, half-waste plot of land dotted with
nall wooden structures was transformed by this architectural genius
to one of the city's most beautiful squares. Surrounded by an architec-
ral composition of bright and classically austere buildings, it brings to
ind the architect's own words that the aim was not an abundance of
rnamentation, but majesty of form, nobility of proportions, and
holeness.

Since 1923, the square (formerly Alexandrinskaya Square) has born
e name of A. Ostrovsky, the great 19th-century Russian dramatist.

HE PAVILIONS OF THE ANICHKOV PALACE

16-1818. Architect—C. Rossi. Statues by S. Pimenov

In his ensemble of the square Rossi included part of the grounds of
e Anichkov Palace (which will be described later) and built two pa-
ions. They are not large, but they are beautifully proportioned and the
tails of the façades have been traced out with great skill. Between

The Pushkin Drama Theatre

Anichkov Brid

the columns stand gigantic sculptures representing ancient Russia
knights. The cast-iron garden railing round the pavilions was also d
signed by Rossi. One of the buildings is used for exhibitions of chi
dren's art.

THE PUSHKIN ACADEMIC THEATRE OF DRAMA
(Formerly The Alexandrinsky Theatre)

1828-1832. Architect—C. Rossi. Sculptured figures on the attic by S. Pimeno
Statues of the Muses from the models by sculptor P. Triscorni. Since 1937, h
been known as the Pushkin Academic Theatre of Drama

The Theatre is the compositional centre of the square.
The function of this building is obvious at a glance.
The external niches are occupied by the statues of four Muses:
the front façade, Terpsichore (lyric poetry and dancing) and Melpe
mene (tragedy); in the rear façade—Clio (history) and Euterpe (m
sic). The original statues, set up when the building was being erecte
quickly began to deteriorate and had to be removed. The niches we
empty for almost a hundred years, but in 1932 the Muses were repr
duced by Soviet sculptors from the model of the originals.
The former Alexandrinsky Theatre (named after Alexandrina, t
wife of tsar Nicolas I) is now the premises of the Pushkin Academ

192

The 'Horse Tamers' sculpture on Anichkov Bridge

Theatre of Drama. Many names are associated with it that have been the glory of Russian acting art: V. Karatygin, M. Savina, V. Komissar-zhevskaya and others. In Soviet times, the history of the theatre is inseparable from the names of such artists as Ye. Korchagina-Alexan-drovskaya, N. Simonov, N. Cherkasov and Yu. Tolubeyev.

ARCHITECT ROSSI STREET (Ulitsa zódchevo Róssi)

1828-1834. Architect—C. Rossi. Length—220 m, width—22 m, height of the build-ings—22 m. In 1923, the street was named after its designer. To the left of the Pushkin Theatre is a building that houses the country's oldest school of choreo-graphy (founded 1738), a museum of theatrical art and a theatrical library, while there are various establishments on the right, including architectural workshops

Rossi laid out a small street behind the Theatre of Drama to Lomo-nosov Square. It is best to walk along it until it ends at the square, which was built almost entirely to Rossi's designs. From here, the view of the street is particularly striking; it is a masterpiece of town plan-ning. Each side is lined with the façades of buildings, with 23 pairs of half-columns raised above the arcades of the ground floors. As you approach the theatre, you have the impression that the columns are beginning to move. Linked in pairs, they alternate rhythmically with the enormous windows. The street looks like propylaea gracing the road to art at its greatest.

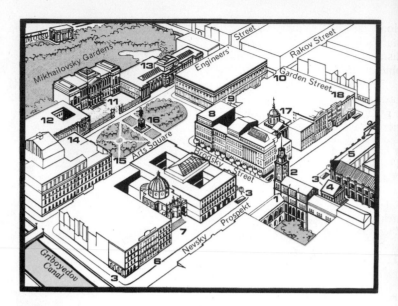

Right Odd-Numbered Side 1. 'Silver Rows' and the City Duma Building—Nos. 31—3
2. Tower of the City Duma **3.** Nevsky Prospekt Metro Station **4.** Portico of Perinnaya Lin
Theatre Tickets Booking Office **5.** 'Gostiny dvor' Department Store—No. 35
Left Even-Numbered Side 6. Maly Philharmonic Hall—No. 30 **7.** Roman Catholic Churc
of St. Catherine—Nos. 32 and 34 **8.** Leningrad State Philharmonic Society. Great Hall—
Brodsky Str. **9.** Theatre of Musical Comedy—13 Rakov Str. **10.** Komissarzhevskay
Theatre of Drama—19, Rakov Str. **11.** Russian Museum (The Mikhailovsky Palace)—4/
Engineers' Str. **12.** West Block of the Russian Museum—2, Griboyedov Canal **13.** Museu
of Ethnography of the Peoples of the USSR—4, Engineers' St. **14.** State Academic Ma
Theatre of Opera and Ballet—1, Arts Sq. **15.** Brodsky Museum-Flat—3, Arts Sq. **16.** Statu
of Alexander Pushkin **17.** Armenian Church—Nos. 40 and 42 **18.** 'Passage' Departmer
Store—No. 48

The Lunacharsky Theatrical Library on Rossi Street is the oldes
and biggest of its kind in the country, containing over 350 thousand
items: manuscripts, books, sketches, letters and memoirs.

This building also houses the Leningrad State School of Choreogra
phy, named after A. Vaganova (an outstanding ballerina and teache
who gave classes at the school from 1921 to 1951). Famous exponent
of the Russian ballet studied here, including Istomina, Pavlova, Vaga
nova herself, Nizhinsky, Fokin, Ulanova, and Chabukiani.

THE STATUE OF CATHERINE II

1873. Artist—M. Mikeshin, sculptors—M. Chizhov, A. Opekushin, architects—
D. Grimm, V. Schröter. Bronze. Height—14 m

This monument in Ostrovsky Square gardens was erected ove
twenty years after Rossi's death. The composition and finish are com
plex and florid. Catherine is in full ceremonial dress with an ermine

194

cloak draped from her shoulders and with a sceptre and crown of laurels in her hands. Her pose is gravely theatrical. Her favourites are distributed round the base: the sculptural treatment is realistic, and the physical likenesses have been reproduced with great fidelity.

The construction is of interest. The monument is of cast metal and has simply been placed on the dome of the granite base. It creates a general impression of majesty, but it interferes somewhat with the view of the theatre façade from the Nevsky Prospekt.

THE ZHDANOV LENINGRAD PALACE OF YOUNG PIONEERS (The Anichkov Palace), No. 39

Foundations laid in 1741. Architect—M. Zemtsov. Completed in 1750; architect—G. Dmitriyev. Subsequently rebuilt many times. Handed over to the Zhdanov Palace of Young Pioneers in 1937

The Department' (the block originally intended as the palace administrative office), No. 39

1803-1805. Architect—G. Quarenghi. Since 1937 has belonged to the Palace of Young Pioneers as a training block

This magnificent palace, the oldest on the Nevsky Prospekt, belonged throughout most of its history to tsarist dignitaries and members of the royal family.

For over forty years now, it has been 'owned' by the city's schoolchildren. The Leningrad Palace of Young Pioneers was the country's first out-of-school establishment to provide children with facilities for recreation, cultural development and the fostering of their talents. They have at their disposal over 300 laboratories, workshops, science study rooms, music studios, graphic art, theatre and choreographic studios, and also lecture and concert halls, cinemas and an excellent library. Two of the rooms in the palace were painted by Palekh craftsmen (Palekh painting is a branch of Russian folk art), one illustrating Pushkin's fairy tales, the other Gorky's. There are sports and other clubs. Members of the International Friendship Club have extensive contacts with foreign countries.

The Palace of Young Pioneers also owns the territory of the Gardens of Rest (the former grounds of the Anichkov Palace), with exhibitions and children's attractions facilities. The Gardens' summer theatre, open to adults in the evenings, puts on plays, shows and concerts.

THE ANICHKOV BRIDGE

1841. Length—54.6 m, width—37 m.
The sculptured groups by P. Clodt were put up in 1850

The River Fontanka, which crosses the Nevsky Prospekt after th Anichkov Palace, was once a city boundary. The first wooden bridg was built in 1715, on Peter I's orders, under the direction of militar engineer M. Anichkov (his name was given to the quarter where th soldiers of the working detachment were stationed and also to th palace and the bridge). The bridge was rebuilt a number of times sub sequently—completely so in 1841.

The bridge is decorated with four groups of sculpture, 'The Horse Tamers'. If the visitor looks at them in succession, he will see in all it dynamic beauty a magnificent representation in stone of four stages i the breaking-in of a horse.

During the blockade years, Clodt's horses were taken from thei granite pedestals and buried in the garden of the Palace of Youn Pioneers to safeguard them from enemy bombs and shells. Had it no been for this precaution, these valuable sculptures would hardly hav survived. A bronze plaque on the granite pedestal reminds us that th enemy poured nearly one and a half hundred thousand shells on to th city.

Left even-numbered side

NOS. 8 AND 10 ARE THE OLDEST HOUSES ON THE PROSPEKT

1768-1780. Architect unknown

Building commenced on the beginning of the Nevsky Prospekt in the 1760s on this side with no departure from the straight line of the Prospekt and the spacing between the separate buildings. Only two houses have been preserved with their elegant moulded vases, garlands, masks, medallions on the façade, and gryphon friezes. House No. 8 is the site of a Permanent Exhibition-Sales of work by Leningrad artists.

SCHOOL, House No. 14

1939. Architect—B. Rubanenko

The wall at the gates of this house bears a pale-blue rectangle with the inscription: 'Citizens! In the event of artillery fire, this side of the street is the most DANGEROUS!'

'This notice has been preserved to commemorate the heroism and courage of Leningrad's citizens during the 900-day blockade' reads the marble plaque affixed in peacetime next to this historic relic of 1941-1943. The fresh flowers here in winter and summer alike show that the ople of Leningrad and visitors to the city will always honour the emory of its heroic defenders.

OTOMIN'S HOUSE', No. 18

12-1816. Architect — V. Stasov

This dwelling house, which has gone down in the history of the ty's architecture bearing the name of its first owner, forms, with o. 15 opposite, a formal setting for the narrowest part (26 m) of the evsky Prospekt. In spite of certain subsequent changes, the façade as preserved the austere beauty of the Doric order.

At the beginning of the 19th century there used to be a confection-'s shop in the corner apartment of the lower storey with its windows verlooking the River Moika Embankment. A very popular rendez-ous for the artistic intelligentsia of Petersburg, it was often visited by lexander Pushkin who lived nearby at No. 12 on the River Moika mbankment. It was from here that fatal morning of January 27, 1837, at he drove off with his seconds to the place of the duel which was to sult in his death. Later, the same house was frequented by Pyotr chaikovsky.

OUSE OF THE DUTCH CHURCH, No. 20

830-1833. Architect — P. Jacquot

The stretch on the East side of the Nevsky Prospekt immediately fter the River Moika was earmarked in the 18th century for the build-g of 'heterodox' churches, as they were then called. The first you ome to as you walk along is the Dutch church.

The part conspicuous with its white-columned portico and its cupo-a served as the actual church, while the side wings were used for ervice and living accommodation by the Dutch mission in Petersburg. here is now a district library in the building.

UILDING OF THE LUTHERAN CHURCH OF ST. PETER, os. 22 and 24

832-1838. Architect — A. Bryullov

The short main façade of the church is decorated with the arch of portal and a colonnade. The three-tier corner towers give the impres-ion that the building is straining upwards. The dwelling houses situat-d symmetrically on either side of it form a small square which inter-upts the regular line of buildings.

BOOK HOUSE (Dom Knígi), No. 28

1907. Architect — P. Suzor. Originally the sales premises of the Singer Sewi
Machine Company. Now the biggest bookshop in the city

The building is decorated with an ornamental tower topped wi
a glass sphere which bears a metal ring inscribed 'Book House'. The
is a bookshop on the first two floors, and above it are the editor
offices of several Leningrad publishers.

THE CHURCH OF THE RESURRECTION OF CHRIST
(Saviour on the Blood)

1883-1907. Architects — I. Malyshev and A. Parland. Height — 79.8 m. The belf
walls are decorated with mosaics depicting the arms of the Russian guberr
cities. The pediments over the entrances are mosaic panels from sketches
artist V. Vasnetsov

A church can be seen from the Nevsky Prospekt some distan
away down the Griboyedov Canal Embankment. Emperor Alexand
III had it built to perpetuate the memory of his father, Alexander
fatally wounded as a result of the attempt on his life in 1881.

The St. Basil's Cathedral in Moscow had a considerable influen
on the architectural and artistic design of this building. The cardin
feature of the 'Saviour on the Blood' church is the extensive use
mosaics for external and interior decoration. The high quality of th
decorative work testifies to the great skill of the Russian builders.

A unique museum of Russian mosaics is to be opened in this churc

THE MALY PHILHARMONIC HALL, No. 30

Mid-18th century. Architect — B. Rastrelli. Rebuilt in 1829 by architect P. Ja
quot, and in 1890 by architect L. Benoit. Suffered heavily in the blockade. R
stored at the end of the 1940s. Since 1949 has been the Maly Hall of the Leni
grad State Philharmonic named after M. Glinka

This is one of the oldest buildings on the Nevsky Prospekt. In th
first half of the 19th century, it was the centre of the city's musical lif
The best singers and musicians of the time used to perform here. 'Mus
House', with its magnificent concert hall, was frequented by Pushk
and Lermontov. Liszt, Wagner and Berlioz gave guest appearance
During the blockade, the building was destroyed by a direct hit fro
a bomb. Restored after the war, it is now Leningrad's second philha
monic hall and is used for chamber music concerts.

BUILDING OF THE ROMAN CATHOLIC CHURCH OF ST. CATHERINE, Nos. 32 and 34

1763-1783. Architect—J.-B. Vallin de la Mothe. The dwelling houses on both sides of the church were built in the 1740s. Architect—D. Trezzini

The Catholic Church and the identical side buildings linked to it by arches depart from the straight line of the Prospekt and form a small square which is reminiscent in composition of the square in front of the Lutheran church. It is only since comparatively recently that this ensemble has had the finished appearance originally planned by the architects. It was reconstructed after the war (the pre-revolutionary modifications which were spoiling the former outlines, were demolished).

ARTS SQUARE (Plóshchad Iskússtv)

A wide street named after the Soviet painter I. Brodsky leads left from the Nevsky Prospekt to the square.

A mere list of the noteworthy buildings on this square is enough to explain why we should interrupt our walk along the Nevsky Prospekt by turning off at this point. Three theatres, The Great Philharmonic Hall, three art museums, the buildings in which they are housed—first-class monuments of architecture—a statue of Alexander Pushkin, the genius of Russian poetry—all these, grouped round the same square, explain why it was given its present name in 1940. And the square itself with the adjoining streets is a model of town planning as an art.

In 1816, C. Rossi was commissioned to build a palace here, which later housed the Russian Museum. He considered it his task not only to do this, but to create another architectural ensemble in the centre of the city.

Arts Square was conceived by Rossi earlier than the Ostrovsky Square ensemble but was the last of his projects to be completed.

The palace, now the Russian Museum, sets the architectural keynote of the rectangular square. There is a good view of it from the Nevsky Prospekt through the central avenue of the oval gardens. The houses fringing the square are more modest in appearance, thus emphasising the majesty of the main building. Rossi worked out standard façades for them in his time. By subordinating their designs to the unified plan, architects subsequently created one of the stylistically most austere of the city's architectural ensembles.

THE LENINGRAD STATE PHILHARMONIC, GREAT HALL (Bolshói zál), No. 2, Brodsky Street

1834-1839. Architect—P. Jacquot. Originally the building of the Noblemen's

Club. Since 1921, the State Philharmonic Society. Suffered heavily during tl
blockade. 1948-1949 saw the reconstruction and restoration of the façades. W:
named after Dmitry Shostakovich in 1976

A Philharmonic Society was founded in Petersburg in 1802. Josep
Haydn was one of its honorary members. The Hall of the Noblemen
Club is in three colours, with white columns, superb acoustics and a
organ. It was often used for the Philharmonic Society's concert
A. Rubinstein and Tchaikovsky performed their own works here. Afte
the October Revolution, the building was handed over to the first stat
concert organisation in the world, the State Philharmonic. Many work
by outstanding contemporary composers such as D. Shostakovicl
R. Gliére and N. Myaskovsky were performed in the Great Hall for th
first time. The best orchestras in the world played here under Stokow
ski, Karajan, Willy Ferrero and others.

The Symphony Orchestra of the Leningrad Philharmonic, whicl
has been under the direction of conductor Ye. Mravinsky for severa
decades, is famous all over the world.

It was from the Great Hall of the Philharmonic on August 9, 1942
that Shostakovich's Seventh Symphony was broadcast by all the radic
stations in the Soviet Union.

> '... I composed nearly the whole of the symphony in my n
> tive Leningrad. The city was being subjected to enemy air raic
> and artillery bombardment...
>
> 'During those days, I kept working on the symphony; I worke
> on it a great deal, intensively and quickly...
>
> 'I dedicate my Seventh Symphony to our struggle with fas
> cism, to our forthcoming victory over the enemy, and to my nativ
> city, Leningrad.'

> DMITRI SHOSTAKOVICI
> March 194

That is the symphony's name—'The Leningrad'. Noticeable on the
composer's score are the letters 'VT'—'vozdushnaya trevoga' (air-raid
warning). Shostakovich would interrupt work on the symphony and go
on fire-watching duty to deal with enemy incendiary bombs. When the
symphony was being performed, the members of the orchestra looked
rather strange. Some were in service uniform—they had just been recalled on a special order from the Leningrad Front. Others played in
the traditional black evening dress, starched shirt-fronts and collars;
but these peacetime clothes looked far too big for the wearers, who
were gaunt with starvation during the blockade. The crystal chandeliers shone brightly in the White-Columned Hall (Belokolónny
zál)—the city had somehow managed to lay on the necessary electric
power from its desperately limited supplies.

This day had been marked out by Hitler as yet another deadline for
the capture of the besieged city. The symphony born within its walls

ang out to the whole world as an anthem to the inflexible courage and invincibility of Leningrad.

THE THEATRE OF MUSICAL COMEDY, No. 13, Rakov Street

Beginning of the 19th century. Architect unknown

The theatre was founded in 1929 and moved to these premises in 1938. The theatre company was the only one in the city that never stopped performing throughout the blockade.

The current repertoire includes contemporary musical comedy and classical operetta.

Two houses further along the same line of buildings there is another theatre—

THE KOMISSARZHEVSKAYA THEATRE OF DRAMA, No. 19, Rakov Street

1846-1848. Architect—R. Zhelezevich

The building's history as a theatre began in the mid—19th century. In 1904-1906, the hall was hired by Vera Komissarzhevskaya, the great Russian actress. She opened a theatre here which reflected the mood of the progressive Russian intelligentsia.

The Komissarzhevskaya Theatre dates back to the last war. It opened for its first season on October 18, 1942. The local people called it the 'Blockade Theatre'. It is now one of the city's leading playhouses, mainly putting dramas by contemporary authors.

THE RUSSIAN MUSEUM (THE MIKHAILOVSKY PALACE), No. 4/2, Engineers' (Inzhenérnaya) Street

1819-1825. Architect—C. Rossi. Length of façade—over 200 m. Frieze of 44 bas-reliefs by sculptor V. Demut-Malinovsky. Since 1917, the State Russian Museum

The big central building of the palace is situated inside the front courtyard, which is separated from the square by tall cast-iron railings. The two-storey palace seems higher owing to the monumental portico and the 20 half-columns of the façade. The two side wings are also two-storeyed, but they are low in height and emphasise the majesty of the main building.

C. Rossi, a master of city ensembles, believed that all the component parts, even down to the minutest details, should go to make a harmonious whole. Consequently, when the Mikhailovsky Palace was being built to his designs, this also meant the total organisation of a big area, the erection of park pavilions and garden fences, and the decora-

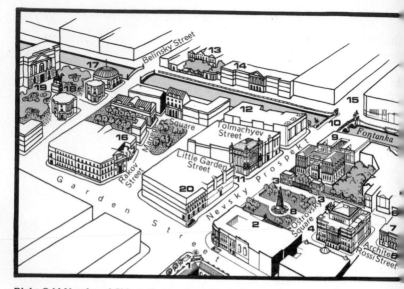

tion of the palace interiors in which not even the door handles were left to chance. Unfortunately, the Mikhailovsky Palace did not survive in its original form beyond the 1890s. Only the front vestibule with its staircase and the White Columned Hall on the second floor escaped later alterations. In the second of the two, it is still possible to see the coloured ceiling, and spaces above the door and the friezes illustrating scenes from the Trojan war, the carved wooden divans and chairs, the chandeliers, the candelabra, the parquet, the fireplaces etc., all executed according to Rossi's designs.

The 'Russian Museum of Emperor Alexander III' was opened in the Mikhailovsky Palace after crude alterations to the building. It was intended by official circles as a memorial to the tsar and its first exhibition included the emperor's personal effects. On the insistence of the progressive public, the best works by Russian artists were obtained from private houses and the Russian department of the Hermitage and also put on display. About 400 pictures, 100 sculptures, 70 drawings and water colours became the basis of the present collection in one of the biggest museums of Russian fine art.

Today, it houses over 300 thousand paintings, sculptures, and works graphic and applied art. Set up on strictly scientific principles, the exhibition in the museum rooms is a visual thousand-year chronicle of Russian art from ancient Russian iconography to the present day art.

The *West Block of the Russian Museum* (2 Griboyedov Canal) was added to the Palace on the canal side in 1910-1912 in accordance with designs by architects L. Benoit and S. Ovsyannikov.

Somewhat earlier, in 1911, the site of the Russian Museum's side wing was used for a massive building (architect—V. Svinyin) which ruined the harmony of the palace composition. It was intended for the Ethnography Section of the Russian Museum. *The Museum of the Ethnography of the Peoples of the USSR* (4 Engineers' Street) has been here since 1934.

This unique museum is engaged in collecting, preserving, studying and popularising the works of culture and applied art of the Soviet peoples. There are in the USSR over 100 big and small nationalities, each preserving, within the framework of the state and social community of the country's population, the characteristics of its own language, writing, manners, customs, cultural traditions and folk art.

Authentic specimens of tools, household implements, arts and crafts, national dress and works of fine art illustrate the history of the multinational Soviet people over the last two centuries.

There are always thematic exhibitions open to the public at the museum.

THE MALY THEATRE OF OPERA AND BALLET,
No. 1, Arts Square

1831-1833. Architect—A. Bryullov. Became the Mikhailovsky Opera Theatre in 1833. In 1918—the Maly Opera Theatre. Has borne its present name since 1963

In defiance of tradition, but in conformity with Rossi's intentions, the exterior of the building suggests an ordinary, unpretentious dwelling house. The interior, however, has been decorated with the sumptuousness typical of the early 19th century.

The former Mikhailovsky Theatre was destined to become the first musical theatre in Soviet Russia. It is considered to have been born on March 6, 1918, when it opened with Rossini's opera 'The Barber of Seville'. The theatre's creative history is associated with the search to create contemporary musical presentations. It is known as the 'laboratory' of Soviet opera.

BRODSKY MUSEUM-FLAT, No. 3, Arts Square
(Plóshchad Iskusstv)

First third of the 19th century. Opened as a museum in 1949

Next to the theatre there is another building with a façade designed by Rossi. It houses the museum-flat of the well-known Soviet artist Isaac Brodsky, where there is an exhibition of many of his canvases and his own collection of works by outstanding, mainly Russian, masters of painting and graphic art. ·

THE STATUE OF ALEXANDER PUSHKIN

Unveiled in 1957. Sculptor—M. Anikushin, architect—V. Petrov. Height of memorial—9 m and of the bronze statue—4 m

For the occasion of Leningrad's 250th anniversary, a monument to Alexander Pushkin was unveiled in the centre of the public garden of Arts Square. Sculptor M. Anikushin, who was awarded the Lenin Prize for his work, said: 'I wanted something out of the ordinary, I wanted a living man to stand on the pedestal, not just a sculpture. There he is as he was and as I imagined him ... A part of the city's spirit. I wanted to represent him as young, of the earth, human.' The sculptor succeeded. The town planning ensemble conceived by C. Rossi, who was Pushkin's contemporary, is superbly rounded off by this monument to the great poet who sang of the city on the Neva. It would be hard to imagine Arts Square without him.

You have finished your tour of the square and are now returning to the Nevsky Prospekt.

BUILDING OF THE ARMENIAN CHURCH, Nos. 40 and 42

1771-1780. Architect—Yu. Felten

The Armenian church forms another composition typical of the Nevsky Prospekt with a recession from the straight line of the buildings. The church itself is notable for lightness and elegance. This outstanding monument of architecture is the work of Yuri Felten, already known to you as the creator of the famous railing in the Summer Gardens.

COMEDY THEATRE, No. 56

1903-1907. Architect—G. Baranovsky. Comedy Theatre since 1929

The elaborate decorations, big stained-glass windows, metal sculptures and abundance of ornamentation on this theatre clash with the harmonious and austere style of the buildings on the Nevsky Prospekt.

articularly with the classical style of Ostrovsky Square opposite the
heatre. Yet it is effective in its way.

The house is widely known as the premises of the comedy theatre
which for over 30 years was run by one of the most talented Soviet
stage-directors, N. Akimov, authority on the art of the theatre, man of
etters, stage designer and artist.

The unusual notices done by this master are preserved in the
heatre museum with his sketches and models for stage sets, cartoons
and other drawings. Like the museums in the other theatres, it is open
during performances.

HOUSE OF FRIENDSHIP AND PEACE
No. 21, River Fontanka Embankment

The 1790s. Architect unknown. Rebuilt in the 1840s and in 1965

This former private house on the River Fontanka Embankment is
now the premises of the Leningrad Branch of the Union of Soviet
Societies for Friendship and Cultural Relations with Foreign Countries.
It cooperates with nearly 500 organisations in over 30 countries.

The building is of interest owing to the carefully preserved and
artistically valuable decorated interiors of the Hall of Columns, the
Golden Reception-Room, the Knights' Hall and so on.

Friendship House arranges concerts and meetings with foreign
delegations. Exhibitions are organised so that the citizens of Leningrad
can get to know about life and culture in foreign lands. Abroad, the
society popularises the achievements of Leningrad figures in science
and culture.

You are back at the Anichkov Bridge. The modern Nevsky Prospekt does not end here. After the bridge, which is approximately in the
middle, more buildings eventually went along the Prospekt, most of
them being the dwelling houses dating back to the end of the 19th
century and the beginning of the 20th. They are of no particular architectural merit, although there are some exceptions.

Before you leave the Fontanka Embankment, it is worth looking
across the river at an old private house (Fontanka Embankment, 34,
1750-1755, architects—F. Argunov and S. Chevakinsky). The composer
M. Glinka visited the house, and O. Kiprensky painted there his well-
known portrait from life of Pushkin, about which the latter wrote in his
poem 'To Kiprensky': 'I see myself as in the mirror'. This is now the
premises of the *Institute of Arctic and Antarctic*, the biggest research
establishment of its kind in the world. In the garden of this 'HQ of two
Poles' stands a bust of the great polar explorer Roald Amundsen, a gift
from the Norwegian government to the Soviet Union.

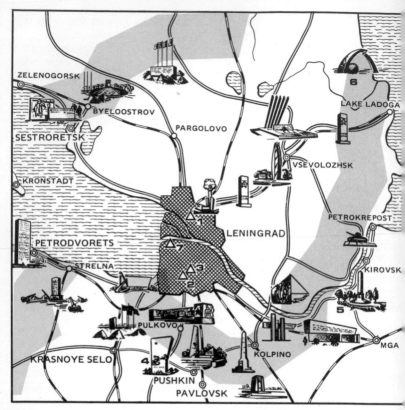

Figures stand for: 1. Piskaryovskoye Memorial Cemetery **2.** Monument to the Heroic Defenders of Leningrad **3.** Moskovsky Victory Park **4.** Monument to Volunteer Corps (11th km of the Leningrad-Pushkin Highway) **5.** Nevsky Pyatachyok (the Neva Foothole) **6.** Broken Blockade Ring Monument **7.** Museum of the History of Leningrad

We would suggest you look round one more square situated not far from the Nevsky Prospekt. You can, in fact, go to Manege Square from the Fontanka Embankment where you are at present. But it would be better for you to retrace your steps a short way along the Nevsky and turn off into Malaya Sadóvaya Street. Then, on the way to the Square, you will see on your left

THE WINTER STADIUM (The Mikhailovsky Manege or Riding School)

1798-1801. Designer unknown, 1823-1824—rebuilt; architect—C. Rossi. Bas-reefs on the façade by S. Pimenov and V. Demut-Malinovsky. In the 1950s, the indoor premises of the Manege were converted into a winter stadium

The general view of the building and the style of the walls have been preserved as they were after Rossi's reconstruction. Taking the Manege façade overlooking the central building and the side pavilions by having high thick stone walls put up.

The Manege is associated with the revolution of 1917. Lenin spoke twice here. In April 1917, at a meeting of the soldiers of the armoured squadron, he made a speech about the imperialist nature of World War I, which was being continued by the Provisional Government. On the second occasion, he spoke at a review of the first detachments of troops about to leave for the front on 1 January 1918, to defend the young Republic of Soviets from the counter-revolution.

The Winter Stadium in the building of the former Manege is a large-scale sports centre. It is used for track-and-field events, basketball, weight-lifting, fencing, wrestling, handball, etc. It is also used for concerts and shows, when it can accommodate about five thousand spectators.

MANEGE SQUARE

The alterations to the Manege (Riding School), which gave its name to the square, was part of Rossi's reconstruction in the 1820s of the land adjacent to the Mikhailovsky Palace, the premises of the present-day Russian Museum, and to the Engineers' Castle.

Manege Square acquired its present look in the 50s after the great Patriotic War. A passage was opened from Manege Square to the Engineers' Castle and the surrounding area was developed. There is now a magnificent view from Manege Square of the main façade of the Engineers' Castle. In front of it stands the *Monument to Peter the Great* (1715. Sculptor—C.-B. Rastrelli; erected in 1800). The model of this monument was made by the sculptor during Peter's lifetime. At the beginning of the Great Patriotic War, the statue was taken down from its pedestal and hidden away. It was re-erected in 1945.

THE ENGINEERS' CASTLE

1797-1800. Designed by architect V. Bazhenov. Built under the direction of architect V. Brenn. Originally the fortress-residence of tsar Paul I. After 1823, the St. Petersburg Military Engineering College. Now the premises of several establishments. Restoration work is currently in progress

It is well worth walking round the Engineers' Castle and studying it from every angle. The original treatment of each façade was organically linked with the surrounding landscape: the austere gravity of the main South façade—with the square, once used for parades and the posting of the sentries; the lyrical grace of the North façade with the Summer Gardens.

> *The palace was built for Paul I as his main residence. Fearing attempts at assassination, he did not want to remain in the Winter Palace and gave orders for the new castle to be converted into an impregnable fortress.*
> *The castle was surrounded with water: on the North side, by the River Moika and on the East by the River Fontanka. Canals were dug on the West and South sides (one was filled in later and the other channelled into an underground conduit). This artificial island was reached by draw bridges protected by cannons and a reinforced watch. In spite of these precautions, however, Paul only had forty days to live in the castle-fortress. He was strangled in his bedroom by officers of his own guard. The castle was never used again as a royal residence. The unoccupied building became a Widows' House and was later converted into a Military College of the Engineering Department.*

In 1838, the great Russian writer Fyodor Dostoyevsky was sent to the Engineering College as a 16-year-old boy. His first attempts at literature date back to his stay there. One of the young Dostoyevsky's favourite places for study was the window-sill in the corner room on the third floor.

The Nevsky Prospekt continues in a straight line as far as Insurrection Square, where the Moscow Railway Station is situated, and then branches off to the right. It ends at Alexander Nevsky Square, where you will see the *Alexander Nevsky Monastery (Lavra)* (see the section 'Museums') and also the new *Intourist Hotel Moskva (Moscow)*. The latter is part of a new architectural ensemble which graces Leningrad's main thoroughfare.

900 Days — the Heroic Defence of Leningrad

The places of interest on this excursion are in widely dispersed parts of Leningrad and its environs.

You can get a detailed picture of Leningrad at the time of the fascist blockade by visiting Museum of the History of Leningrad (at 44, Red Fleet Embankment (Náberezhnaya Krásnovo flóta).

Public transport: Trolleybuses—5, 6, 14; Buses—6, 49, 50, 90; Trams—1, 5, 8, 11, 15, 21, 24, 26, 31, 33, 42.

All visitors to Leningrad, whether Soviet or foreign, invariably visit the Piskaryovskoye Memorial Cemetery and pay tribute to the magnificent heroism of Leningrad's defenders who lie buried there. The Piskaryovskoye Memorial Cemetery is at 72, Avenue of the Unconquered (Prospékt Nepokoryónnykh).

Public transport: Trolleybus—30; Buses—9, 102; Trams—46 and 51.

Visitors arriving in Leningrad by car from Moscow, Kiev or from Leningrad airport will pass Victory Square (Plóschad Pobédy) from which Moscow Avenue starts. A magnificent memorial complex, the Monument to the Heroic Defenders of Leningrad, stands in the centre of the square.

Public transport: Buses—3, 11, 13, 16, 39, 50, 55, 56, 67, 130; Trolleybuses—2, 27, 29, 35; Metro station—Moskovskaya.

We advise you to visit the Moscow (Moskóvsky) and Maritime (Primórsky) Victory Parks, laid out to immortalize the heroes of Leningrad war-time epic. The Moscow Victory Park is at 138, Moscow Avenue.

Public transport: Trolleybuses—2, 15, 24, 26; Buses—3, 16, 50, 63, 64, 67; Trams—3, 16, 29, 35, 45; Metro station—Park Pobedy.

The Maritime Victory Park is at 2, Krestovsky Avenue.

Public transport: Trolleybus—69; Buses—45, 71; Trams—12, 17, 25.

On their way to Pushkin, Petrodvorets and the Karelian Isthmus, the tourists will see compositions reproducing, in artistic form, episodes from the Leningrad siege and marking the front line during the Battle of Leningrad. These are the monuments of the 'Green Belt of Glory'.

Of course, there are many more places associated with the defence of the city than are given in this chapter, and you are sure to pass them during other excursions and walks round Leningrad and its environs.

In order to get acquainted with the 900 Days of Leningrad's Heroic Defence, one can count on the services of Intourist or the City Excursions Bureau.

MUSEUM OF THE HISTORY OF LENINGRAD

1826-1827. Architect—V. Glinka. Formerly a private mansion. Rebuilt to house the museum in the 1950s

> *Oh, this great city! How they tortured it*
> *From earth and sky with freezing cold, with fire,*
> *And with starvation ...*
>
> *VERA INBER*

The 12 exhibition halls on the first floor feature items illustrating the main stages of the Battle for Leningrad.

Hitler planned to take Leningrad eight weeks after the beginning of the Blitzkrieg on the Soviet Union. Apart from the strategic considerations, the nazi leaders attached tremendous political importance to the seizure of Leningrad. To accomplish this task, the Wehrmacht threw in the Army Group North supported by the Army Group Centre—in all, some 42 divisions (about 725 thousand officers and men), 1,200 aircraft, 13 thousand of guns and mortars, and 1,500 tanks.

The fascist hordes broke through into the Leningrad Region in early July 1941. The city was in deadly peril.

Civilian Defence Corps whose numbers totalled some 160,000 citizens joined the regular army units and the partisan movement to fight

The Piskaryovskoye Memorial Cemetery

the enemy. Among the museum exhibits there are applications — whole families wanted to be sent to the front. The citizens, women and schoolchildren among them, went out to build a ring of defences. In a short space of time, they dug 625 kilometres of anti-tank ditches, constructed many thousands of weapon emplacements and built 400 kilometres of escarpments. Scenes of these heroic labour efforts can be viewed in the display of photographs.

All Leningrad's plants and factories switched over to munitions. The museum exhibits include cartridges, mines, grenades, weapons, military uniforms and other munitions bearing the trade-marks of former confectionary, footwear, clothing, printing and tobacco factories.

On September 25, 1941, the defenders of Leningrad halted the enemy and forced them to go over to the defensive. From that day on, the fascist armies could not advance by an inch.

When the nazi command realised that their attempts to take the city by assault had ended in failure, they decided to strangle Leningrad by an all-round blockade. On display in the museum there is a copy of the nazi Navy Headquarters top-secret directive, dated September 29, 'On the Future of the City of Petersburg' which reads: '... the Führer has decided to wipe Petersburg off the face of the earth. After Soviet Russia's defeat, there will be no reason for the further existence of this large inhabited area ...

Part of the monument to the
heroic defenders of Leningrad on
Victory Square

The 'Boundary Stone' at the Green
Belt of Glory

'It is proposed to blockade the city tightly and raze it to the ground
by means of all-calibre artillery fire and continuous bombardment from
the air ...

'For our part, we are not interested in preserving even a part of this
big city's population...' Many documents on show illustrate how meth-
odically and on what scale this order was executed. The mass starvation of the blockade-stricken city in the winter of 1941-1942 became
a weapon of mass destruction in the enemy's hands. On September 8,
the last land route connecting Leningrad with the rest of the country
was cut off, and this was the beginning of the 900-day heroic epic of the
city's defence. In the autumn, the daily food ration was reduced five
times until it became a tiny slice of bread weighing only 125 grammes.
Museum visitors can see samples of this bread and the recipe for bak-
ing it, in which almost 50 per cent of the ingredients are artificial. In
November of that year alone, 10,000 died of dystrophy in Leningrad.
The situation was catastrophic. The most tragic days were in December, since the winter was exceptionally severe.

> *Time softens, conceals and even obliterates the most horrible
> events in man's life. However, when an especially frosty, foggy
> night falls on Leningrad, then, if you spent at least one tragic night
> there in 1941-1942 you can imagine yourself walking round the
> blockade-stricken city again ...'*

> *... Ice-bound trams and trolleybuses, broken and grotesquely*
> *tangled wires hanging from above ... In the dusk hours, figures*
> *would pass here and there, pulling a hand-made sledge loaded*
> *with something swathed like a mummy. This is how the people*
> *who died from starvation made their last journey. Or you could*
> *see a group of people heaving a big sledge piled with pots and*
> *buckets filled with ice-cold water from the Neva or the Fontanka*
>
> *'It is impossible to list all the heroic deeds performed by the*
> *city's defenders. It would take many volumes to tell how Leningrad*
> *lived, fought, worked and held out.'*

MIKHAIL DUDIN
a poet who took part
in the defence of Leningrad

At the Nürnberg trials the chief nazi criminals faced the accusation, confirmed by documents, of having caused the deaths of 632,000 Leningrad citizens by starvation alone. However, this was not the complete roll of casualties.

But Leningrad did not simply hold out. The city believed in final victory and fought for it. Among the museum's priceless exhibits are hand-printed books and newspapers, posters announcing shows and concerts during the blockade, designs for the future Triumphal Arch drawn by an architect who was dying of starvation, photographs of the 'Lifeline'. This was the road which played a vital role in the Leningrad epic. It ran across icebound Lake Ladoga and was under constant energy shellfire. But this thin artery kept the weakening pulse of the starving city going. There are also photographs of trains of the horse-drawn carts with which the partisans brought food to the city after breaking through the front lines. There are also documents on display which depict the heroic labour efforts of the people who, despite the apalling conditions, carried on working at the plants and factories and provided the Army with armaments of all kinds. Also on display in the museum are photographs of citizens who saved the lives of old people, the disabled and children.

Special hospitals were opened to care for the starving, and orphanges for children who had lost their parents. Volunteers from the Komsomol 'home-help teams' assisted the weak and the sick with such chores as fetching water and keeping the stoves burning. Schoolchildren continued with their lessons, but during air-raids or artillery bombardments they helped the grown-ups to put out fires and also assisted the weak and the ill.

Another exhibit depicts the Victory Salute over the Neva on 27 January 1944 — the triumphal climax telling the whole world that the blockade had been lifted and the fascist armies had been completely smashed at the walls of Lenin's city.

The museum shows documentary films on the heroic defence of Leningrad.

THE PISKARYOVSKOYE MEMORIAL CEMETERY

1955-1960. Architects—A. Vassilyev and Y. Levinson. Area—26 hectares. Monument of the Mother-Country by sculptors V. Isayeva and R. Taurit. Height of monument—12 m and of bronze figure—6 m. The memorial wall is 150 m long and 4.5 m high

Lowered state flags of the Soviet Union on the tall flag-posts near the entrance. Museum pavilions on either side of it. Verses by Mikhail Dudin on the friezes. A display of documents in the pavilions. Concealed lighting in one of the halls illuminates a row of war-time photographs: anti-air-raid trenches in the public parks, apartments ripped open by explosions, a wounded child, bodies on the Nevsky Prospekt after the latest artillery bombardment, the haggard faces of the starving ... The Piskaryovskoye Cemetery register, open at a page bearing the entries for February 1942: on the 18th—3,241 bodies brought for burial; on the 19th—5, 569; on the 20th—10,043 ...

And here is another document which will haunt the memory: beside a photograph of little Tanya Savicheva are some pages from her blockade diary. In a child's large script, Tanya recorded on the pages of her ABC book the dates and times as the members of her family—sister, brother, grandmother, uncle, mother—died one after the other. Finally come the tragic lines: 'The Savichevs have died. Everybody's died. Only Tanya's alive.' Tanya was evacuated, but she was too weak to recover from the effects of starvation ...

In the other pavilion, there is a documentary chronicle of the city's struggle and the achievements of its defenders—heroic trips by convoys of lorries bringing foodstuffs along the 'Lifeline', the link-up of the Volkhov and Leningrad Fronts which smashed the blockade ring in 1943, the jubilant city celebrating victory over the enemy ...

Between the museum pavilions is a raised terrace, in the centre of which an Eternal Flame is burning in a black granite surround. This flame was lit from the one in the Field of Mars (Mársovo pólye) where there is a monument to the heroes of the Revolution.

There is a good view from this terrace of the whole memorial complex. To the left and right from the terrace run the flat low gravestones of common graves, no names are given—just the years: 1941, 1942, 1943, 1944. Here lie over 500,000 inhabitants of Leningrad who gave their lives for the happiness of the future generations.

The central avenue leads to the only monument in the Piskaryovskoye Cemetery. It is a statue of the Mother-Country holding out towards the graves of her sons a wreath of oak leaves, symbol of eternal glory. To the strains of solemn funeral music, visitors go up to the frontal wall which serves as a background for the monument. Some lines of verse are engraved on the wall. They were composed by Olga Bergholts, who remained in the besieged city throughout the blockade.

Here lie the people of Leningrad,
Here are the citizens — men, women, children ...
They gave their lives
Defending you, Leningrad,
Cradle of Revolution.
We cannot number all their noble names here,
So many lie beneath the eternal granite,
But know as you look upon these stones,
That no one has been forgotten, and nothing
has been forgotten.

MONUMENT TO THE HEROIC DEFENDERS OF LENINGRAD

1974-1975. Architects — S. Speransky and V. Kamensky. Sculptor — M. Anikushin

This magnificent Monument to the Heroic Defenders of Leningrad was unveiled on the new Victory Square on 9 May 1975 to commemorate the 30th Anniversary of the Victory over fascism. Thousands upon thousands of Leningrad people of various age and trades voluntary spent their spare time on the construction of this memorial.

The monument faces south, where the front line once ran. Wide steps of pink granite lead to a granite oval. The stairs are flanked by massive stone blocks which serve as a background for dark bronze groups of statuary and sculptures of the city's defenders. In the centre there is a 48-metre obelisk, which stands inside a gap in a circle to symbolise the breaking of the blockade ring. There is the bronze figure of Soldier and an Eternal Flame at the foot of the obelisk. On the insides of circular walls are bronze bas-reliefs of decorations awarded to Leningrad and the texts of the relevant decrees by the USSR Supreme Soviet. Solemn funeral music can be faintly heard in the background.

Only the first stage of this monument has been completed. According to the original design, the ground floor of the base will serve as a museum exhibiting documents and photographs illustrating the defence of Lenigrad.

THE MOSCOW VICTORY PARK
(Moskóvsky park Pobédy)

Architects — Y. Katonin and V. Kirkhoglani. Total area — 68 hectares

... Early in the morning, the people
of Leningrad went out
In huge crowds to the sea-shore,
And each of them planted a tree
Up on that strip of land, marshy, deserted,

*In Memory of that great Victory Day,
Look at it now—it is a comely orchard...*

ANNA AKHMATOVA

The war ended in spring 1945, and in autumn, two public parks, called Victory Parks, had been laid out according to the ancient tradition. Hundreds of thousands of people lent a hand in the work. The parks are cheerful monuments to the city's defenders. They combine the formal style with landscape gardening. Ponds and lakes add beauty and variety to the view.

The Victory Park in the Moscow district is located in the south part of Leningrad.

The central feature of the layout is the Alley of Heroes, which runs from the main entrance. It is flanked with the busts of citizens who became twice Heroes of the Soviet Union.

The Decree on the Award of Medals and Orders of the USSR stipulates that all who receive this title twice shall be commemorated by a monument in their birthplace erected in their lifetime. And so the Alley of Heroes immortalizes the names of combat pilots, sailors and tankmen.

In the side avenues stand two symmetrically placed sculptured monuments to two national heroes of the Soviet Union who gave their lives in the fight against fascism: Zoya Kosmodemyanskaya (1951, by M. Manizer) and Alexander Matrosov (1951, by L. Eidlin).

THE GREEN BELT OF GLORY

A memorial complex extending for some 230 km along the 1941-1944 front line from the south shore of the Gulf of Finland to Sestroretsk

Monuments, memorial pillars, bridges, tanks and guns erected on pedestals, memorial groves and avenues and museum pavilions are all there to remind future generations of those who defended the city of Lenin from the fascist invaders during the Great Patriotic War.

The defence lines ran across fields, marshes, woods and so 'The Green Belt of Glory' is not, of course continuous. The principal monuments stand at points where the blockade ring is crossed by roads, railways and bridges, in towns and villages, and also by rivers and lakes in the Leningrad Region.

...At the 11th kilometre of the Leningrad-Pushkin road, you will see what appears to be a banner fluttering in the breeze. This is part of a 12-metre high monument with bas-reliefs depicting a worker from the people's volunteer corps, a navy man, a soldier and a girl machine-gunner, erected in the memory of the home guards of the Hero City.

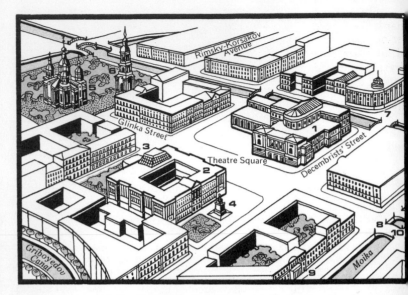

1. Kirov Opera and Ballet Theatre (Mariinsky Theatre) **2.** Rimsky-Korsakov State Conservatoire **3.** Statue of Glinka **4.** Statue of Rimsky-Korsakov **5.** Nikolsky Marine Cathedral **6.** Dome of the Nikolsky Marine Cathedral **7.** First Five-Year Plan Palace of Culture **8.** Potseluev Bridge **9.** Education Workers' Palace of Culture **10.** To Labour Square, Palace of Labour and Museum of the History of Leningrad

... In September 1941, Soviet troops succeeded in recapturing a tiny 3-kilometre-deep stretch of land. This *Nevsky pyatachok* (the Neva foothold) was perhaps the 'hottest' along the entire Leningrad front. It was surrounded on the three sides by the enemy and cut off from the main land by the river. Every square metre was continuously shelled and bombed...

... The obelisk is surrounded by railings and poplar trees have been planted nearby. A tank and a gun stand on pedestals, and there is a 'Boundary Stone' with a picture of soldiers in combat. An epitaph is carved on the stone:

> *You*
> *The living*
> *Know*
> > *that from this land*
> *We did not mean to go*
> *We made our stand*
> *By the Neva*
> *We did not fear to give*
> *Freely of our lives*
> *That you might live*
> > > *ROBERT ROZHDESTVENSKY*

216

Another obelisk, which can be seen on the way to Petrodvorets, marks the position from which the Soviet troops launched their counter-offensive in 1944. Nearby are the remains of a wall, which was part of an ancient palace, rows of young poplar trees, and the common grave of the sapper troops who were killed while clearing mines in Petrodvorets, at which we marvel so much today.

...All these go to make the 'Green Belt of Glory,' preserved in eternal memory of those who died for the sake of posterity.

Theatre Square and Places of Interest in the Vicinity

Theatre Square (Teatrálnaya plóshchad) can be the subject of a separate tour, in which case it will be quite a short walk, or it could serve as the point for a tour of, say, St. Isaac's Square and the vicinity.

You already have some idea of your way round Leningrad and know that you can easily get to Theatre Square by crossing from the right to left bank of the Neva over Lieutenant Schmidt Bridge; or by going along the Red Fleet Embankment and through Labour Square (Plóshchad Trúda) after visiting the State Museum of the History of Leningrad; or from the Central Post Office on Communications Union (Soyúz svyázi) Street. The Moika Embankment and Glinka Street also lead to Theatre Square. Finally, you will find yourself on Theatre Square if your tour programme includes visit to the Kirov Opera and Ballet Theatre or the Rimsky-Korsakov Conservatoire.

Or you can travel to Theatre Square by taking the following *public transport* routes: Buses—2, 3, 22, 27, 43, 49, 50, 100; Trams—1, 5, 8, 11, 15, 21, 24, 31, 33, 36, 42 to the stop named 'Theatre Square'.

A large tract of land, virtually a waterlogged field, remained undeveloped some distance away from the capital's aristocratic centre. This was the place where public festivities, carnivals and fairs were held, which accounted for the booths, unsophisticated amusements and merry-go-rounds everywhere. In the 18th century, it was actually called Merry-Go-Round Square (Karusyélnaya plóshchad).

A wooden theatre was built on the site of the present Conservatoire, to be replaced in 1783 with the Bolshoi (Stone) theatre, in its heyday considered to be one of the finest of its kind in Europe, since the main auditorium had three tiers and could seat some 2,000 spectators. Dramas, ballets and operas were performed there.

In 1836, the drama company broke away to form the Alexandrine Theatre, now known as the Pushkin Academic Drama Theatre. A new building was put up in 1860 on the opposite side of the square for the musical theatre, which became known as Mariinsky Theatre (now the Kirov Opera and Ballet Theatre).

THE KIROV OPERA AND BALLET THEATRE
(Mariinsky Theatre)

1860. Architect—A. Kavos. Rebuilt in 1883-1896 and 1969. In 1935, named afte
S. Kirov, a prominent figure in the Communist Party of the Soviet Union an
the Soviet Government

The excess of small and pretentious details on the façades deprive
building of true monumentality.

However, the interior decorations—gilded mouldings, blue velve
and a handsome plafond—give the theatre a festive appearance. The
Theatre permanent troupe is considered to have been founded in 1783
when the Bolshoi (Stone) Theatre was built on the square.

Brilliant artistes performed there in Pushkin's time. The theatre hac
a great deal to do with the foundation of the Russian ballet. Tchaikovs
ky's world-famous 'Sleeping Beauty', 'Swan Lake' and 'Nutcracke
Suite' were all staged there. Marius Petipa, the brilliant balletmaste
and teacher, was a leading figure in the Petersburg ballet for over hal
a century. L. Ivanov and M. Fokin made great contributions to the
development of choreography. The world-famous ballerinas Istomin
and Pavlova danced on its stage.

From the very beginning the Mariinsky Theatre developed the tra
ditions of Russian national art. It launched operas by Russia's grea
maestros, Glinka, Tchaikovsky and Mussorgsky. Chalyapin and Sobin
ov sang here.

Since the Revolution, the theatre's traditions have continued in per
formances of works by Dmitri Shostakovich, Sergei Prokofyev and
Dmitri Kabalevski, and in the magnificent interpretations of Ulanova
Semyonova and Dudinskaya. The Kirov Theatre orchestra is known as
one of the finest in the world. The theatre's tours abroad are always
a great triumph.

The Fyodor Chalyapin Memorial Room, where the great singer's
photographs, papers, sketches and personal belongings are on display
is open to visitors during performances.

THE RIMSKY-KORSAKOV STATE CONSERVATOIRE

1891-1896. Architect—V. Nicolas. Named after Nikolai Rimsky-Korsakov i
1944

At the end of the 19th century, this building housed the first Russiar
advanced school of music, founded in 1862 on the initiative of Anton
Rubinstein, the famous pianist, composer and conductor.

Many fine Russian musicians and composers studied here. One of
the first graduates in 1865 was Tchaikovsky, later to become one of the
world's greatest composers. Rimsky-Korsakov taught a whole galaxy

of Russian musicians, including Prokofyev, Myaskovsky, Asafyev and Glazunov. In 1923, an opera studio opened at the Conservatoire. It has the use of the Rubinstein Great Hall. The finest Soviet and foreign artistes appear on its stage.

To the right, if you stand facing the Conservatoire, is the monument to the great Russian composer Mikhail Glinka, and on the left is the one to Nikolai Rimsky-Korsakov.

THE NIKOLSKY MARINE CATHEDRAL

1753-1762. Architect—S. Chevakinsky

There is a good view from Theatre Square of this cathedral, which stands at the intersection of the Kryukov and Griboyedov canals. The talented S. Chevakinsky, a contemporary of B. Rastrelli, gave the cathedral a festive appearance.

Simple in architectural composition, the two-storey building is crowned with five widely-spaced gilded domes. White columns against the pale-blue walls create a picturesque interplay of light and shade. The frames of the large windows on the both floors are decorated with intricate mouldings.

A graceful four-tier bell tower, standing apart in the garden, is mirrored in the waters of both canals.

The interior decorations are of great artistic value—a handcarved wooden iconostasis and icons painted by gifted 18th-century Russian artists.

The Nikolsky Marine Cathedral is one of the 19 places of worship open in Leningrad (15 Orthodox churches, one Catholic church, a Baptist church, a synagogue and a mosque).

Behind the Kirov Theatre, the Kryukov Canal Embankment is overlooked by the First Five-Year Plan Palace of Culture.

THE FIRST FIVE-YEAR PLAN PALACE OF CULTURE

1929-1930. Architects—N. Miturich and V. Makashev. Rebuilt 1953-1957

This is one of several Palaces of Culture built in Leningrad during the first ten years of Soviet power. It has seven halls for theatre performances, concerts, film shows and lectures.

EDUCATION WORKERS' PALACE OF CULTURE

The 1830s. Architect—A. Mikhailov Jr. Teachers' House since 1925

Behind the Conservatoire building on the bank of the Moika you will see a bright yellow building with a white-columned portico. This former residence of the Counts Yusupov, is a Palace of Culture, known in the city as Teachers' House.

The entrance hall, the ceremonial rooms, the White-Columned (Belokolónny) Concert Hall and the Blue and Red Rotondas are lavishly decorated. The former private theatre with its tiers, boxes, mouldings, painting and gilt is an exact miniature replica of the interior of the Mariinsky Theatre.

There are various hobby groups and societies, amateur stage companies. There is considerable popular science teaching activity. Concerts and dances are also held. The drama group has been performing foreign plays in the original language for many years.

As you leave Theatre Square and walk towards the Neva, you will come to Labour Square.

LABOUR SQUARE (Plóshchad Trudá)

This square (formerly Annunciation Square) was formed in the middle of the 19th century. A monumental building was erected there, the present Palace of Labour.

PALACE OF LABOUR (Dvoréts Trudá)

1861. Architect—A. Shtakenshneider. From 1885, a Girls' Private Boarding School. Became the Trade Union Regional Council in 1919. In 1962, the ceremonial rooms were taken over by the Trade Unions Palace of Culture

The magnificent iron railings round the palace are particularly worthy of attention.

The main entrance consists of a columned portico surmounted by a balcony. Inside, the entrance hall and the main stairs decorated with columns, are the most interesting features.

In March 1919, V. I. Lenin made a speech at the First Petrograd Regional Congress of Agricultural Workers, which was held in the assembly hall.

The reception halls of the palace are used for meetings of the city's youth with distinguished people living in Leningrad or the Leningrad Region, as well as for receptions of foreign guests and for balls and musical concerts.

Labour Square borders on the Red Fleet (Krásny flót) Embankment which is joined by Lieutenant Schmidt Bridge to Lieutenant Schmidt Embankment, familiar to you from your first sightseeing tour of Leningrad.

The New Maritime (Primórsky) District on Vasilyevsky Island

The western part of Vasilyevsky Island, washed by the waters of the Gulf of Finland, is a new development area quite near the city centre. It only takes 10-15 minutes by a car from Palace (Dvortsóvaya) Square.

Public transport to Marine Glory Square (Plóshchad Morskóy slávy): Trolleybuses — 10, 12; Buses — 50, 128, 151, 152.

Though the mass housing construction in progress here is on a smaller scale compared with northern and southern parts of Leningrad, you can gain an impression of how the basic ideas of the city's General Development Plan are being carried out.

Public transport to Housing Estate No. I, only a few stops from Marine Glory Square: Trolleybus — 10, 12, 46; Buses — 30, 41, 44, 47, 50, 128, 151, 152; Trams — 26, 40.

Another reason for visiting this area is the splendid view over the Gulf of Finland and the sight of the seagoing ships at their moorings. You feel that you really are in a city on the sea-coast.

Public transport to the sea-shore (known as the city's Waterfront): Buses — 30, 41, 128, 151, 152.

And now, as on the first day of your stay in Leningrad, you are on Vasilyevsky Island — the place where the city began and which is still ageless...

In the last century, one Leningrad writer wrote as follows about this district known as Galley Harbour: 'The poorest and remotest town in Russia cannot be compared unfavourably with this wretched suburb ... it's impossible to believe that this is part of magnificent Petersburg.'

Only under Soviet power was this outlying area properly developed: running water and sewage systems were provided, the streets were paved and public gardens laid out. Even before World War II, however, there were wooden houses on the street nearest to the shore. There were no buildings at all further to the west — just a marshy seashore dotted with scrub.

In 1963, a new square was laid out on the sea-front at the end of Grand Avenue. It was later named Marine Glory Square.

In 1968, several exhibition pavilions, each covering an area of 2,500 sq m were built in Galley Harbour to house the international exhibition 'Inrybprom-68'. However, not all the exhibits were on display in the plate-glass pavilions — the fishing vessels of many countries were moored at the jetties. Since that time, a feature of the many interna-

tional exhibitions here has been the sight of the different national flag
fluttering from the tall masts in the exhibition grounds.

MARINE GLORY SQUARE (Plóshchad Morskóy slávy)

There is a good view from this square of the Neva estuary. Th
river is over a kilometre wide here, and as a result, the water for a goo
twenty kilometres in the Gulf is fresh, provided there is no wind fror
the sea.

On the left bank of the Neva can be seen the Marine Harbour a
which, until 1963, all sea-going vessels, including passenger ships, use
to arrive. Nowadays, only big ocean liners and cargo ships tie up ther
Other ships moor at the jetties by Marine Glory Square.

Note the bright dwelling houses on little Kanonersky Island to th
right of the Marine Harbour. Until recently, the only way to the islan
from the city was by ferry across the Sea (Morskóy) Canal, since it wa
not feasible to build a bridge over a shipping route. A tunnel abou
a kilometre long now runs under the Canal. It can take pedestrians an
two-way vehicular traffic.

A new transport tunnel is to be driven under the Neva some dis
tance upstream from the estuary.

Further to the right from the Kanonersky Island and visible fror
the mooring at Marine Glory Square lies the man-made White (Bély
Island. It grew up on a spot referred to on maps as the White Sand
bank until quite recently. It was a tiny piece of land, not more than ha
a square kilometre. The soil used to make the island was taken fror
the bed of the Gulf. A complex of high-capacity plants for the biologi
cal treatment of sewage is being built on the new island, which is joine
to Kanonersky Island by a bridge.

If you stand facing the Gulf, you can see on your right two absolute
ly identical little towers crowned with pointed domes. Since the tim
of Peter the Great, they have been called 'observation towers' o
'Kronspiz'. Once upon a time, cannons stood near the towers with thei
muzzles trained on the Gulf to defend the approaches to the mooring
of the galley fleet. By the mid-18th century, the wooden structures ha
rotted away and were replaced with new ones of stone. A big construc
tion project is to be carried out on this section of the sea-shore. Th
two 'Kronspiz', however, will be preserved as monuments of the pas

Extending for over 400 km, the Gulf of Finland is called 'the cyc
lone road'. The cyclone, usually travelling from west to east, generate
what is known as a 'long' wave reaching all the way from one side o
the Gulf to the other. Forming a considerable distance away the city a
times, the wave rolls towards Leningrad, if it is propelled by a follow
ing wind, at the speed of a fast passenger train. Cramped by the nar
rowing banks at the river estuary, it rapidly gains height.

The city is warned of the approaching 'long' wave several hour beforehand. All the buildings in the city have been designed with due allowance for this danger. At Marine Glory Square, you can see the high quay walls of the upper part of the embankment.

The General Plan for the Development of Leningrad envisages measures which will thoroughly protect the city from floods. A long pier of earth and stone will run across the Gulf, linking the southern and northern shores well out to sea. The proposed length is 26 km, and work is now in progress on the technical aspects of the project.

HOUSING ESTATE No. I

The street names in this area remind the visitor that this is a seaside district. The road nearest to the Gulf is called Shipbuilders' Street (Ulitsa Korablestroítelei). It will eventually be extended south and north. The city's first seaside embankment will run parallel to it. Both thoroughfares will be linked by Skippers' (Shkíperskaya), Sailors' (Marósskaya), Midshipman's (Míchmanskaya), Boatswair's (Bótsmanskaya) and Captain's (Kapitánskaya) Streets, while the embankment will bear the name Maritime (Morskáya náberezhnaya).

A ride round the housing estate will give you some idea of the basic principles underlying a modern giant construction programme. The area of the estate is over half a square kilometre. The first building went up here in 1969. Nine-storey and twelve-storey blocks alternate in the middle of the estate. The buildings are placed so as not to throw shadow on each other. The south side of the estate is fringed with picturesquely designed buildings, most of which are faced with coloured tiles, and finished with decorative glass and wood. There are many open or glazed balconies, bows, and loggias. There are children's playing grounds near the houses.

Inside the estate are two large, interestingly designed school buildings with eye-catching façades. The stadiums are adjacent. There are also shopping and service centres, a children's polyclinic, kindergarten and nurseries.

Avenues of young poplar-trees and beds of flowers delight the eye in summertime. There is plenty of space inside the estate, and in winter the residents can go skating and skiing as well as tobogganing not far from their homes.

The international-class *Pribaltiysky* Hotel, capable of accommodating 2,400 guests, towers over the waters of the Gulf. The Maritime (Primórsky) Civic Centre is to be constructed soon.

THE CITY WATERFRONT

A highway, the continuation of Shipbuilders' Street, leads to the shore of the Gulf.

In conformity with the General Plan for the Development of Leningrad a waterfront over 25 km long will fringe the waters of the gulf like a gigantic horseshoe. Embankments will run along the north and south shores. The central part of the seaside town will be on Vasilyevsky Island. It will consist of ten- or twelve-storey apartment blocks whose line will be interrupted by squares fringed with public buildings. The embankment will be faced with stone and there will be steps going down to the water at regular intervals. Nearby them will be jetties for high-speed hydrofoils travelling round the Gulf, and there will also be rowing-boat stations. The total width of the embankment, including the esplanade, will be 160 m. Three tree-lined streets will run from the centre of the Island to the embankment.

A large-scale hydraulic engineering project was completed on this part of Vasilyevsky Island, mainly in 1972. A few years ago, the waters of the Gulf covered an area where today there are motor roads and apartment blocks. Over 3.5 sq km were reclaimed from the sea. The shore-line of all three islands was raised to a safe height as a precaution against flooding and was also levelled off, which meant that in some places it had to be moved out into the Gulf by as much as a kilometre. Prior to housing construction, hollow reinforced concrete piles over 1 m in diameter are driven 30 m deep into the ground. This completely ensures the safety of the foundations for all types of structure.

Several years ago, the narrow, meandering River Smolenka debouched into the Gulf just near the place where there is now a motor road leading to the Gulf. A new river-bed was dug out for the Smolenka, over 2 km long and 24 m wide.

One of the five widest (70 m) bridges in the city was built recently at the point where Nalichnaya Street crosses the Smolenka. Massive obelisks decorate the approaches to the bridge. Work on a Metro station has begun here. The new October (Oktyábrsky) Avenue will run along the Smolenka River, thus forming a fine esplanade. Construction is already under way. The new avenue will be flanked by 22-storey buildings.

At the place where October Avenue reaches the Gulf, there is to be a spacious square, with a wide-open view of the sea. A granite-clad pier will run from the shore out into the Gulf. It is to be decorated with a magnificent group of monumental statuary. A big team of Leningrad architects and sculptors is now working on the project. A model of this monument was exhibited in the Russian (Rússki) Museum in 1977, and was widely discussed by the public. A foundation stone was ceremonially laid on the site of the future main square. An inscription on the stone reads: 'A monument will be erected here in honour of the Great October Socialist Revolution and the military and labour victories won by the people of Leningrad under the guidance of Lenin's party.'

ENVIRONS OF LENINGRAD

he map gives the suburbs of 'Greater Leningrad'. Each suburb will probably equire a separate tour. Places of interest can be viewed in any order that seems onvenient. Our recommendations are given with the description of the places f interest in each chapter.

ublic transport to Razliv: By electric train from Finland Railway Station (going)wards Sestroretsk).

ublic transport to Petrodvorets: By electric train from the Baltic Railway tation or by river-boat from the Hermitage jetty.

ublic transport to Pushkin and Pavlovsk: By electric train from Vitebsk Railay Station.

ublic transport Repino Village ('Penates' — the Repin Museum-Estate): by ectric train from Finland Railway Station (going towards Vyborg).

Razliv

In the summer of 1917, Lenin was hiding in Razliv from the persecutions by the counter-revolutionary Provisional Government.

After the shooting down of people taking part in the peaceful work-s' demonstration on July 4 (17), 1917, in Petrograd, the bourgeois rovisional Government launched an open campaign of counter-revo-tionary terror. An order was issued for Lenin's arrest and trial on charge of treason.

The Central Committee of the Bolshevik Party consequently took l possible measures to save its leader, who was in peril of his life.

It was decided to hide Lenin in the house of the Bolshevik worker . Yemelyanov who lived in a village near the railway station of Razliv the region of Sestroretsk.

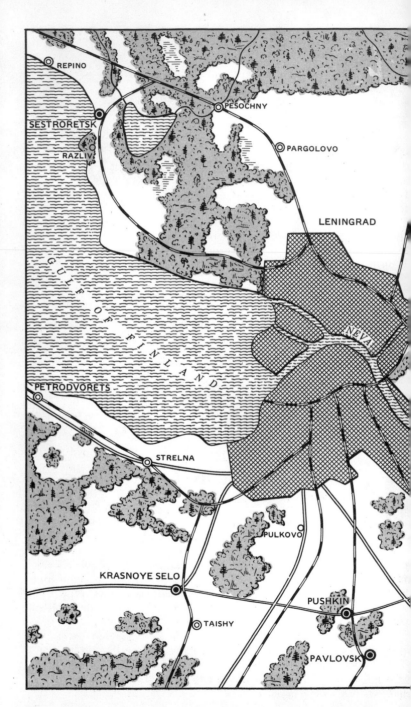

Nikolai Yemelyanov met Lenin and his party at the agreed spot. He
ok Lenin to the train across some side-tracks. It was safer that way.
nin left on the last suburban train and sat on the steps of the last
rriage all the way to Razliv so as to be able to jump down in an
ergency.

'After the July days I had occasion, thanks to the particular solici-
de lavished on me by Kerensky's government,' wrote Lenin sarcasti-
lly about that time, 'to go underground. I was hid, naturally enough,
a worker.'

IE YEMELYANOVS' MEMORIAL HOUSE AND THE 'SHED' ARÁI') MUSEUM

Nikolai Yemelyanov, a worker at munitions plant, and his wife
ned the Party in early 1900s and had considerable experience of
rking in the underground.

The documents, photographs, diagrams and drawings on display in
Yemelyanovs' Memorial House tell how Lenin left Petrograd and
ed in hiding with them.

During that memorable summer of 1917, Yemelyanov's house was
ing repaired and the large family had moved to the shed, temporarily
ed as living quarters. Lenin lived in the loft of the shed.

The 'Shed' memorial museum, opened by decision of the Central
mmittee of the Bolshevik Party in 1925, re-creates the atmosphere
that time. To ensure the preservation of this historical and
volutionary relic, the shed is enclosed in a glass case.

Lenin did not stay in the Yemelyanovs' shed for long. The place was
t safe enough, and it was decided to hide the leader of the revolution
mewhere really safe. It was a deserted spot on swampy land beyond
ke Razliv and could only be reached by a rowboat.

HE 'HUT' ('SHALÁSH') MONUMENT-MUSEUM

27 — granite monument, architect — A. Gheghello, 1964 — museum pavilion,
chitects — V. Kirkhoglani and others

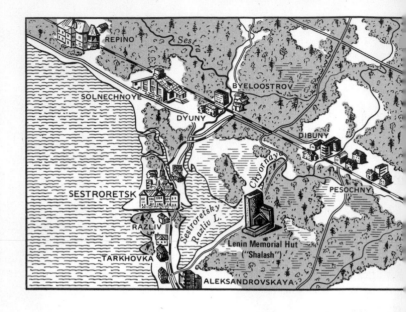

Disguised as a haymaker, Lenin took his abode in a hut made of branches covered with hay. The hut stood beside a haystack in which a cavity was hollowed to serve as a sleeping-place on cold nights.

Beside the hut, a small clearing was made in the thick bush to which Lenin referred jocularly as 'my green study'. The 'furniture' of the 'study' consisted of two blocks of wood, the higher one serving as a desk and the lower one as a chair.

It was from here that Lenin directed the preparations for the October Socialist Revolution and prepared material for the Sixth Communist Party Congress which decided on an armed uprising. In July and August of 1917, while living in the meadow beyond Lake Razliv, Lenin wrote dozens of articles and booklets. He wrote in his 'green study' most of his fundamental work, *The State and Revolution,* in which he gave the fullest and most systematic exposition of the Marxist teaching on the state.

This small clearing, surrounded by alders, aspens, willows and young birches, was to become one of Lenin's first memorials. On the 10th anniversary of the October Revolution in 1927, a granite monument was erected here. It consisted of two walls of different height standing at a right angle. In the corner thus formed was a stylised representation of the historic hut. The memorial bore a brief inscription 'To Lenin' and a memorial plaque:

228

he 'Hut' (Shalash) Museum in Razliv

'On the spot where, in July and August, 1917, the leader of the world ꞌctober hid in a hut of branches from the persecutions of the bour-ꞓoisie and wrote his book *The State and Revolution*—we have erected granite hut. The workers of the city of Lenin. 1927.'

A semicircular concrete-and-glass pavilion houses an exhibition of bjects, documents, photographs, first editions of Lenin's works at that me, pictures and sculptures.

Lenin stayed in Razliv until the Central Committee of the Party ꞓcided that he should go abroad, to Finland.

After studying all the possible ways of getting Lenin to Finland ꞓcretly, the comrades suggested that he go on a locomotive disguised ; a stoker. He agreed to this plan, and they made arrangements with ꞷ engine driver H. Galava to smuggle Lenin across the border.

Late in the evening of August 8, Lenin left the hut. They had to alk some 10 kilometres under cover of darkness to the nearest station ꞷ the Finland Railway line. Lenin's guides lost their way in the dark ꞷd came to a river which they had to ford. They wandered for several ore hours, found themselves in a burning forest and finally, exhausted ꞷd hungry they came to a station on the frontier. Lenin barely had ꞷe to hide at the bottom of the railway embankment. Yemelyanov, ho had gone off to check the lie of the land and buy tickets, was ꞷmediately detained by a patrol. When the train came in Lenin and

229

a comrade got into one of the rear carriages and safely reached Ude‌l‌naya station.

Lenin's trek from the moment he left the hut beyond the lake an‌d until he reached Helsingfors (Helsinki) is shown on a big relief ma‌p exhibited in the museum pavilion.

You have already learned on previous tours how Lenin returned t‌o Petrograd to head the preparations for the armed uprising and how h‌e directed it.

Petrodvorets — a Town of Fountains

PETRODVORETS (former Peterhof)

Founded in 1710 as a summer residence o‌f the tsar. Original designer unknown. The fu‌r‌ther building involved architects J.-B. L‌e‌blond, P. Yeropkin, M. Zemtsov, B. Rastrel‌l and A. Voronikhin, among others. Since the October Revolution, has bee‌n a place of recreation and a museum complex. Situated 29 km west of Leningra‌d. Was occupied by the Hitlerite forces from September 1941 to January 1944 an‌d nearly razed to the ground. Rebuilt after the war. Restoration work continue‌s.

Petrodvorets, the gem of the Leningrad environs, has been admire‌d for more than two hundred years. There are beautiful examples o‌f architecture, sculpture, painting, and landscape gardening and founta‌in design.

For two centuries, the Peterhof palaces and gardens had been th‌e property of the royal family, the palatial summer residence of the Rus‌sian monarchs. After the October Revolution, the masterpieces of Pe‌t‌rodvorets became the property of the people and were placed unde‌r state protection. Petrodvorets was converted into a complex of pictur‌e galleries and history museums.

After the fascist invasion, Petrodvorets virtually ceased to exist a‌s a work of art.

The Grand Palace and the Grand Cascade of fountains were blow‌n up: the Marly Palace, the Catherine block of the Monplaisir Palace an‌d the Greenhouse were burnt down; part of the Hermitage Palace an‌d he whole of the English Palace, the Pink Pavilion and Olga's Pavilion were completely destroyed. Some of the main statues of the Grand Cascade were stolen and disappeared without a trace. Some 34,000 objects of painting, sculpture and handicraft were pillaged or destroyed. The fountains and the entire waterpipe system were put out of action. Some 10,000 trees, or more than one third of the landscape garden, were cut down. The lawns, avenues and remaining buildings were mined.

Restoration work began immediately after Petrodvorets was recaptured. The first stage (1944-1945) was preparatory: the mines were cleared, the rubble removed, trees planted, etc. The second stage (1945-1951) way the restoration of the fountains and the restoration of the decorative sculpture. Finally, the rebuilding of the palace and the landscape architecture (1952-1960). The masterpiece that had taken over a hundred years to create rose from its ashes in fifteen post-war years. The miracle of Petrodvorets was born again.

Petrodvorets owes its uniqueness above all to its geographical position.

The town lies on the coast of the Gulf of Finland, on a series of rising terraces. The high ground overlooking the uppermost terrace is abundant with spring waters which supply the fountains.

The waterpipe system of the Petrodvorets fountains is a unique monument of Russian engineering skill.

THE GRAND CASCADE

1715-1723. Architects—J.-B. Leblond, J. Braunstein, N. Michetti and M. Zemtsov. Sculptors—M. Kozlovsky, V. Shchedrin, F. Shubin and others

There is a magnificent view from the terrace in front of the Grand Palace. There are 37 gilded statues, 150 small decorative sculptures, 29 bas-reliefs, two cascade staircases, 64 fountains and a majestic grotto on the hill-slope, all part of the Grand Cascade. Many of the sculptures are masterpieces of Russian art. Below, in the centre of a large semicircular pool, rises huge gilded stature of Samson Rending the Jaws of the Lion (height—3 m, weight—5 t). The most powerful jet of water in the park shoots up from the lion's mouth to a height of 20 m.

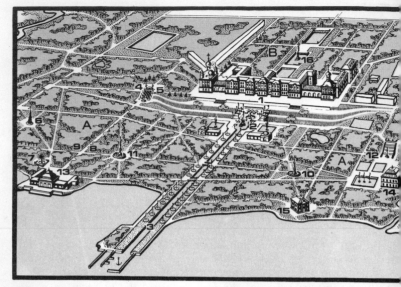

Figures stand for: **A.** Lower Park **1.** Grand Palace **2.** Samson Fountain **3.** Samson Canal **4.** Chess Hill Cascade **5.** Roman Fountain **6.** Pyramid Fountain **7.** Sun Fountain **8.** Oak Fountain **9.** Umbrella Fountain **10.** Eve Fountain **11.** Adam Fountain **12.** Golden Hill Cascade **13.** Monplaisir Palace **14.** Marly Palace **15.** Hermitage Pavilion **B.** Upper Gardens **16.** Neptune Fountain

Samson has earned world-wide fame for its creator, sculptor M. Kozlovsky. During the war the statue was taken away by the invaders. It was recast by Soviet sculptors V. Simonov and N. Mikhailov.

The Marine (Morskóy) Canal going down to the Gulf used to be a ceremonial approach to the Royal Palace: yachts with guests on board used to arrive along the canal via a lock. The granite-clad banks of the waterway are decorated with twenty-two marble cups spurting jets of water—an alley of fountains.

THE LOWER PARK

Begun early 18th century. Area 102.5 hectares. Nearly 150 fountains. More than 2,000 jets of water. Consumption—30,000 litres per sec.

The Lower Park is the green garden surrounding the Samson Pond. Here are the main cascades, fountains and architectural beauties of Petrodvorets. The Park was laid out in the geometrical style which was fashionable in the 18th century and is distinguished by its perfect symmetry.

In the eastern part of the Park there is a cascade called Chess Hill

Shákhmatnaya gorá). Here water falls slowly down sloping terraces faced with black and white marble squares. The chequer pattern sets off the quaint shape of the mountain rocks ornamenting the cascade grottos. The top grotto is surmounted with three dragons. The steps on both sides of the cascade are flanked with marble statues of the Greek gods. The Chess Hill cascade was built in 1721 by architect N. Michetti and rebuilt in the 1830s from designs by architect M. Zemtsov and others.

Two powerful fountains play on the spacious square in front of the Chess Hill. Built in 1739 by architects. I. Blank and I. Davydov, redesigned in the late 18th century by architect B. Rastrelli, they are called the Roman Fountains because, before they had been modified at the end of the 18th century, they were reminiscent in shape of the fountains in front of St. Peter's in the Italian capital.

Conspicuous in one of the avenues leading down from the Roman Fountains is the Pyramid Fountain. Five hundred and five jets of varying heights form a seven-step pyramid, snowy white because of the churning water. It is a highly ingenious example of hydraulic engineering: the height of each step depends on the water pressure in one of the seven supply chambers. The closer the jet to the centre of the pyramid, the higher it is.

There is another elaborately designed fountain called the Sun also in the eastern part. In the middle of a rectangular pool, sixteen bronze gilded dolphins, arranged in a circle, blow curving jets of water which form a transparent, lacy goblet. In the middle stands a tall pillar topped with a gilded disc, rotating slowly round its vertical axis while the rim throws out fine jets of sparkling water in imitation of the sun's rays.

The fountain designers showed much imagination so that Petrodvorets should not only be a beautiful ornamental park, but should be a place of amusement as well. They built a number of Jester Fountains, or *Shutikhi* in the Russian. They are always surrounded by crowds of laughing visitors.

Jester Fountains or Shutikhi. *Attracted by a cosy nook in the park, a visitor decides to have a rest on a broad garden bench. But as soon as he sits down, mischievous jets of water spring up and form a spherical canopy over his head (the Bench Fountain). Or there is the gravel that squirts fine jets of water as soon as anyone steps on it. Then there is the 'The Mushroom' arbour in which the unwary visitor is trapped by a circular curtain of water falling*

The ruins of the Grand Cascade in a 1944 photograph of wartime Petrodvorets

from the roof. There is also a six-metre-high oak surrounded b
a bed of tulips. Its trunk, green branches and leaves, like the flo
ers round it, are made of metal and conceal tiny nozzles. Th
inquisitive visitor who steps too close to it will find himself i
a mist of water droplets. 'The Oak' was erected in 1735 from a de
sign by Rastrelli. After the last war it was rebuilt from the so
surviving branch.

West of the Sea Canal, the Park's central axis, the other half of th
Lower Park geometrically repeats the plan of the eastern part. Yet i
seems quite different owing to the inventiveness of the architects.

True, the big Adam Fountain is balanced by the Eve Fountain
These two marble statues were commissioned by Peter the Great from
the Italian sculptor G. Bonazza to a design by architect N. Michetti.

But the Chess Hill is symmetrical to a quite different cascade of the
Golden Hill (by architects N. Michetti and M. Zemtsov). It consists of
a twenty-two step staircase tiled with gold leaf, a balustrade, a parapet
decorated with statuary.

The two columns of water are called 'Les menagères' (i. e. economic) and look remarkably powerful. This effect is achieved by a minimal
consumption of water owing to the ingenuity of the craftsmen. Water
spurts through the ring-shaped interstice between two pipes of differ-

234

The restored Grand Cascade in Petrodvorets

ent diameters with a common centre. The column of water is 30 cm in diameter and hollow, but this is not noticeable from outside.

At present, the Leningrad restorers are having to add to the Lower Park the features lost since the mid-18th century. The elaborate outlines of the original avenues have been discovered in one part of the western maze. To the east of the Sun Fountain, archaeologists have uncovered an oval pond. The specialists are being assisted in the excavations by volunteers from the All-Russia Society for the Protection of Historical and Cultural Monuments.

A stroll through the Lower Park will also take you to the Monplaisir, Marly and Hermitage Palaces, described at the end of this chapter. The Lower Park affords a generous view of the 300-metre-wide façade of the Grand Palace.

THE GRAND PALACE

1714-1724. Architects—J.-B. Leblond and N. Michetti. Completely rebuilt 1747-1754, architect—B. Rastrelli. Façade—275 metres long. Since 1917, Museum of history and the fine arts. Destroyed by the fascist invaders in 1944. Restoration work began in 1951. Partly open to visitors

The building of the original Palace which was called Uphill (Nagórny) began in the reign of Peter the Great. The new Palace, erected to the design of architect B. Rastrelli, retained in the original only Peter' study with the carved oak panelling and a carved oak staircase leading to the study. The Grand Palace was distinguished for its luxurious interior and exterior decoration. Its façades were adorned with pilaster and window plasterwork. The complex and elaborately contoured roof gave the building a highly unusual silhouette. The grand façade was flanked by two symmetrical wings surmounted by richly decorated gilded domes.

The inner ceremonial halls, reception rooms and royal chambers vied with one another in luxurious and imaginative mouldings, gilt carvings, mosaic floors, crystal, mirrors, and painted ceilings and wall panels.

After the October Revolution the Grand Palace was opened as a museum of history and the fine arts.

During the war, the Palace was reduced to ruins by the invaders. Everything moveable—works of art, palace utensils and furniture—was evacuated at the beginning of the war. The rest was destroyed by the enemy. The work of restoration was done from old plans sketches, photographs and the surviving fragments of the decorations The grand façade, the roof, the domes, the wrought-iron railings enclosing the balconies and also the main interior were restored. The first reconstructed museum rooms, including the double-lighted hall exhibiting, as before, 368 works by the 18th-century Italian painter P. Rotari, Peter's study and other features were opened to the public for the 250th anniversary of Petrodvorets in 1964. Restoration work is still in progress.

The Grand Palace features an extensive exhibition of works of decorative and applied art that were preserved in evacuation. A display of photographs illustrates the state of ruin in which the Palace and gardens were found by the Soviet troops when they liberated the town in January 1944.

MONPLAISIR

1714-1717. Architects—J. Braunstein, J.-B. Leblond and N. Michetti. Since 1917, a museum of history and the fine arts

In the eastern half of the Lower Park, not far from the Jester Fountains and very close to the sea, there is a light one-storey structure, the Monplaisir. It was Peter's favourite little palace built to his own sketches. Peter the Great used to enjoy the beautiful view from the terrace overlooking the sea. To decorate the Monplaisir, Peter collected Russia's first picture gallery—over 170 paintings, mainly by Dutch masters. Since the October Revolution, it had been a historical museum of domestic life.

During the years of war and occupation, Monplaisir also severely suffered. It was used by the Germans as an artillery site to shell Leningrad at close range. Carvings, mouldings, wall and ceiling paintings and other decorations were destroyed. In 1950, the work of restoration began on the exterior and the adjacent garden. The palace interiors were reproduced, including the carvings, the tiles, the Chinese lacquer room, the galleries and the Ceremonial Hall. The furniture, paintings and household utensils saved during the war were returned to their original places. The garden behind the Monplaisir is quiet and attractive. Fountains play here too, amid the fragrant flower-beds.

THE MARLY PALACE

1723. Architect—J. Braunstein

Another small palace, the Marly, stands not far from the western edge of the park near the sea. One façade overlooks a large rectangular pond, the other—a semicircular pool.

The palace was also luxuriously decorated with carvings, majolica, paintings, mouldings and lacquered panels. Next to it stood an orchard, hot-houses, poultry pens, cellars and other household premises. Fish were bred in the ponds. This palace was the tsar's private residence. Before the war, the Marly Palace had retained its original appearance both inside and outside. It was blown up by a fascist delayed-action mine, but some of the interior decorations were saved. In 1955, the façades and roof were restored. Work on the interior decorations which is rather difficult continues.

THE HERMITAGE PAVILION

1724. Architect — J. Braunstein

Also situated in the western corner of the park, this Pavilion wa designed to receive the cream of society. Surrounded by water, it coul only be reached by a small foot bridge. Its ground floor had a vestibul a kitchen and a room with an elevator mechanism. From here, th visitor could be taken up to the first floor in a special chair. In this wa the tsar and his intimates could meet in private. The whole first floc was a ceremonial hall with an oval table standing in the middle. Ther were chairs and covers for fourteen persons at the most. They wer served from below with the help of a lift. The central part of the tab and the wells for plates round the edge could be lowered to the kitche on the ground floor and then, at a prearranged signal, sent up agai with everything required.

Literary soirées were held at the Hermitage Pavilion. It was her that Dmitri Fonvizin, the famous Russian satirist, read his play *Th Brigadier* for the first time.

THE COTTAGE PALACE IN ALEXANDRIA

In the 19th century, several landscape gardens were laid out in th area adjacent to the Lower Park. The Alexandria Park group is th most famous of them. It harmoniously incorporates a number of palac buildings, including the Cottage Palace. Artistically, it is remarkable fo its interior decorations — wall and ceiling paintings, the graceful mould ings on the cornices and ceilings, and wood carvings which are master pieces of Russian applied art.

The palace exhibits works of Russian and European art dating bac to the first half of the 19th century.

Pushkin and Pavlovsk

THE TOWN OF PUSHKIN

Founded early in the 18th century as a country mansion. In 1710 Peter the Great presented it to his wife Catherine. In 1716, it acquired the name of Tsar's Village (Tsárskoye Seló). By the mid-19th century it was developed into a palace and garden complex with the participation of architects M. Zemtsov, A. Kvasov, S. Chevakinsky, B. Rastrelli, I. Neyelov, Y. Felten, G. Quarenghi, Ch. Cameron, V. Stasov and others. Named Children's Village (Détskoye Seló) in 1918. Renamed in honour of Pushkin in 1937. Situated 25 km from Leningrad. Occupied by the fascists from September 1941 to January 1944 and almost completely devastated. Largely restored since the war. Work still in progress

Today's tour is not just an opportunity to learn a few facts about the historical and architectural monuments of the Leningrad environs. It is a chance to meet a great poet. Everything here is reminiscent of Pushkin: the 'beautiful park in Tsarskoye Selo', which was extolled in so many wonderful poems; the town itself, where he used to feel himself 'surrounded by a host of recollections'; and finally, the modest building of the Lycée, where he spent six of his adolescent years and which, in the words of a schoolmate, Pushkin illumined with the 'light of his fame' for centuries to come.

THE LYCÉE

1789-1791. Architect—I. Neyelov. Originally, a wing of the Catherine (Yekaterí-ninsky) Palace and was connected to it with a passage in the form of an arch over the street. Redesigned by architect V. Stasov in the early 19th century. From 1811 to 1843, a private school for the nobility. The Lycée was destroyed in the last war. Restored and opened to the public as a memorial museum in 1949, to mark the 150th anniversary of Pushkin's birth

Alexander Pushkin was in the Lycée's first intake. He studied here from 1811 to 1817.
... When the town was liberated from the enemy on January 24, 1944, none of the houses was fit for habitation. The Lycée and the

239

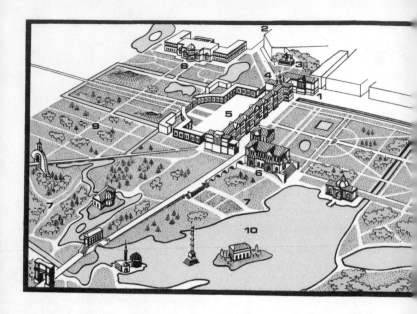

Catherine Palace had been gutted by fire. The first window to be glazed in the town was the one in Pushkin's room in the Lycée.

Today, the memorial museum at the Lycée houses classrooms, living quarters and the Assembly Hall. It was in this Hall on January 8 (Jan. 20 Old Style), 1815, that the young Pushkin recited his widely known poem, *Recollections in Tsarskoye Selo,* to the famous poet Gavriil Derzhavin and the board of examiners.

Not far from the Lycée, you will surely come across Pushkin himself sitting on a garden bench and lost in thought. This is one of best monuments to Pushkin (erected 1900; architect—R. Bach), a veritable symbol of the 'town of muses', and has often been painted or drawn by artists.

Several buildings in the town are associated with Pushkin. One of them is Pushkin's Country House.

PUSHKIN'S COUNTRY HOUSE

1827. Architects—V. Stasov and A. Gornostayev. A dwelling house. Opened as a memorial museum in 1958

Pushkin rented this house for the summer in 1831 after his marriage. Inspiration visited him here and he spent the whole autumn in

The Lycée where Alexander Pushkin
studied in Pushkin

Tsarskoye Selo. He wrote a number of lyrical poems (one of them was dedicated to the Lycée's 20th anniversary), continued working on *Eugene Onegin,* and wrote two fairy-tales for children. His friends came to visit him here, including such famous writers as Zhukovsky, Gogol and Vyazemsky.

The museum exhibition gives a detailed picture of this period of Pushkin's life. The rooms are furnished in the style of the period.

THE CATHERINE (YEKATERÍNINSKY) PALACE

Built 1719-1723 as chambers for the monarch and converted into a palace which was itself rebuilt many times. Architects included M. Zemtsov, A. Kvasov and S. Chevakinsky. The present version was built between 1751 and 1756 to the designs of architect B. Rastrelli. The façade is 306 m long. In the 1880s-1890s the Tsarskoye Selo ensemble took shape with the participation of architects I. Neyelov, G. Quarenghi and Ch. Cameron. (Between 1792 and 1794 the Cameron Gallery was built). Since 1917, has been a museum of Russian decorative and applied art. Destroyed by the fascist invaders during the war. Restored. Work still in progress

The Catherine Palace is abundantly decorated with columns, pilasters, mouldings and statuary. In the mid-18th century, some of the

Catherine Palace in the town of Pushkin

decorations were covered with pure gold. The combination of gold, azure walls, white columns and silvery roof was so breathtaking that one visitor had good reason to exclaim: 'All this jewellery needs now is a casket!'

The interior decoration was even more staggering. The doors were covered with delicate gilt woodcarving. The walls looked as if they had been hung with gold lace. The Throne Room (also called the Grand Gallery) with over 900 square metres of floor space, was particularly splendid: the walls were decorated with golden lace curtains and the interior of the dome was richly painted. The Palace owned an immense collection of paintings, sculptures, china, tapestry and Chinese art objects.

As a result of the war, almost nothing was left of the interior decorations and the façade. Immediately after the liberation, everything that remained intact was carefully preserved. Restoration work began first on the exterior and then on the interior.

Today, fourteen rooms are open to the public. Some look exactly as they did before, but others will never recover their former magnificence, which can only be judged from the surviving fragments and from photographs.

... According to Rastrelli's contemporaries and successors, the designer of the Winter and Peterhof Palaces surpassed himself

this time. His architectural inventiveness is astounding. It is not just that he managed to avoid even a hint of monotony in the great line of façades and to sing (there is no other word for it) a powerful and flowing melody . . . . He threw open this residence of dreaded monarchs to light, air, trees and sky. In the accurately found rhythms and exquisite baroque proportions, Rastrelli alternates an imposing line of columns with spacious windows, and the structure seems almost weightless without any loss of grandeur.

The story goes that Charles Cameron, who designed the gallery named after him, took off his hat every time he passed by Rastrelli's masterpiece. This cannot be attributed to good manners alone . . . . The Cameron Gallery is itself unique and has a special place in the architectural ensemble. It forms a natural extension to the Palace by joining the façade that overlooks the Catherine Park. This Park is so vast that any architectural structure might be expected to be swallowed up by it; yet the delicate and comparatively small Gallery is positioned in such a way that it dominates the whole park with its green sea of trees and its ponds, canals, bridges, monuments and many pavilions.

. . . Time is the best healer, but it cannot erase from memory what happened in the last war. How can one forget the shattered marble and the charred walls on those thirty-year-old photographs? This only serves to highlight the tremendous achievement of those who returned to us these gems of architecture in their original beauty.

The second floor of the Palace's former church annexe accommodates

THE NATIONAL PUSHKIN MUSEUM

Founded 1949. Accommodated in the Catherine Palace since 1967

Displays unique portraits of Pushkin and his contemporaries, rare publications, more than 1,200 manuscripts and drawings by the poet and objects that belonged to him and his friends.

Regular exhibitions devoted to aspects of Pushkin's life and work are held in the Cameron Gallery.

The Pushkin's Country House, The Lycée and also *Pushkin Museum-Flat* on the River Moika Embankment in Leningrad are all branches of the *National Pushkin Museum.*

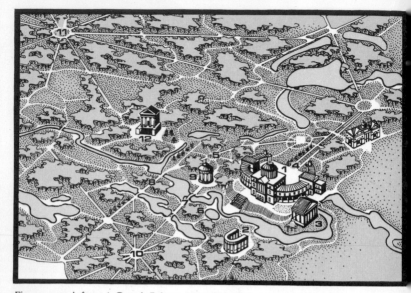

Figures stand for: **1.** Grand Palace **2.** Apollo's Colonnade **3.** Three Graces Pavilion **4.** Triple Lime Avenue **5.** Large Rings **6.** Cold Bath Pavilion **7.** Bridge of Centaurus **8.** Iron Gates with Vases **9.** Temple of Friendship **10.** Big Star **11.** 'White Birches' Clearing **12.** Mausoleum

THE CATHERINE (YEKATERÍNINSKY) PARK

Time went by bringing new tastes and new generations of architects, new features were added to the architectural complex of Tsarskoye Selo. Today, the green landscape gardens extend over a vast area of 600 hectares, combining into a unified whole the palaces, the monuments to Russia's victories on land and at sea, the park pavilions, arbours, decorative ruins, gates, bridges and administrative premises in various architectural styles. In more than two hundred years, the trees have grown into veritable giants, but their regular rows are still a reminder of the original layout of the parks.

The poetic beauty of the gardens in the town of Pushkin is enhanced by the many ponds, lakes and canals. All of them are man-made. Tsarskoye Selo is situated on high ground (over 65 metres above sea-level). Water was so scarce that it had to be brought from Petersburg in large wooden barrels. Later, ponds were dug and connected by canals, and these were spanned by fantastic bridges lined with marble statuary and ornamental fountains.

Use the services of Intourist and other travel agencies in Leningrad and Pushkin if you wish to acquaint yourself with the sights of the town in a fairly short space of time. But even a casual stroll on your own round the parks, Leningrad's favourite place of recreation, can also be a source of great aesthetic enjoyment.

PAVLOVSK

The park-and-palace ensemble took shape from 1778 to the early 19th century. Architects — Ch. Cameron, G. Quarenghi, C. Rossi and A. Voronikhin. Paintings and decorations — P. Gonzaga. Sculptors — M. Martos, M. Kozlovsky, F. Gordeyev, M. Prokofyev and others. A museum complex since 1917. Situated 29 km from Leningrad beyond the town of Pushkin. From September 1941 to January 1944, occupied by fascist forces and destroyed. Restored by 1970

At the time when the Catherine Palace already stood in all its beauty and splendour in Tsarskoye Selo, there was still only forest here, used by the tsars for hunting.

In 1777, Catherine II gave the lands along the River Slavyanka to the crown prince, Pavel. First, two palaces were built, followed by the Grand Palace, which Pavel I, after succeeding to the throne, had extended and decorated. Many beautiful objects of art by Russian and foreign masters were commissioned and bought. Originally, the park surrounding the Palace had been laid out in the so-called landscape style to create the illusion that it was the work of nature. The new sections were designed in a formal style that gave the park an atmosphere of holiday festivity. The lawns and avenues were decorated with bronze and marble statuary. The leading masters of park design attained the zenith of their art at Pavlovsk. The noted architects invited to work at various times on the project achieved a harmonious blend of the old and the new. As a result, Pavlovsk grew into a remarkably unified architectural complex.

The Pavlovsk concert hall at the railway station is famous for the popular recitals. Thousands of citizens used to attend these festivals of music. Johann Strauss and Glazunov appeared as conductors; Chalyapin, Sobinov and Nezhdanova sang to packed houses.

When the last war broke out, most of the works of art were evacuated or hidden away. For example, the sculptures, heavy stonework and other treasures were walled up in the Palace cellars. And although the fascists set fire to the building as the Soviet troops advanced, these collections survived.

But the Palace, its dome and roofs gone, was in ruins.

More than 40,000 fragments of plaster were reassembled by experts, who succeeded in restoring the sumptuous decorative mouldings.

During the occupation, the nazi cut down over 70,000 trees in the Pavlovsk Park, and before retreating, blew up many pavilions, bridges and the Slavyanka Dam. Soviet sappers uncovered some 250 concealed mines and a dozen high-explosive bombs.

There seemed to be no hope of restoring the Park. Those who visited the suburbs of Leningrad when the blockade ended said that there could only be ruins here as a reminder of the genius of the architects and the barbarism of the fascists.

Yet Pavlovsk rose once again as if from the dead. Restoration work is still in progress.

THE GRAND PALACE

1782-1786. Architect—Ch. Cameron. Extended 1798-1799. Architect—V. Brenna. Restored after the fire of 1803, with new buildings added and interior decoration, architects—A. Voronikhin and C. Rossi. In plan, the Palace resembles that of a broken oval. Two semicircular galleries with 64 columns branch out from the central cubic structure. In the middle of the courtyard stands a monument to Pavel I (erected 1851, sculptor—I. Vitali). Restored in 1970 from the ruins left by the nazis. Fifty rooms with Russian palace furniture and the interior decoration of the late 18th-early 19th centuries are open to the public

The visual impression created by the Pavlovsk Palace depends on the direction from which it is viewed.

From the River Slavyanka, the domed building looks airy and lofty, standing on its steep bank. Seen from the courtyard, it is solemn and formal. The northern side, overlooking the Park, is almost hidden by trees. The southern side, facing the street and overlooking the so-called Private Garden, looks almost dainty with its balconies and terraces. The Palace is a veritable treasure-house, for it houses a collection of priceless paintings, sculptures, stone, wood and bone carvings, glassware, bronzes, china and furniture.

The Ballroom, the Drawing Room, the Billiards Room, the Dining Hall, Pavel's studies etc, are on the ground floor.

The architectural composition on the first floor centres on the Italian Hall. It is two storeys high and culminates in a domed lantern. There

The Grand Palace in Pavlovsk

is a collection of antique sculptures here second only to that of the Hermitage in size and value.

The suite of rooms to the left served as Pavel's private chambers; those to the right were occupied by his wife.

Thematic exhibitions are usually open to the public on the second floor of the main building.

There are experienced guides available to show visitors round the Palace.

THE PAVLOVSK PARK

The largest landscape garden in the USSR. Area—600 hectares. Laid out 1777-1828

You see a park that has undergone vast restoration work since the liberation of Pavlovsk from the fascists in 1944. Many avenues, lawns, pavilions and foot-bridges have been reproduced in their original form. New trees have been planted in place of those cut down.

The total length of all the paths and avenues is nearly equal to the distance from Leningrad to Moscow, and a one-day tour is not enough to see everything. But many curious pavilions and park interiors are within walking distance of the Palace.

From its windows, overlooking the winding Slavyanka below, one can see the Apollo's Colonnade on the opposite bank (erected 1782-1783, architect—Ch. Cameron). The Colonnade was built as a double ring. In 1817, part of it collapsed as a result of a violent thunderstorm. The breach gave such a picturesque view of Apollo's statue that it was decided to leave the ruins exactly as they were.

At the far end of the tiny and delicate Private Garden the visitor will find the Three Graces Pavilion (built 1800, architect—Ch. Cameron, sculptor—P. Triscarni). This group of statuary, which stands in the centre of the 16-columned Pavilion, was carved of a single block of marble.

During the war, the sculpture was buried in the ground and grass was sown on top. But the fascists found it and planted a time-bomb right inside the case in which it had been packed. The bomb was defused by Soviet sappers.

The Palace's main gates open on to the Triple Lime Avenue, the lay-out axis for the front courtyard and the adjacent Park. There are several pavilions along the Avenue. To the left, on the bank of the Slavyanka, stand the so-called Large Rings (built 1799, architect—V. Brenna), round tufa terraces with marble statues on granite pedestals in the middle and green turf and flower-beds around.

Also on the bank of the Slavyanka is the Cold Bath Pavilion, the Bridge of Centaurs, the Iron Gates with Vases, the Temple of Friendship and many other items of interest.

The Karelian Isthmus

The Karelian Isthmus lies to the north-west of Leningrad between Lake Ladoga and the northern coast of the Gulf of Finland. It is crossed by part of the international tourists' motorway from Finland.

The coastal road winds tortuously through the dense forest, which parts in places to give a view of the sea and picturesque lawns. The Ice Age has left its imprint on the Isthmus in the form of rocky seaside

terraces, mány enormous polished boulders that split off from the gla-
cier's granite bedrock and hundreds of lakes, many of them in the
forest.

The air is pure and fragrant with the resinous tang of conifers.
Leningrad and its environs are in the taiga climatic zone, but in addition to firs and pines there are oaks, limes and hazel trees. You can see
fearless squirrels bounding from tree to tree, and elks roam through
the forest.

The Karelian Isthmus is a health resort area with sanatoriums, rest
homes and holiday hotels, where more than 250,000 visitors stay every
year. There are 14 sanatoriums for children and 200 crèches, kindergar-
tens and Young Pioneer camps. The many hiking centres are very popular with lovers of this kind of vacation. Building and development
work continues along the 70-kilometre coastal strip which spreads as
much as six kilometres inland. There is enough room here for each
health centre to have spacious grounds of its own. Moreover, there are
public parks and woods which are open to all and where the silence is
disturbed only by the singing of the birds.

Some of the beaches are covered with fine sand, as is the sea-bed.
The woods and parks come right down to the beaches.

The Karelian Isthmus also boasts spas of sodium chloride and fer-
rous waters and curative muds.

The natural ionization of the air is another feature of this part of
the country. Holiday makers and victims of hypertension and a nervous
break-down restore bodily vigour and psychological balance.

THE DUNES (DYUNY) HOLIDAY HOTEL

41 km from Leningrad. Founded 1966. Grounds — 20 hectares. Capacity — 600
foreign tourists

The Dunes, a seaside resort
The Dunes, a forest resort
The Dunes, a resort which is
not too near the city, and not too far away
The Dunes, a resort for sport, for leisure,
for pleasure, and learning Russian for good measure

The *Dunes* holiday hotel

True to its name, the resort is situated among sand dunes over-grown with pine and fir-trees. One of the blocks takes visitors from Leningrad all the year round, most of them with vouchers bought at reduced prices, the difference being paid by the trade unions from their social insurance funds.

From June to September, five two-or three-storey blocks cater for foreign tourists. The *Dunes* is much in demand by holiday-makers and so it is advisable to reserve in good time. Many families with children spend their vacations here.

The *Dunes* Holiday Hotel stands 70-80 metres back from the sea. It has a sandy beach, an aerosolarium, a boat station, shower cubicles, summer cafés and a dance pavilion.

Intourist is represented at the hotel and offers a wide choice of excursions around the Karelian Isthmus, Leningrad and its environs.

The musically minded are invited to attend the *Sonata* Club, and there is the *Lesovik* Club for nature-lovers. The *Globe* Club provides travel-films and lectures. For each intake, amateur stage concerts are organised and a sports festival is held at the stadium.

Students of Russian are offered a chance to improve their know-ledge in twelve-day seminars during the summer.

The Penates Museum-Estate in Repino

THE PENATES (PENÁTY): REPIN MUSEUM-ESTATE

45 km from Leningrad. From 1900 to 1930, Repin's country house. A memorial museum since 1940. Burnt down in 1944 by the fascist invaders. Restored in 1962

The great Russian artist, Ilya Repin, lived in this house for 30 years, died here, and was buried close by. Repin called his little country house *The Penates* in honour of the ancient Roman household gods. When he bought this plot of land, there was only the usual one-storey log cottage. Little by little, the house and grounds came to look, thanks to Repin's designs, almost like something out of a fairy-tale. He added verandas, porches, lanterns over the studios, and small towers, while all kinds of arbours, bridges and so forth appeared in the grounds.

Repin's endless interest in everything new and his passionate love of the arts drew famous contemporary poets, musicians and scientists to *The Penates*. The Repins' Wednesdays were frequented by Gorky, Mayakovsky, Chalyapin and Yesenin among others.

It was in this house that Repin worked on their portraits and such famous canvases as 'Ceremonial Session of the State Council', 'Pushkin's Examination at the Lycée', 'What Space!', 'Black Sea Cossacks', 'The Hopak' and others. It was here, too, that he wrote his memoirs, 'Far Is Near'.

251

The Repin Museum exhibits copies of the many works by him now preserved in the Russian Museum (Leningrad), the Tretyakov Gallery (Moscow) and other national museums.

The visitor can also see several original Repins including his last self-portrait. He worked furiously all his long life, dying at the age of 86. When he was too old and weak to hold the palette (now a museum exhibit), he fastened it to his belt. When his hands were too weak to hold the brush, he used a pen and even a match as a substitute. The remarkable drawings done in this way are also exhibited here.

All the eleven rooms of the Penates seem lived-in and every detail adds to the story about the Repins and the artist's self-sacrificing service to art. '... I'm more interested in art than in my own life,' he wrote in a letter to Lev Tolstoy's daughter.

There are three rooms in the Museum with exhibits that give a stage-by-stage account of Repin's life and creative work.

The Penates were burnt to the ground by the fascists before their retreat. Nothing left except cinders, part of the foundations and the brick stove chimneys. The estate was restored from photographs and the reminiscences of those who had visited the artist.

The new Penates received the paintings, drawings, and some of the furniture and personal belongings that had been evacuated when the front began to draw nearer. Many citizens of Leningrad presented the Museum with old photographs, letters and drawings which were being kept in the family archives and were connected one way or another with Repin or his numerous friends who had visited The Penates. Repin's distant relations sent from his flat in town certain pieces of furniture similar to the ones that had been used at The Penates. An old leather-covered chest arrived from Finland. It was sent by a woman who had received it from Repin as a gift when she worked as a charwoman at The Penates.

The great artist was buried here on the estate. He chose the spot himself and planted a juniper nearby. In accordance with his will, a young oak-tree was planted at his grave.

THE LENINGRAD METRO

While sightseeing in Leningrad, you have probably used the underground. At any rate, you cannot consider yourself fully acquainted with the city unless you have had a ride on the Metro railway.

Due to Leningrad's specific geological conditions, driving tunnels at small depths was found to be technically more difficult than laying them at great depths.

All three lines of the Leningrad Metro pass under the bed of the Neva so that there are ships sailing overhead as you travel under the river.

The Leningrad Metro is internationally famous as a brilliant engineering achievement, from the original conception to the construction and operating techniques used. Underground builders from different countries come to consult Leningrad specialists and study their experience. Leningrad builders have taken part in the construction of underground railways in other cities of the Soviet Union and abroad.

The construction of the Leningrad Metro began in 1940, but was interrupted by the war. The first line began running in 1955.

The lines of the Metro cross the city in three directions with several transfer stations in the centre. At present, the total length of the Leningrad Metro is more than 50 km, but it is planned to treble this figure by 1990.

Each of the 36 stations has a distinctive architectural style which, in one way or another, reflects the history of the locality.

We advise you to make a special point of viewing the following stations:

KIROVSKO-VYBORGSKAYA LINE

Ploshchad Vosstaniya (Insurrection Square) (1955)

The station faces the Moscow Railway Terminal, the scene of important events during the February Revolution of 1917 and, later, during the preparations for the October armed uprising. The numerous bronze bas-reliefs depict Lenin and scenes

Entrance to the metro on Nevsky Prospekt

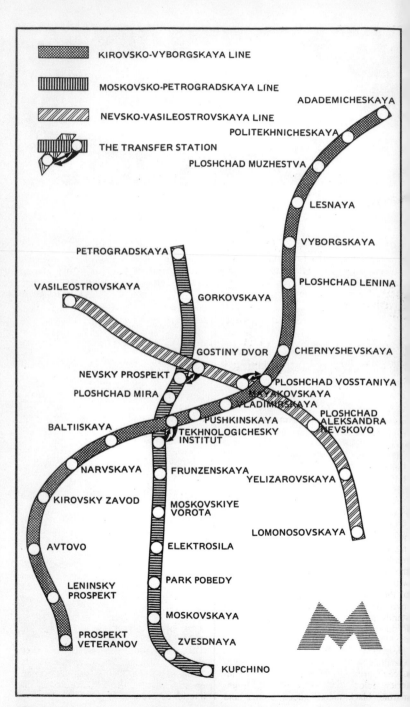

KIROVSKO-VYBORGSKAYA LINE

MOSKOVSKO-PETROGRADSKAYA LINE

NEVSKO-VASILEOSTROVSKAYA LINE

THE TRANSFER STATION

ADADEMICHESKAYA

POLITEKHNICHESKAYA

PLOSHCHAD MUZHESTVA

LESNAYA

VYBORGSKAYA

PETROGRADSKAYA

VASILEOSTROVSKAYA

GORKOVSKAYA

PLOSHCHAD LENINA

GOSTINY DVOR

CHERNYSHEVSKAYA

NEVSKY PROSPEKT

PLOSHCHAD VOSSTANIYA

PLOSHCHAD MIRA

MAYAKOVSKAYA

VLADIMIRSKAYA

PUSHKINSKAYA

PLOSHCHAD
ALEKSANDRA
NEVSKOVO

BALTIISKAYA

TEKHNOLOGICHESKY
INSTITUT

NARVSKAYA

FRUNZENSKAYA

YELIZAROVSKAYA

KIROVSKY ZAVOD

MOSKOVSKIYE
VOROTA

LOMONOSOVSKAYA

AVTOVO

ELEKTROSILA

LENINSKY
PROSPEKT

PARK POBEDY

MOSKOVSKAYA

ZVESDNAYA

PROSPEKT
VETERANOV

KUPCHINO

M

254

The Pushkinskaya Metro station

rom the revolution. The halls are faced with red marble and bronze.

Underground passages connect the station with the platforms of the Moscow Railway and with Mayakovskaya Metro station.

Pushkinskaya (1956)

The street-level hall of the station has been incorporated in a three-storey building. It is situated in the vicinity of the Vitebsk Railway Terminal. A branch-line of the Vitebsk Railway connects Leningrad with the town of Pushkin, and the interior of the station has been decorated accordingly. At the end of the underground hall stands a bronze sculpture of Alexander Pushkin by M. Anikushin, also sculptor of the Pushkin monument in Arts Square (Plóshchad Iskússtv). The bust occupies a shallow niche, with a lyrical landscape of Lycée Gardens as the background. The interior colour scheme combining bright marble, black metal, gilded bronze and white tiles, creates a mood of dignified solemnity.

Tekhnologíchesky Institút (The Technological Institute) (first station—1955, second—1960)

This is the main transfer station of the Leningrad Metro. It consists of two underground stations with a common street-level hall.

The station is situated beside one of the city's biggest and oldest higher educational establishments—the Lensoviet Technological Institute (49, Suburban Avenue, 1820—1831; architects—A. Postnikov and E. Anert). This determined the stations' interior decorations: bronze medallions with bas-relief portraits of prominent Russian scientists in one hall, and, in the other, inscriptions of white polished marble commemorating the conquest of the North Pole, the commissioning of the world's first atomic power station, the launching of the Earth's first artificial satellite and other achievements of Soviet science and technology.

Baltíiskaya (Baltic) (1955)

The street-level pavilion adjoins the Baltic (Baltíisky) Railway Terminal and its impressive six-column portico looks out onto the square.

The underground decorations are inspired by the sea and the history of the port of Leningrad. The walls are faced with blue-gray marble, the vaults are reminiscent of billowing sails, the bronze medallions bear portraits of distinguished Russian admirals. The mosaic panel '1917' is dedicated to the revolutionary sailors of the Baltic Fleet.

Avtovo (1955)

During the war, the front line passed quite near where this station now stands. This is illustrated on the bas-relief panels on both sides of the entrance and in the interior decorations.

MOSCOW-PETROGRAD (Moskóvsko-Petrográdskaya) Line

Párk Pobédy (Victory Park) (1960)

This architecturally austere station is dedicated to the victory of the Soviet people in the Great Patriotic War of 1941-1945. The street-level hall stands in the Moscow Victory Park (Moskóvsky Párk Pobédy).

Moskóvskiye Voróta (Moscow Gates) (1960)

The interior colour-scheme is determined by a combination of russet marble and snow-white ceilings. There is a sculptural composition of war trophies which decorate the Moscow Triumphal Gate in whose vicinity stands the underground station.

Nevsky Prospekt (1960)

The street-level ticket-hall of the transfer station is situated in the city's main thoroughfare. An impression of festivity is created by the bright decorative materials, white pylons, strips of polished aluminium and crimson walls faced with small transparent glass tiles.

NEVSKO-VASILEOSTROVSKAYA LINE

Mayakovskaya (1967)

The entrance has been incorporated in a house in Nevsky Prospekt opposite Mayakovsky Street. A mosaic portrait of Vladimir Mayakovsky in the underground hall was executed by M. Engelke.

Plóshchad Alexándra Névskovo (Alexander Nevsky Square) (1967)

The station is of interest because of its luminous effect and lay-out decorated with a bas-relief, 'Prince Alexander Nevsky with his Troops'.

NAME INDEX

SUBJECT INDEX

SOME USEFUL RUSSIAN WORDS AND PHRASES

SUBJECT INDEX

SOME USEFUL RUSSIAN WORDS AND PHRASES

ARRIVAL

Porter!	Носильщик!	Nasee'l'shchik!
Where can I get a taxi, please?	Скажите, пожалуйста, где стоянка такси?	Skazhee't'e, pazhah'lsta, gd'e stayah'nka taksee'?
Where is the Intourist representative (office)?	Где представитель (отделение) 'Интуриста'?	Gd'e pretstavee'tel' (od'ele'neeye) 'Eentooree'sta'?
Where is the . . . hotel?	Как проехать в гостиницу . . .?	Kahk praye'khat v gastee'neetsoo?
I am a foreigner.	Я иностранец (иностранка)	Yah eenastrah'nets (eenastrah'nka)
I am a tourist.	Я турист	Yah tooree'st

CUSTOMS

I have nothing to declare.	У меня нет ничего, что подлежит пошлинной оплате	Oo min'yah n'et neechevo', shto padlezhi't po'shleennoy aplah't'e
These things are for personal use.	Это вещи личного пользования	E'ta v'e'shchee lee'chnava po'l'zavaneeya.
Here is my money.	Вот моя валюта	Vot mayah' valyoo'ta
This is all my luggage.	Весь этот багаж мой	Ves'e'tat bagah'sh moy
Where do I pass through customs?	Где будет таможенное оформление?	Gd'e boo'det tamo'zhennoye afarmle'neeye?
This is my suitcase. This is someone else's suitcase.	Это мой чемодан. Это чужой чемодан	E'ta moy cheemadah'n. E'ta choozhoi' cheemadah'n
How much duty must I pay?	Какую пошлину я должен уплатить?	Kakoo'yoo po'shleenoo yah do'lzhen ooplatee't'?
Is the inspection finished?	Досмотр окончен?	Dasmo'tr ako'nchen?
Is my baggage overweight?	Есть ли лишний вес?	Yest' lee lee'shneey v'es?
How much must I pay for overweight baggage?	Сколько я должен уплатить за лишний вес?	Sko'l'ka yah do'lzhen ooplatee't' zah lee'shneey v'es?

HOTEL ACCOMMODATIONS

I want a single room with bath/shower.	Мне нужен номер для одного человека, с ванной (с душем)	Mn'e noo'zhen no'mer dlyah adn'avo' chelave'ka s vah'nnoy (s doo'shem)

My wife and I would like a double room.	Нам с женой нужен один номер на двоих	Nahm s zhenoy' noo'zhen adee'n no'mer nah dvaee'k
May I have the key to my room?	Дайте мне, пожалуйста, ключ от номера	Dai'te mn'e, pazhah'lsta, klyooch at no'mera
Please take my baggage to my room.	Доставьте, пожалуйста, мой багаж в номер	Dastah'vt'e, pazhah'lsta, moy bagah'sh v no'mer
What is my room number?	Какой номер моей комнаты?	Kakoy' no'mer mayey' ko'mnaty?
Where can I have breakfast (lunch, dinner)?	Где я могу позавтракать (пообедать, поужинать)?	Gd'e yah magoo' pazah'vtrakat' (paab'e'dat', paoo'zheenat')?
Where can I buy foreign newspapers?	Где я могу купить иностранные газеты?	Gd'e yah magoo' koopee't' eenastrah'nniye gaz'ety?
Please wake me at ... o'clock.	Разбудите меня, пожалуйста, в ...часов ...минут	Razboodee't'e min'yah', pazhah'lsta, v ...chaso'f ...minoo't
Where is the elevator (service bureau, restaurant, café)?	Где находится лифт (бюро обслуживания, ресторан, кафе)?	Gd'e nakho'deetsa leeft (byooro' apsloo'zheevaneeya, restarah'n, kafe')?
I stay at the ... hotel. I live in room ... on the ... floor.	Я остановился в гостинице. Я живу в ... номере на ...этаже	Yah astanavee'lsya v gastee'neetse ... Yah zheevoo' v ... v ... no'mere nah ...etazh'e'
Wait a minute!	Одну минуту!	Adnoo' meenoo'too!
Come in.	Войдите!	Vaidee't'e!
Can I change money here?	Можно ли здесь обменять валюту?	Mo'zhna lee zd'es' abmenyah't' valyoo'oo?
Where can I make a phone call?	Где можно позвонить по телефону?	Gd'e mo'zhna pazvanee't' pa t'elefo'noo?
Please buy me a ticket (two tickets) to the theatre for tomorrow's performance of ...	Купите, пожалуйста, мне билет (два билета), в театр на завтра, на спектакль...	Koopee't'e, pazhah'lsta, mn'e beele't (dvah beele'ta v tyah'tr nah zah'ftra, na spektah'kl' ...
Is there any mail for me?	Нет ли для меня корреспонденции?	N'et lee dlyah minyah' karrespand'e'ntsee ee?

AT THE BANK

| Where is the nearest bank? | Где находится ближайший банк? | Gd'e nakho'detsa bleezhai'sheey bahnk? |

272

I should like to change money and one traveller's cheque.	Я хотел бы обменять валюту и один чек	Yah khat'el'l bih abmenyah't valyoo'too ee adee'n chek
What documents do I need to change money?	Какие требуются документы, чтобы обменять валюту?	Kakee'ye tr'e'booyootsa dakoome'nti, shto'bi abmenyah't' valyoo'too?
Can you change a ten-ruble (a five-ruble, a three- ruble) note?	Разменяйте, пожалуйста, десять (пять) рублей, три рубля	Razmenyai't'e, pazhah'lsta, de'syat' (pyaht') rooblei', tree rooblyah'

GREETINGS, GETTING ACQUAINTED, RELATIONS, PROFESSIONS

Hello!	Здравствуйте!	Zdrah'stvooit'e!
Good morning!	Доброе утро!	Do'broye oo'tro!
Good afternoon!	Добрый день!	Do'briy d'en'!
Good evening!	Добрый вечер!	Do'briy v'e'cher!
Goodbye!	До свиданья!	Da sveedah'neeya!
Mr.	Господин	Gaspadee'n
Mrs./Miss	Госпожа	Gaspazhah!
Comrade	Товарищ	Tavah'reeshch
Let me introduce myself. My name is ...	Разрешите представиться, меня зовут ...	Razr'eshee't'e pretstah'veetsa, menyah' zavoo't ...
What's your name?	Как вас зовут?	Kahk vahs zavoo't?
How old are you?	Сколько вам лет?	Sko'l'ka vahm l'et?
I am from ...	Я приехал из ...	Yah preeye'khal eez ...
Father	Отец	At'éts
Mother	Мать	Maht'
Brother	Брат	Braht
Sister	Сестра	Sestrah'
Son	Сын	Sin
Daughter	Дочь	Doch
Boy	Мальчик	Mah'lcheek
Little girl	Девочка	D'e'vachka
Girl	Девушка	D'e'vooshka
Man	Мужчина	Moozhshchee'na
Woman	Женщина	Zhe'nshcheena

Husband, spouse	Муж, супруг	Moozh, sooproo'k
Wife, spouse	Жена, супруга	Zhenah', sooproo'ga
Worker	Рабочий (работница)	Rabocheey (rabo'tneetsa)
Peasant	Крестьянин (крестьянка)	Krestyaneen (krestyah'nka)
Office or professional worker	Служащий	Sloo'zhashchee
Public figure	Общественный деятель	Apshchestvenniy d'e'yatel'
Journalist	Журналист	Zhoornalee'st
Writer	Писатель	Peesah'tel'
Teacher	Учитель (учительница)	Oochee'tel' (oochee'tel'neetsa)
Actor/actress	Актер (актриса)	Aktyo'r (aktree'sa)
Student	Студент (студентка)	Stood'e'nt (stood'e'ntka)
Engineer	Инженер	Eenzhen'e'r
Doctor	Врач	Vrahch
Miner	Шахтер	Shakhtyo'r
Mechanic	Механик	Mekhah'neek
Artist	Художник	Khoodo'zhneek
Interpreter	Переводчик	Per'evo'tcheek
Group	Группа	Groo'pa
Excursion	Экскурсия	Ekskoo'rseeya

REQUESTS, EXPRESSION OF GRATITUDE, EXCUSES, WISHES

Please get an interpreter.	Позовите, пожалуйста, переводчика	Pazavee't'e, pazhah'lsta, per'evo'tcheeka
Please help me!	Помогите, пожалуйста!	Pamaghee't'e, pazhah'lsta!
Please take me to . . . (meet me at) . . .	Прошу вас проводить (встретить) меня	Prah'shoo vahs pravadee't' (fstr'e'teet') menyah'
I am very grateful to you!	Благодарю вас!	Blagadaryoo' vah's!
Thank you!	Спасибо!	Spasee'ba!
Please forgive me!	Извините, пожалуйста!	Eezveenee't'e, pazhah'lsta!
Excuse me!	Простите!	Prastee't'e!
I want to rest (to eat, to drink, to sleep).	Я хочу отдохнуть (есть, пить, спать)	Yah khachoo addakhnoo't' (yest', peet', spaht')

274

I'd like to see the city (exhibition, ... museum).	Я хочу осмотреть город (выставку, музей)	Yah khachoo' asmatre't' go'rot (vi'stafkoo, moozey)
I'd like to go to the theatre (to the cinema, to a park).	Я хочу пойти в театр (в кино, в парк)	Yah khachoo' paitee' f t'eah'tr (f keeno', f pahrk)
I want to buy a souvenir.	Я хочу купить что-нибудь на память	Yah khachoo' koopee't' shto'-neebood' nah pah'myat'
I agree.	Я согласен (согласна).	Yah saglah'sen (saglah'sna)
I don't object.	Не возражаю	N'e vazrazhah'yoo
Yes, of course!	Да, конечно!	Dah, kane'shna!
With pleasure!	С удовольствием!	S oodavo'l'stveeyem!
I don't want to.	Я не хочу	Yah n'e khachoo'
I can't.	Я не могу	Yah n'e magoo!
No, thank you!	Нет, спасибо!	N'et, spasee'ba!
Unfortunately, I am busy.	К сожалению, я занят (занята)	K sazhale'neeyoo, yah zah'nyat (zah'nyata)
I don't agree with you.	Я не согласен (не согласна) с вами	Yah n'e saglah'sen (n'e saglah'sna) s vah'mee
Congratulations!	Поздравляю вас!	Pazdravlyah'yoo vahs!
To your good health!	За ваше здоровье!	Zah vah'she zdaro'vye!
I wish you happiness (health, success).	Желаю счастья (здоровья, успеха)	Zhelah'yoo shchah'stya (zdaro'vya, oospe'kha)
I don't understand you.	Я не понимаю вас	Yah n'e poneema'yoo vahs
I (only) speak ...	Я говорю (только) по-...	Yah gavaryoo' (to'l'ka) pa ...
Please repeat what you said.	Повторите, пожалуйста, еще раз	Paftaree't'e, pazhah'lsta, yeshcho' rahs
Please speak a little slower.	Говорите, пожалуйста, медленнее	Gavaree't'e, pazhah'lsta, me'dlenn'eye

DAYS OF THE WEEK, MONTHS, SEASONS

What day is it?	Какой сегодня день?	Kakoi' sevo'dnya den'?
Monday	Понедельник	Ponede'l'neek
Tuesday	Вторник	Fto'rneek
Wednesday	Среда	Sr'edah'
Thursday	Четверг	Chetve'rk
Friday	Пятница	Pyah'tneetsa

275

Saturday	Суббота	Soobo'ta
Sunday	Воскресенье	Vaskres'e'nye
A working (non-working) day	Рабочий (нерабочий) день	Rabo'cheey (n'erabo'cheey) d'en'
Week	Неделя	Ned'e'lya
Month	Месяц	Mes'yats
January	Январь	Yanvah'r'
February	Февраль	Fevrah'l'
March	Март	Mahrt
April	Апрель	Apre'l'
May	Май	Mai
June	Июнь	Eeyoo'n'
July	Июль	Eeyoo'l'
August	Август	Ah'vgoost
September	Сентябрь	Sentyah'br'
October	Октябрь	Aktyah'br'
November	Ноябрь	Nayah'br'
December	Декабрь	Dekah'br'
Winter	Зима	Zeemah'
Spring	Весна	Vesnah'
Summer	Лето	L'e'ta
Autumn	Осень	O'seen'
Holiday	Праздник	Prah'zneek
New Year	Новый год	No'veey got

TIME

What time is it?	Который час?	Kato'riy chahs?
Nine a.m. (p.m.)	Девять часов утра (вечера)	D'evyat' chaso'f ootrah' (v'e'chera)
Nine-thirty	Половина десятого	Palavee'na d'esyah'tava
At seven o'clock	В семь часов	V sem' chaso'f
At ... hours ... minutes	В ... часов ... минут	V ... chaso'f ... meenoot
Morning, in the morning	Утро, утром	Oo'tro, oo'tram
Evening, in the evening	Вечер, вечером	V'e'cher, v'e'cheram
Afternoon, in the afternoon	День, днем	Den', dnyo'm
Night, at night	Ночь, ночью	Noch, no'chyoo

276

Minute	Минута	Meenoo'ta
Hour	Час	Chahs
Half-hour	Полчаса	Po'lchasa
Today	Сегодня	Sevo'dn'ya
Tomorrow	Завтра	Zah'ftra
Yesterday	Вчера	Fcherah'
The day before yesterday	Позавчера	Pozafcherah'
The day after tomorrow	Послезавтра	Posl'ezah'ftra
Last (next) week	На прошлой (следующей) неделе	Nah pro'shloy (sl'e'dooshchei) n'ed'e'l'e
Next month (year)	В будущем месяце (году)	V boo'dooshchem me'syats'e (godoo')

COUNTING

How much (many)?	Сколько?	Sk'ol'ka?
1—one	1—один	1—adee'n
2—two	2—два	2—dvah
3—three	3—три	3—tree
4—four	4—четыре	4—cheti'r'e
5—five	5—пять	5—pyaht'
6—six	6—шесть	6—shest'
7—seven	7—семь	7—s'em'
8—eight	8—восемь	8—vo'sem
9—nine	9—девять	9—d'e'vet'
10—ten	10—десять	10—d'e'syat'
11—eleven	11—одиннадцать	11—adee'nnatsat'
12—twelve	12—двенадцать	12—dvenah'tsat'
13—thirteen	13—тринадцать	13—treenah'tsat'
14—fourteen	14—четырнадцать	14—cheti'rnah'tsat'
15—fifteen	15—пятнадцать	15—pyatnah'tsat'
16—sixteen	16—шестнадцать	16—shesnah'tsat'
17—seventeen	17—семнадцать	17—semnah'tsat'
18—eighteen	18—восемнадцать	18—vasemnah'tsat'
19—nineteen	19—девятнадцать	19—devyatnah'tsat'
20—twenty	20—двадцать	20—dvah'tsat'

30 — thirty	30 — тридцать	30 — tree'tsat'
40 — forty	40 — сорок	40 — so'rak
50 — fifty	50 — пятьдесят	50 — pyadesyah't
60 — sixty	60 — шестьдесят	60 — shezdesyah't
70 — seventy	70 — семьдесят	70 — se'mdesyat
80 — eighty	80 — восемьдесят	80 — vo'semdesyat
90 — ninety	90 — девяносто	90 — d'eveno'sta
100 — one hundred	100 — сто	100 — sto
200 — two hundred	200 — двести	200 — dve'stee
300 — three hundred	300 — триста	300 — tree'sta
400 — four hundred	400 — четыреста	400 — cheti'resta
500 — five hundred	500 — пятьсот	500 — pyatso't
600 — six hundred	600 — шестьсот	600 — shesso't
700 — seven hundred	700 — семьсот	700 — semso't
800 — eight hundred	800 — восемьсот	800 — vosemso't
900 — nine hundred	900 — девятьсот	900 — devet'so't
1,000 — one thousand	1000 — тысяча	1,000 — ti'syacha

MONEY, PRICES

1 (one) kopeck	1 (одна) копейка	1 (adnah') kapey'ka
2 (two) kopecks	2 (две) копейки	2 (dv'e) kapey'kee
3 (three) kopecks	3 (три) копейки	3 (tree) kapey'kee
5 (five) kopecks	5 (пять) копеек	5 (pyat') kape'yek
10 (ten) kopecks	10 (десять) копеек	10 (de'syat) kape'yek
15 (fifteen) kopecks	15 (пятнадцать) копеек	15 (pyatnah'tsat') kape'yek
20 (twenty) kopecks	20 (двадцать) копеек	20 (dvah'tsat') kape'yek
1 (one) ruble	1 (один) рубль	1 (adee'n) roobl'
3 (three) rubles	3 (три) рубля	3 (tree) roobl'yah'
5 (five) rubles	5 (пять) рублей	5 (pyat') roobley'
10 (ten) rubles	10 (десять) рублей	10 (de'syat') roobley'
25 (twenty-five) rubles	25 (двадцать пять) рублей	25 (dvah'tsat' pyat') roobley'
50 (fifty) rubles	50 (пятьдесят) рублей	50 (pyadesya't) roobley'
100 (one hundred) rubles	100 (сто) рублей	100 (sto) roobley'

How much does it cost?	Сколько стоит?	Sko'l'ka sto'eet?
Please write down the price.	Напишите, пожалуйста, цену	Napeeshee't'e, pazhah'lsta, tse'noo
Change	Сдача	Zdah'cha

CHARACTERISTICS

Good	Хорош/ий (-ая, -ее)	Kharo'sh/eey (-aya, -eye)
Bad	Плох/ой (-ая, -ое)	Plakh/oy' (-ayah', -o'ye)
Pretty, beautiful	Красив/ый (-ая, -ое)	Krasse'v/iy (-aya, -a'ye)
Ugly	Некрасив/ый (-ая, -ое)	N'ekrasee'v/iy (-aya, -a'ye)
Interesting	Интересн/ый (-ая, -ое)	Eentere'sn/iy (-aya, -a'ye)
Uninteresting	Неинтересн/ый (-ая, -ое)	N'e'eenteresn/iy (-aya, -a'ye)
Expensive (dear)	Дорог/ой (ая, -ое)	Darag/oy' (-ah'ya, -o'ye)
Cheap	Дешев/ый (-ая, -ое)	D'esho'v/iy (-aya, -a'ye)
Quick	Быстр/ый (-ая, -ое)	Bi'str/iy (-aya, -a'ye)
Slow	Медленн/ый (-ая, -ое)	Me'dl'enn/iy (-aya, -a'ye)
Gay	Весел/ый (-ая, -ое)	Vesyo'l/iy (-aya, -a'ye)
Dull	Скучн/ый (-ая, -ое)	Skoo'shn/iy (-aya, -o'ye)

SIGNS

Attention!	Внимание!	Vneemah'neeye!
Stop!	Стоп!	Stop!
Crossing	Переход!	Per'ekho't!
Bus (trolley, tram) stop	Остановка автобуса (троллейбуса, трамвая)	Astano'fka afto'boosa (traley'boosa, tramvah'ya)
Look out for cars!	Берегись автомобиля!	B'er'eghees' aftamabee'lya!
Taxi stand	Стоянка такси	Stayah'nka taksee'
Phone box	Телефон-автомат	T'el'efo'n-aftamah't
Information bureau	Справочное бюро	Sprah'vachnoye byooro'
Lavatory (Gents, Ladies)	Туалет (м)(ж)	Tooal'e't
Washroom (Gents, Ladies)	Уборная (м)(ж)	Oobo'rnaya
Chemist's	Аптека	Apt'e'ka
Post office. Telegraph office	Почта. Телеграф	Po'chta. T'el'egrah'f

Beauty parlour, barber's shop	Парикмахерская	Pareekmah'kherskaya
Box office (for a theatre)	Театральная касса	Teatrah'lnaya kah'ssa
Restaurant	Ресторан	Restarah'n
Café	Кафе	Kafe'
Bakery	Булочная	Boo'lachnaya
Confectionery	Кондитерская	Kondee't'erskaya
Grocery store	Гастроном	Gastrano'm
Grocery shop (for dry goods: flour, sugar, grains, etc.)	Бакалея	Bakale'ya
Meat/fish	Мясо-рыба	Myah'sa-ri'ba
Closed	Закрыто	Zakri'ta
Open	Открыто	Atkri'ta
Dinner break	Перерыв на обед	P'er'eri'f na ab'e't
Self service	Самообслуживание	Samaapsloo'zheevaneeye
Entrance (exit)	Вход (выход)	Fkhot (vi'khot)
No Entrance	Входа нет	Fkho'da n'et
Milk	Молоко	Malako'
Beer/soft drinks	Пиво-воды	Pee'va-vo'di
Fruit and vegetable juices/mineral water	Соки-воды	So'kee-vo'di
Wines/liqueurs, alcoholic drinks	Вина-ликеры, алкогольные напитки	Vee'na-leekyo'ri, alkoho'l'niye napee'tkee
Vegetables/fruit	Овощи-фрукты	O'vashchi-froo'kti
Florist's	Цветы	Tsv'e'ti
Perfumery	Парфюмерия	Parfyoome'reeya
Tobacco shop	Папиросы-табаки, сигареты	Papeero'si-tabah'k, seegar'e'ti
Bookshop	Книги	Knee'ghee
Articles for cultural and recreational needs	Культтовары	Kool'ttavah'ri
Furniture store	Мебель	Me'b'el'
Clothing store	Одежда	Ad'e'zhda
Shoe store	Обувь	O'boof'
Hats	Головные уборы	Galavni'ye oobo'ri
Haberdasher's	Галантерея	Galanter'e'ya

| Detsky Mir (a store selling goods for children) | Детский мир | D'etskeey meer |
| Department store | Универмаг | Ooneevermah'k |

THE METRO (M)

Entrance	Вход	Fkhot
Exit (To the street)	Выход (выход в город)	Vi'khot (vi'khot v go'rot)
No exit	Выхода нет	Vi'khada n'et
Ticket office	Кассы	Kah'si
Drop 5 kopecks in the slot.	Опустите 5 копеек	Apoostee't'e 5 kape'yek
Stand to the right, pass through on the left side.	Стойте справа, проходите слева	Stoy't'e sprah'va, prakhadee't'e sl'e'va
To the trains	К поездам	K payezdah'm
Transfer to ... line	Пересадка на ...	Peresah'tka nah ...

SHOPPING

Where is the nearest ... shop/store?	Где ближайший магазин?	Gd'e bleezhay'shee magazee'n?
I would like to see ... please.	Покажите, пожалуйста!	Pakahzhee'te, pazhah'lsta!
Do you have ...?	У вас есть ...?	Oo vahs yest' ...?
Another colour	Другого цвета	Droogo'va tsv'e'ta
Another style	Другой фасон	Droogoi' faso'n
A larger (smaller) size	Больший (меньший) размер	Bol'sheey (me'n'sheey) razm'e'r
I'll take that.	Я это куплю	Yah, e'ta kooplyoo'
Where can I pay for this?	Где я могу оплатить покупку?	Gd'e yah magoo' aplatee't' pakoo'pkoo?

MEDICAL AID

| I am unwell. | Я нездоров (нездорова) | Yah n'esdaro'f (n'ezdaro'va) |
| I don't feel well. | Я плохо себя чувствую | Yah plo'kha sebyah' choo'stvooyoo |

Please call a doctor (first aid). | Вызовите, пожалуйста, врача (скорую помощь) | Vi'zaveet'e, pazhah'lsta, vrachah'

I have a temperature. | У меня температура | Oo menyah' t'emperatoo'ra

My head (heart, stomach, throat, eye, hand, arm, leg) hurts/aches. | У меня болит голова (сердце, желудок, горло, глаз, рука, нога) | Oo menyah' boleet galavah (se'rtse, zheloo'dak, go'rla, glahs, rookah', nagah')

Do you have something for a cold? | Есть ли у Вас что-нибудь от простуды? | Yest'lee oo vahs shto'-neebood' at prastoo'd

DINING OUT

Please bring me a menu. | Дайте, пожалуйста, меню! | Dai't'e, pazhah'lsta, menyoo'!

Please bring me one serving (two servings) of ... | Принесите, пожалуйста, одну порцию (две порции)... | Preenesee't'e, pazhah'lsta, adnoo po'rtsiyoo (dv'e po'rtseeee)...

Please bring me a bottle of beer (wine, mineral water, cognac, champagne, vodka). | Принесите, пожалуйста, бутылку пива, (вина, минеральной воды, коньяку, шампанского, водки) | Preenesee't'e, pazhah'lsta, booti'lkoo pee'va (veenah', min'erah'lnoi vodi, kanyakoo', shampah'nskava, vo'tkee)

Glass | Стакан | Stakah'n

Wine-glass | Рюмка | Ryoo'mka

Plate | Тарелка | Tar'e'lka

Knife | Нож | Nosh

Fork | Вилка | Vee'lka

Spoon | Ложка | Lo'shka

Napkin | Салфетка | Salf'e'tka

Tablecloth | Скатерть | Skah't'ert'

Salt | Соль | Sol'

Pepper | Перец | Pe'r'ets

Mustard | Горчица | Garchee'tsa

Sugar | Сахар | Sah'khar

Butter | Сливочное масло | Slee'vachnaye mah'sla

Cigarettes | Сигареты | Seegar'e'ti

Matches | Спички | Spee'chkee

Please give me the bill. | Дайте, пожалуйста, счет! | Dai't'e, pazhah'lsta, schot!

ON THE STREET

Can you tell me how to get to the ... hotel?	Скажите, пожалуйста, как пройти к гостинице ...?	Skazhee'te, pazhah'lsta, kahk proitee' k gastee' neetse ...?
straight ahead, to the right, to the left, ahead, back	Прямо, направо, налево, вперед, назад	Pryah'ma, naprah'va, nal'e'va, fperyo't, nazah't
street, square, alley, crossroads, avenue, highway	Улица, площадь переулок, перекресток, проспект, шоссе	Oo'leetsa, plo'shchat', per'eoo'lak. per'ekryo'stak, prasp'e'kt, shase'
Can you tell me what bus (trolley, tram) I should take to get to the city centre (to .. hotel, ... station)?	Скажите, пожалуйста, каким автобусом (троллейбусом, трамваем) я могу доехать до центра города (гостиницы, вокзала)?	Skazhee'te, pazhah'lsta, kakee'm afto'boosam (traley'boosam, tramvai'yem) yah magoo' daye'khat' da tse'ntra go'rada (gastee'neetsi, vogzah'la)?
Where is the trolley stop, please?	Скажите, пожалуйста, где остановка троллейбуса?	Skazhee'te, pazhah'lsta, gd'e astano'fka traley'boosa?
Where is a taxi stand?	Где стоянка такси?	Gd'e stayah'nka taksee'?
Please show me on the map where I am	Покажите, пожалуйста, на карте, где я нахожусь	Pokazhee'te, pazhah'lsta, nakah'rt'e, gd'e yah nakhazhoo's'
I am lost.	Я заблудился (заблудилась)	Yah zabloodee'lsa (zabloodee'las')
Militiaman	Милиционер	Meeleetsian'e'r
How can I get (in a vehicle) to ...?	Как мне доехать до ...?	Kahk mn'e daye'khat' da ...?
Where is the transfer for ...?	Где пересадка на ...?	Gd'e peresah'tka nah ...?
How many stops to ...?	Сколько остановок до ...?	Sko'l'ka astano'vak da ...?

DEPARTURE

I am leaving tomorrow at ... o'clock	Я ыезжаю завтра в ... часов	Yah ooyezhah'yoo zah'ftra v ... chaso'f
Please have my bill ready to be paid.	Приготовьте мне, пожалуйста, счет	Preegato'ft'e mn'e, pazhah'lsta, schot
When does the train for ... leave?	Когда отходит поезд на ...?	Kagda' atkho'deet po'yest nah ...?
Where can I look at a train (plane, boat) time-table?	Где можно посмотреть расписание поездов (самолетов, пароходов)?	Gd'e mo'zhna pasmatr'e't' raspeesah'neeye payezdo'f (samalyo'tof, parakho'dof)?

283

When does the flight ... for ... leave?	Когда вылет самолета на ... рейс ...?	Kagdah' vilye't samalyo'ta nah ... reis ...?
Please call me a taxi!	Вызовите, пожалуйста, такси!	Vi'zaveet'e, pazhah'lsta, taksee'!
Where do I board the train ... for ...?	Где посадка на поезд номер ... до ...?	Gd'e pasah'tka nah po'yest no'm'er ... do ...?
Where do I board the flight ... for ...?	Где посадка на самолет рейс номер ... до ...?	Gd'e pasah'tka nah samalyo't no'm'er ... do ...
What track does the train ... for ... leave from?	С какой платформы отходит поезд номер ... до ...?	S kakoi' platfo'rmi atkho'deet po'yest no'm'er ... do ...?

FOR NOTES

FOR NOTES